Researching Everyday Childhoods

ALSO AVAILABLE FROM BLOOMSBURY

Celebrity, Aspiration and Contemporary Youth, Aisha Ahmad, Kim Allen, Laura Harvey and Heather Mendick

Rethinking Children and Research, Mary Kellett

Research Methods for Education in the Digital Age, Maggi Savin-Baden and Gemma Tombs

Researching Everyday Childhoods

Time, Technology and Documentation in a Digital Age

**RACHEL THOMSON,
LIAM BERRIMAN
AND SARA BRAGG**

Bloomsbury Academic
An imprint of Bloomsbury Publishing Plc

B L O O M S B U R Y
LONDON · OXFORD · NEW YORK · NEW DELHI · SYDNEY

Bloomsbury Academic

An imprint of Bloomsbury Publishing Plc

50 Bedford Square	1385 Broadway
London	New York
WC1B 3DP	NY 10018
UK	USA

www.bloomsbury.com

BLOOMSBURY and the Diana logo are trademarks of Bloomsbury Publishing Plc

First published 2018

British Library Cataloguing-in-Publication Data
A catalogue record for this book is available from the British Library.

ISBN: HB: 978-1-3500-1174-8
PB: 978-1-3500-1173-1
ePDF: 978-1-3500-1175-5
ePub: 978-1-3500-1176-2

Library of Congress Cataloging-in-Publication Data
A catalog record for this book is available from the Library of Congress.

Cover image © Carol Yepes / GettyImages

Typeset by Newgen KnowledgeWorks Pvt. Ltd., Chennai, India
Printed and bound in Great Britain

To find out more about our authors and books visit www.bloomsbury.com.
Here you will find extracts, author interviews, details of forthcoming events
and the option to sign up for our newsletters.

Contents

Figures

Foreword

David Buckingham

Public debates about children and media are often infused with sweeping claims about social change. Of course, childhood is always a focus for hopes and fears about the future; and when we combine this with ideas about the power of media and technology, we have the makings of a powerful popular mythology. Childhood, it seems, has been comprehensively transformed by media, if not (as many suggest) utterly destroyed.

Those of us who have studied this area for many years might be forgiven a certain sense of *déjà vu* here. Claims about the powerful influence of the media – for good or ill – have been around for many decades, if not centuries. There's a kind of endless recurrence about this: as each new medium appears on the scene, similar claims are rehearsed about its magical powers, whether to liberate and empower children or to corrupt and harm them.

The problem with these claims is not simply that they are so often overstated, or unduly polarized. Perhaps more significantly, they rest on a separation between children, on one side, and media, on the other. Media are seen as somehow external to childhood and to children's everyday lives. They come along, uninvited and as if from nowhere, yet they instantly exercise an almost mesmeric power. Children, meanwhile, are typically seen as innocent and vulnerable, easy prey for manipulation and exploitation. The relationship is understood as one of cause and effect: the media are seen to impact on children's consciousness and behaviour, and that influence is seen to flow only in one direction. In this account, children have very little agency: they are seen merely as victims or passive recipients.

Of course, this is not to imply that media have *no* effects, or that they are somehow insignificant. It is merely to suggest that such notions of cause-and-effect are a simplistic and inadequate way of understanding children's experiences of media. This approach leads us to ignore the diverse ways in which children interpret media, and the diverse roles they play in their lives. Media may do things *to* children, but children also do things *with* media. Media are not outside children's lives, impacting upon them, but deeply embedded within them.

This is even more apparent in an age where media have effectively become ubiquitous. With the proliferation of digital platforms and the advent of mobile media, media have become ever more deeply entangled with our social and personal lives. Through media, we can be connected at any time, and in any location. Easy distinctions between the online and offline have become increasingly difficult to maintain. For most of us, media are an inextricable part of the texture of our everyday lived experience: we live with and through them, moment by moment. They are fundamental to how we communicate, how we represent ourselves to others, and how we understand the wider world. To separate out the media, and to ask simplistic questions about their influence or effects, is thus to misinterpret the nature of contemporary social life.

These observations are particularly pertinent to children. Yet there is also a risk of romanticism here. Today's children, we are often told, are a 'digital generation'; today's childhoods are mediated childhoods. Adults, meanwhile, are struggling to catch up. While children are 'digital natives', born into a world of digital media, adults are apparently 'digital immigrants', who must struggle to learn a new language and a new culture. Such assertions represent children as exotic and alien beings. While waxing sentimental about their apparently spontaneous competence with media, they ignore the increasingly complex demands that children have to negotiate, and the learning that this requires. They also underestimate the continuities across generations, and the opportunities for communication between them that media can afford.

This book was originally to be entitled *Digital Childhoods,* and when I was invited to write the foreword, I recalled the fact that I had written a contribution for a book of exactly the same name (albeit published in Norwegian, as *Digital Barndom*) no less than twenty years ago. It would be good to imagine that this might be the *last ever* book about 'digital childhoods', although publications with similar titles are continuing to appear today.

Part of the problem here is with the technological term 'digital' – at a point when the distinction between digital and analogue (or non-digital) no longer has very much significance. Pretty much everything is now 'digital', or involves digital technology in some way. The fact that things are digital seems so banal that it is hardly worth saying. Yet such expressions also invoke vestiges of technological determinism, as though technology is an alien force that is now somehow colonizing or defining contemporary childhood. If we talk about technology in this way, we not only exaggerate its power, but also marginalize more important and complex questions about representation, communication and culture.

Recent discussions of 'participatory culture' have begun to take us beyond this deterministic approach, although they have raised further problems. It is undoubtedly true that new social media do provide greater opportunities for participation. This book provides many instances where children have effectively become media producers rather than mere consumers: they are using media to communicate their own perspectives, and to represent their own lives, in ways that were much more difficult to achieve before.

However, we need to beware of romanticism here too. The distinction between media 'production' and 'consumption' is always a little tenuous, especially once we acknowledge that children are actively making meaning from media of all kinds, and are rarely a passive audience, even for 'old' media like television or books. Furthermore, we should not forget that social media platforms are almost invariably commercial: they may appear to be free, but they make enormous profits by gathering data about their users, which is then used to target them with personalized advertising and other commercial appeals. Each medium, and each platform, inevitably exerts constraints on how it can be used. Children may be actively participating and communicating in new ways, but that activity does not necessarily mean that they have greater agency or social power.

This book brings a range of new empirical and theoretical perspectives to bear on these questions. The research that is reported here comes close to the rich detail of lived experience in ways that only in-depth, long-term ethnographic studies can do. The authors look across different settings – the family home, the school, and the peer group – and explore the different functions that media serve in each of them. They consider the role of media not just in private 'memory work' and in communication among friends and family, but also how they are used as means of surveillance in the public context of schooling. As these examples show, 'new' social media are often inextricably connected with 'older' media; and they are very much embedded within the wider dynamics of relationships among the family and the peer group. In this world of constant connectivity, it makes even less sense to consider media as an alien, external influence.

In analysing these different uses of media, the book also draws on broader theoretical debates. It considers how media use is implicated in children's sense of time and place, in their establishment of identity and their performance of childhood itself. The book resists the temptations of a media-centred or technology-centred approach, and refuses easy distinctions between mediated and non-mediated communication. It draws on 'post-digital' approaches, and notions such as 'polymedia' and 'intensive materialities', to capture the contemporary proliferation of media and the comprehensive mediation of everyday life. It also explores the diverse opportunities children have to create, curate and circulate media content, and what this tells us about the changing nature of 'communicative capitalism'.

Rather than conceiving of these developments in terms of cause-and-effect, the book also seeks to explain how children themselves understand and experience the various media cultures in which they are immersed. Amid the continuing public debate about children and media, there has been little attempt to access children's voices and perspectives. The research presented here seeks to address this absence, but it does so in a careful and nuanced way. Children's voices and perspectives are not simply out there in the world, awaiting the observation of researchers. On the contrary, research also actively constructs 'the child' in specific ways; and good research is explicit and reflexive about how it does this.

What is especially innovative about this book, however, is that it addresses the constitutive role of media in this process. The studies reported here use a range of media as means of generating and gathering data; and, more importantly, they enable children to make creative use of these media themselves – in effect, to play a greater role in determining how they are to be represented, and in how 'their' data is to be produced, circulated and interpreted. Using such creative, media-based methods has become somewhat fashionable in social research in recent years; but there is often a degree of naivety in how such methods are applied, and the claims that are made about them. As this book makes clear, such methods are by no means straightforward, and they should not be seen simply as a matter of 'empowering' or 'giving voice' to children. On the contrary, as several of the chapters here suggest, these methods raise complex methodological and ethical questions that are probably incapable of easy resolution. Yet in this respect, the book goes beyond simply problematizing, to provide concrete and helpful suggestions for future researchers.

The ways in which academic research plays into public debate are often indirect and mysterious. Yet, if this book can contribute to the demise of simplistic claims about 'digital childhoods', and to the development of a more thoughtful, empirically grounded account of the role of media in children's lives, it will have achieved a very important and necessary aim.

Professor David Buckingham
London, July 2017

Acknowledgements

This book has been an ensemble performance, involving many people working in collaboration over time. We would first like to acknowledge the vital and generous contribution of the young people and families that made the research possible. We would also like to acknowledge both the Economic and Social Research Council (grant reference 512589109) and the Arts and Humanities Research Council (H/M002160/1) for funding our work. The Centre for Innovation and Research in Childhood and Youth and the Sussex Humanities Lab at University of Sussex and the Education Research Centre at the University of Brighton provided a supportive and creative environment for this work. We are also grateful for joint project funding from the Communities and Cultures Network + in support of our Hackathon. An Open Access version of this publication was made possible by the generous support of a Research Councils UK Open Access block grant provided to the University of Sussex.

The project was enriched by our advisory group which includes David Buckingham, Janet Boddy, Ann Phoenix, Jette Kofoed, Susie Weller and Carey Jewitt, as well as our collaborators: Fiona Courage at the Mass Observation Archive and Susi Arnott of Walking Films and photographer Crispin Hughes. We also extend thanks to our hackathon collaborators – Chris Kiefer, Suzanne Rose, Kirsty Pattrick, Anthony McCoubrey, Thanos Liontiris, Ben Jackson, Sarah Leaney and Cathy Grundy. The research team have all been involved in the book in different ways, but we would like to thank Kate Howland, Sue Sharpe, Lucy Hadfield, Ester McGeeney and Mary Jane Kehily for the rich data that they co-produced for the archive and the book. Finally, we acknowledge the contribution of our 'in house' children who have in different ways inspired, critiqued and encouraged our interest in this research area: Milica, Lyra and Isaac. Nothing would be possible without the endless patience and support of Mark Erickson, Louise Berriman and Sean Arnold.

Chapter 4 is based on a journal article originally published as Berriman, L. and Thomson, R. (2015) 'Spectacles of intimacy? Mapping the moral land-scape of teenage social media' *Journal of Youth Studies*, 18(5): 583–597.

Rachel Thomson, Liam Berriman and Sara Bragg

1

Everyday Childhoods: Time, Technology and Documentation

Rachel Thomson, Liam Berriman and Sara Bragg

FIGURE 1.1 *Lucien's Lego camper van*

I ask Lucien to show me something that is more about his past and he takes me upstairs to the room that he and his sister share. Bright colours, fabric, stuff. A beautiful space. He puts onto the spotted bed a camper van made out of Lego. He still plays with Lego, but less than in the past. It used to be his big thing. He made things with his dad. He evaluates the camper van as a car (good quality but slow) rather than as a piece of construction kit. Lucien plays with the van, shows how the interior works, the faults in the design. While in his room, we talk about play. If his friends come over, they tend to play in his room. He explains that he is not the kind of boy that plays online. He is 'calm and quiet'. His mum doesn't like him spending time on his PlayStation and he doesn't understand why. His mum thinks that his dad becomes a kid when he plays on it. Lucien wants to stay a child, he is in no hurry to grow up. He likes to play. But adults also have freedom. They are allowed to go fast. He maps his life so far in terms of speed: starting with buses, moving on to trains and now cars. He expects that next time I see him, he will be into jet fighters. I check whether this is all linked to future careers? No, it's about now. He wants to stay a kid. [Researcher field note, RT]

We begin this book with an extract from a research field note written after a visit with 7-year-old Lucien. The researcher has known Lucien since before he was born, having collaborated with his mother Monica in a study of new motherhood in 2005. Over 12 months, our research followed Lucien between home and school, and shared in his excitement in discovering online search and the computer game Minecraft. Like many parents, Monica expressed concerns about Lucien's 'screen time' and the complicated tangle of educational, social and hedonistic dimensions of digital culture. At the same time, Lucien observed and questioned the boundaries his parents made. Through our research, we observed how Lucien's experiences at home and school shaped his discovery and engagement with technology in his everyday life.

Researching Everyday Childhoods: Time, Technology and Documentation in a Digital Age is a book that explores the role of research in understanding children's lives in a digital age, and the opportunities and challenges this raises. Everyday Childhoods is also the title of a collection of material held in digital form at the Mass Observation Archive. It was made possible by two publicly funded research initiatives that combine methodological and sub-stantive aims (see Appendix 1 for the story of the study). The book explores the dataset, reflects on the methods used to generate it and the insights that arise from thinking with and through it. As a group of researchers, our experience spans the analogue and digital transition, and we are attuned to how recalibrations can be felt in the settings and practices of children's lives. Our endeavour expresses something of the spirit of the age, where researching and curating have become popular practices and where we are challenged to find ways of speaking across the many and ephemeral publics enabled by digital methods. We have attempted to work with the affordances of digital data and methods in order to create a text that is scholarly and analytical, yet which allows the reader to navigate the material on their own terms in conjunction with the archive to which it is so closely connected. For example, if you want to see Lucien's bedroom and hear his own words, you can look at the multimedia animations that are part of this project.[1] The images and the audio provide access to the texture of Lucien's everyday life with an immediacy that text alone does not; however, making meaning of and from such documents is a longer, slower and often painstak-ing task. In this opening chapter, we outline some of the key ideas guiding the interpretations we present in this book, including the idea of the 'every-day' in a digital age, and themes of time, technology and documentation, which provide a focus for our analysis.

Childhood and digital culture

> A decade ago our first multiple-signatory 'toxic childhood' press letter described how children's health and wellbeing were being undermined by the decline of outdoor play, increasingly screen-based lifestyles, a hyper-competitive schooling system and the unremitting commercial-isation of childhood. Despite widespread public concern, subsequent policymaking has been half-hearted, short-termist and disjointedly ineffective.
>
> [extract from multiple signed letter to the *Guardian* newspaper 25 Dec. 2015]

---

[1]See http://modernmothers.org/favs/L/Lucien.html.

We call for research to capture the nuance and detail of engagement with technology and understand *HOW* rather than *HOW MUCH* new technologies should be used. We call for technology developers in the commercial sector to work with academics, educators and families to create digital worlds where children can play and learn in a way which meets their needs and expands their experiences. We call for anyone making pronouncements on child development to support their arguments with quality evidence. We call for parents not to *switch off*, but instead to *switch on* to technology, and engage with their child's digital learning and play.

['A response to "Screen based lifestyle harms children's health"', Fletcher-Watson & Fletcher-Watson, 2016: http://www.dart.ed.ac.uk/ guardian_letter/]

These two extracts come from a letter to *The Guardian* newspaper and a blogged response to that letter. The first is signed by leading UK child psychologists and educationalists and captures how technology has become a focus of concern in relation to child wellbeing, suggesting a causal connection with a range of trends, including rising obesity and declining mental health. Concerned for the future, the commentators look back to past, 'healthier' and outdoor childhoods. The second extract is a critical response to this letter, produced by researchers working in the field of autism, who observe how children's lives can be positively transformed by technology. Challenging the blanket notion of technology's 'toxicity' for childhood, they call for greater 'nuance' and 'detail' in accounts of how children engage and live with digital technologies. These extracts each provide important insights into contemporary debates about children's lives in a digital age within the UK: first, that discussions about children and digital technology have become highly politicized and are routinely contested within the public sphere; second, that these discussions are experienced and responded to by parents and children; and finally, that research can play a vital mediating role in documenting children's everyday experiences in and of a digital world.

Children are the focus of much of the public debate on the impact of digital culture, with anxiety clustering around physical passivity, brain development, sociality, privacy and risk (see Buckingham 2011 for an overview). The speed of technological innovation results in uncomfortable lags and snags between adult claims to authority and the uneven expertise of the young – who are the most intensive users of new media and who can be understood to power much of its content and circulation (Livingstone & Haddon 2009). Moral panics about digital childhoods, grounded or not, become part of a fabric of everyday parenting, schooling and play. Public anxieties about children's digital culture are international in scope – even though children's digital media practices vary across cultural settings (Miller et al. 2016), as do the concerns to which they give rise (Livingstone and Third, 2017). Our study seeks to develop a methodological perspective that is attentive to, and grounded within, the everyday contexts of children's lives and digital practices. Through a focus on 'the everyday' in a UK context we propose a methodological and theoretical framework that can provide a nuanced perspective on children's lives across a range of local-global contexts. Our approach to thinking about the everyday is inspired by a range of intellectual resources that includes both material worlds and the stories we tell about them. The rediscovery of the 'everyday' appears to mark a new interest in the empirical world as a starting point for the generation of theory (Neal & Murji 2015), characterized by a focus on 'moments' (Gabb & Fink 2015), objects (Rinkinen et al. 2015) and specificity (Back 2015). Our approach is particularly indebted to anthropological (Pink 2012) and interactionist (Scott 2009) traditions that focus on the material and phenomenal as the 'stuff' through which sociality and structure are enacted. A focus on the everyday also draws attention to temporality and processes of continuity and rupture though which certain practices travel and others disappear. Duration is one of the main ways that we classify the everyday, tracing the micro-temporalities of the 'craze', through the meso-temporalities of the 'experience', through to the macro-temporalities that underpin habits, routines, demeanours and collective formations such as curricula and traditions.[2]

Documentation also plays a vital mediating role in our experience of time and is a key component of contemporary governance, be it self-administered or institutionally driven. Within childhood studies, it has been argued that there has been an explosion in 'documentalization' of childhood, with growth charts, progression logs and various kinds of portfolios entering streams of interaction, shaping personal and professional practice (Alasuutari & Kelle 2015). Documents give rise to predictive logics that shape as well as reflect behaviour; in Lindsay Prior's terms, documents *do* things as well as contain things.[3] In this project, we are interested in the documentation of childhood in its widest sense: the formal reporting documents created by teachers and social workers, the informal documents created by children and parents (e.g. family albums), the documents and objects that span the home-school-leisure divide. We also recognize ourselves as part of a post-empirical moment within the social sciences, where the documents created with and by researchers (such as field notes) must also be understood as a part of a wider culture of documentation demanding the same kinds of interrogation (Lury & Adkins 2009).

---

[2] See Shove et al. (2009); Gergen (1984).
[3] See Prior (2008); Alatuusari & Kelle (2015); Williamson (2016).

Documentation has also been digitalized. Writing, photography and film each in its time constituted a revolution in documentation, and their democratization over the twentieth century (accelerated by digital methods) shapes how memory is externalized and organized. As the means to document become available to more of us, the structures of feeling that shape our expectations adapt. Roland Barthes's (1981) analysis of 'punctum' – the emotional arrow that connects him and his mother through a single treasured photograph – speaks of a particular moment in the history of the media. Its present-day equivalent might be one of the many 'time-lapse' films now on YouTube that animate a child's maturation from birth to adulthood or condense years' worth of thousands of 'a photo a day' images into a matter of minutes.

From the earliest days of social media, commentators have noted how new opportunities for documentation are associated with unfamiliar temporalities that give rise to new kinds of awkwardness, embarrassment and exposure. A series of moral panics around 'happy slapping' (using the mobile phone to record and display physical assaults), 'fraping' (having one's online identity taken), 'sexting' and 'revenge porn' (sharing and potentially losing control of explicit material) warn of the new kinds of risk associated with the documenting and publishing of self. Each is associated with a temporal lag – and a failure of empathy – expanding the space between a trusting relationship and the moment of regret and humiliation.[4] Commentators have drawn attention to the importance of *non-synchronicity* as an important characteristic of cyberbullying, as well as the problem of *indelibility*, as digital footprints created in the moment accumulate over time, challenging our ability to forget or be forgotten, or simply to shape and reshape our story.[5] As quickly as new technologies of display appear to solve these problems (such as Snapchat, which disappears after a few seconds), so too do technologies of capture (the screenshot) evolve to foil them.

While the risks of personal exposure associated with social media have generated much public concern, there is also growing interest in how the aggregation of self-documentation makes personal privacy vulnerable in new ways.[6] Alice Marwick (2013) has coined the term *attention economy* to characterize teenage social media use, usefully alerting us to the complexity of real and imagined audiences associated with the kinds of documentary practice that appear to be at the centre of young people's culture. Also useful is danah boyd's (2014) idea of *context collapse*, which refers to how the public nature of social media cuts across the moral communities that shape young people's

---

[4]See Turkle (2011, 2015).
[5]For non-synchronicity, see Kofoed (2014). For indelibility see Mayer-Schönberger (2009); Kofoed & Larsen (2016).
[6]Tifentale & Manovich (2015).

worlds (relationships with friends, parents, teachers/ professionals, strangers and acquaintances). The affective power of social media appears to be rooted in the dynamic collisions it can create between concrete local embodied relationships and more mediated relationships online.

We are interested in the ethical hotspots encountered by children, young people and teenagers as they engage in the documentation of everyday life in what Jodi Dean calls an era of communicative capitalism (Dean 2005). By focusing on ordinarily awkward moments as well as more spectacular exposures, we aim to generate tools and methods that may prove useful to others. In Chapter 4, we propose a model of teenage social media use that maps an imperative to participate against an imperative of in/visibility. Social media constitutes a universe in which value is generated by participation and the circulation of content. Such participation may be relatively passive, lurking and liking, or it may be much more active and extend into the creation of content. Once content is created, the question is whether content is controlled and who reaps the reward of the value embedded within it. In the case of sexting for example, the victim loses control of her image and the value is assumed by and between the persons who circulate the image and whose reputations are enhanced by this.[7] However, it is possible to use oneself as content and to gain some of the value that accrues from your audience's attention as the YouTube celebrities demonstrate. There are also less visible forms of participation associated with content creation that are both high status and involve some control over self-image.

Description, as Claudia Castañeda has noted, is a form of ontological politics; it makes a claim to the real (Castañeda 2002: 142). Some of the language we have already used indicates how acutely any attempt to describe children's lives is caught up in such politics. Are we dealing with gaming, friendship and flirting, or addiction, bullying, sexting and porn culture, for example? Our very vocabularies can pathologize, objectify or depoliticize. We recognize how the figure of the child can operate within popular and public culture, mobilized in reactionary ways to secure an idealized and normative future. In this respect, we embrace the queering of childhood studies and the disentangling of notions of development and growth from ideas of becoming and experimentation (Stockton 2009). Any engagement with children's culture is caught within what David Oswell (2013) describes as a double paradigm, in which we are preoccupied by portraying the child as having agency while at the same time understanding that child as caught within a compelling nexus of material and social relations. The approach we have taken in this project does not resolve this tension, but works with a post-empirical but materialist

---

[7]See Ringrose et al. (2013).

orientation to recognize intra-action (Barad 2007) between bodies, identities and material/cultural resources, showing what young people do with these resources and what these materials might do to them, without slipping into a moralizing register. The task is to navigate a path through a contemporary landscape in which cultures are – often highly self-consciously – mediated by class and other social differences. Our methods as well as our theoretical and ethical orientations incline us away from the spectacular (the explicit or idealized images shared on Snapchat and Instagram respectively, for example), or the isolated focus on single products (such as push-up bras for tween girls), towards the creative and often unpredictable improvisations of children's everyday lives in context, in order to emphasize complexity and contingency.

Concepts for a post-digital age

From school whiteboards and tablets to portable game consoles and home televisions, the screen has become a ubiquitous presence in children's everyday spaces and routines. From the outset, the social and moral functions of screens became a focus of our research. As screen technologies have changed, so do the battle lines of fighting over the remote control, sharing devices, negotiating 'screen time', managing the presence of multiple screens, and extending the boundaries of the personal through mobile media that enable us to manipulate our sense of intimacy through sound and vision. As we describe in Chapter 2, the proliferation of screens also shaped our research methodology – prompting choices in our use of mobile devices and the representation of the documents captured by these devices back to participants, forming the basis of a highly layered, reflexive and mediated data set.

Though the term 'screen' is largely identified with electronic media, it also has meaning that is older and broader – referring both to acts of obfuscation (to hide or protect) and presentation (to display or show). These definitions also proved highly pertinent to our study, enabling us to imagine the screen as both a noun ('the screen' as a surface) and as a verb referring to acts of 'screening'. This helped us to interrogate and move beyond assumptions that young people overshare by 'broadcasting' their lives on social media or become socially isolated and awkward by 'hiding behind screens'.[8] Instead, we looked at the ways that screens enable both display and concealment – for example, by sharing photographs taken with friends and family or using a pseudonym whilst publishing fanfiction. Screens also facilitate both connection and disconnection – such as when 'sonic bridges' are forged with friends over Skype whilst playing Minecraft or when the world is

---

[8]In 'Alone Together' (2011), Sherry Turkle claims that digital media provide only an illusion of togetherness and companionship and instead have created greater social disconnection and isolation.

blocked out listening alone to a favourite playlist through a set of headphones. We suggest that the idea of the screen – in all its complexity and ambiguity – helps us to think about young people's lives with flexible affordances of filtering, blocking, distracting, focusing and projecting all potentially in play. The idea of the screen inevitably brings with it questions of audience, reception, public and private, and these themes are elaborated on throughout this book.

The study design on which we draw is both qualitative and longitudinal, capturing both the fast-moving business of discovering and enjoying new toys or crazes, and the slower-moving aspects of changing bodies, changing family formation, moving house and school. It involves two groups of young people: one group of 7/8-year-olds whom researchers have followed since birth and a newly recruited group of teenagers whom we followed over a year. We characterize these as our 'extensive' and 'intensive' panels respectively, a shorthand for the timespans that we access through their participation in the research. Yet this distinction goes beyond our research design, connecting with an analytic vocabulary for understanding how children may be caught up in a digital economy. Here, we draw on the writings of Scott Lash (2010), who uses the distinction to think about how value is created and circulated in a digitally saturated culture. Lash points to brands as an example of how value is generated by 'intensive' acts of creativity and meaning making which are then circulated via extensive systems (e.g. social media channels) which homogenize what was once unique. We can illustrate this idea by looking at ecologies of social media that rely on the creation and circulation of user-generated content. Children and teenagers not only generate much of the content of platforms such as YouTube, but they also power its circulation and the advertising that relies on this.

The language of extensity and intensity can also help us navigate the contours of academic literature on children's digital cultures, which tends to fall into two camps. On one side, we find an alertness to the spectre of 'creeping connectivity' and a concern with how digitization operates as a mode of governance, often in the form of metrics which in turn drive action. This concern with the extensive dimensions of digital childhood can be found in research on the data-driven school that produces children as data subjects.[9] On the other hand, there is a body of work that encourages us to follow the volatile traces of digital practices and the affective qualities of digital temporalities that shape teenage sociality.[10] A vocabulary of *intensity* helps us to tune into moments and practices that are affectively thick and redolent with potential, while a vocabulary of extensity alerts us to practices, connections and classifications

---

[9]For example, see Beer (2016); Finn (2016); Lupton & Williamson (2017).
[10]For example, see Staunæs & Kofoed (2015); Harvey & Ringrose (2015); Davies (2015).

that connect us to larger grids and systems of meaning. In our analyses, we notice both these aspects of digital culture as well as their entanglements in the everyday lives of children and young people.

Lash argues that today's global informational culture is characterized by coming together of intensive and extensive systems with a 'substance becoming system' and the emergence of 'intensive materialities' (2010: 69). Digital culture is no longer contained by screens, it saturates all aspects of everyday life and increasingly will be embedded in the everyday through the internet of things. One way of capturing this has been through the concept of the *post-digital*, which moves our attention away from technology, the screen and representations towards new forms of life and environment.[11] Madianou and Miller (2012) use the concept of 'polymedia' to capture how everyday life has become saturated by the multiplication of screens and media platforms. They argue that in a polymedia culture, the choice of medium for interpersonal communications is no longer determined by location or cost, but by 'the implications ... for personal and moral responsibility' (2012: 171). These are ideas that move us away from questions of access and the language of 'media poor and rich' or 'natives and immigrants', in order to imagine a near future where unlimited WIFI connections and a multiplicity of devices enable constant connection and the emergence of a range of practices that assume contactability and co-presence through a digital leash.

Polymedia and post-digitality are provocative ideas rather than empirical realities, with access and uptake continuing to be uneven and shaped by both national infrastructure and parenting culture.[12] While most of the younger children in this study had some access to digital devices, their social and play worlds were predominantly embodied and face to face. The teenagers, however did enjoy the kinds of privacy and separation that online forms of communication provided, as well as engaging with the kinds of research potential made available by digital search facilities. For this generation, something happens between 7 and 13, and our longitudinal design allowed us to capture how these new spaces and possibilities were encountered. Timing matters, and the pegging of 'development' to technology is highly contingent. Family interviews revealed the perceived inequities experienced by siblings complaining that rules for an eldest child had become less lenient when others reached the same age. Birthdays and other gift-giving festivals often heralded

---

[11]See Berry & Dieter (2015).
[12]The EU Kids Online project, which carried out survey research with 25,000 children across 25 European countries, found that the opportunities and risks of children's technology use were dependent on factors ranging from existing national infrastructures (e.g. availability of broadband), curricula in schools (e.g. ICT and e-safety) and parenting styles/relationships (see Livingstone & Haddon 2009).

a new stage of life; old forms of sociality became redundant as new devices irrevocably changed the cultural landscape for individuals and families.

Starting with the archive

We are living in an age of 'archival proximity', where easy access to vast digital archives transform our relationship with knowledge and the past. Within both popular and academic culture, this is associated with a 'turn to time', including 'retro-mania' and a new enthusiasm for archival practices, methods and ethics.[13] In this project, we have started rather than ended with the archive, collaborating with young people and their families to create public documents of their everyday lives. We have also invited them into the archive to see how their data is stored and to imagine future users and audiences. Together, we are involved in what Noortje Marres (2012) calls 'redistributed' networks of knowledge production that in our case involves funders, participants, their families, researchers, archivists, readers and secondary users. This book attempts to make all these stakeholders visible. Our aim has been to create a text that works as a stand-alone volume, yet which operates in connection and conversation with the Everyday Childhoods archive. The digital dataset has two forms: the open access multimedia case studies that were compiled, edited and published online in collaboration with our participants[14] and the full data set which is deposited at the Mass Observation Archive, both in an anonymized format (available on request) and in a non-anonymized form, embargoed for future use. By exploring the potentialities of the e-book form, we have been able to integrate some multimedia into the text, yet are aware of the problems that this may produce in terms of functionality and potential obsolescence linked to the propriety formats within which the material is presented.

In thinking about how the material for this project is mediated, we have worked with ideas of raw and cooked data as a continuum. Raw data refers to documents in their most basic state. For us, this involves audio recordings, visual records and field notes – all of which we have endeavoured to capture in the highest quality formats that are less vulnerable to decay or obsolescence. This is the data that cannot and arguably should not be anonymized, access to which is restricted to the primary research team until the expiry of an embargo. To be 'raw' does not mean that this data is 'naturally occurring' – interviews

---

[13]For `archival proximity', see Eichhorn (2013). For the `turn to time', see McLeod & Thomson (2009). For `retromania', see Reynolds (2011). For new academic interest in archives, see McLeod & Thomson (2009); Savage (2010); Moore et al. (2016).
[14]The multimedia case studies and other materials can be accessed on the project's website: http://blogs.sussex.ac.uk/everydaychildhoods.

and research encounters are complicated and staged interactions that demand deconstruction in their own right. The terminology of 'cooking' refers to the process through which documents are selected, compiled and edited into larger wholes.[15] So, for example, the multimedia case studies are 'cooked', meaning that they are synthetic texts created with and through content management software (such as Prezi) to present one particular 'story' from the 'archive' of material on which they draw. These 'cooked' texts fix material in a moment in time, revealing the tools available to researchers, the wider genres on which they draw and the preoccupations that shape academic agendas. In self-consciously creating a data set for posterity, we have paid particular attention to the lessons emerging from the secondary analysis of archived data sets: for example, that the researcher is a key part of the data set and that future researchers are likely to read the archive in very different ways than the original research team.[16] In Chapter 9, Jette Kofoed with Rachel Thomson, a member of the project advisor panel, engages with some of the Everyday Childhoods material as a secondary analyst to demonstrate some of the challenges this can entail.

In writing this book, we are attempting to negotiate several tasks and a complicated timeline – speaking to contemporaneous audiences about children's everyday cultures and engaging with emergent debates about digital methods for social research, while also imagining the afterlife of this project as a historical resource for future researchers. In extending our imagination in this way, we – like teenagers concerned (or warned) that their social media activity might intervene in a future job interview – are vaguely aware of future audiences, our senses heightened by a sense of the difference that time makes to the relationship between context and object/subject.[17]

---

[15]The distinction between the raw (natural) and cooked (cultural) is taken from the anthropology of Lévi-Strauss (1969), and was taken up within digital history by Daniel Cohen (2004) to distinguish between the raw 'documents, information and communications that are heterogeneous and that have little, if any, organization' and cooked 'digital history takes such historical materials and adds helpful markings and a measure of homogeneity' (2004: 337). We encountered this idea through the work of historian Lucy Robinson in discussion of the digital learning resource 'Observing the 80s' https://blogs.sussex.ac.uk/observingthe80s/. The distinction between raw and cooked as an aspect of digital data is subject to vociferous debate in that it can hide the post-structural insight that the raw is always already cooked (see, e.g., Gitelman (2013).

[16]For revisiting studies, see Burroway (2003); Savage (2011); Salmon and Reissman (2008). For discussions of the ethics arising from this, see Mauthner (2012); Gillies & Edwards (2012); Crow, G. (2012); Morrow et al. (2014).

[17]For discussion of the practices of recontextualization that is part of the historical method and how this is s site of tension between historical and sociological epistemologies, see Niamh Moore (2006).

The book is made up of a series of chapters that are inspired by the dataset, and which make original contributions to a series of substantive themes in the study of children's cultures as well as demonstrating methodological innovation. There is no neat demarcation between methodology and findings in this project. We are attuned to what our methods allow us to see – maintaining this reflexivity and specificity in the way we present our insights. The chapters are also polyvocal, reflecting the insights and interests of the broad research team involved in this project. Individual researchers write in their own name, focusing attention on a particular analysis that they have made of the data set or reflecting on a concept or theme on which the project sheds light. Chapters also take different formats, including conversations between collaborators and more discursive analyses in which data and interpretation are integrated. Our vision for this project is that the Everyday Childhoods archive can operate as a platform around which a community of interpretation can form and develop. In making the data set open and transparent in the way we have, we invite others to interrogate the material and to contribute to methodological and conceptual debate. While the book is a highly resilient, flexible and enduring form, it tends not to invite collaboration, interaction or debate. We encourage readers to explore the full range of multimedia case studies that sit alongside the book and to access the data set themselves – either as a resource for teaching or secondary analysis – and to contribute themselves to the Everyday Childhoods collection. The book that follows offers a new direction for childhood studies in the twenty-first century, making sense of how children are at the heart of new ways of living and researching. It makes its claims based on a unique and significant data set and an exceptional body of methodological and conceptual development. While the moment at which we have captured children's cultures will soon pass, we hope that the ideas and approaches forged in this book will have an enduring relevance for the field.

2

Recipes for Documenting Everyday Lives and Times

Rachel Thomson with Susi Arnott, Lucy Hadfield, Mary Jane Kehily and Sue Sharpe

During our event at the Mass Observation Archive at which we invited parents and young participants to reflect on what it meant to preserve their data for the future, we asked the young people, by way of a warm up exercise, to tell us their favourite food. Nathan (14) said 'pizza', to which his mother reacted with an exclamation somewhere between hurt, anger and disappointment. Catching my eye, she said 'not his mother's cooking!'
[Researcher reflective memo, SB]

A cooking metaphor runs throughout this book, with the distinction between 'raw' and 'cooked' helping us think about how lives are documented, and how these documents are then represented having their own material effects. As the opening extract suggests, cooking is not an innocent metaphor: choices are laden with moral meaning and market romance. Nathan may have preferred the relative anonymity of locating himself within globalized youth food cultures than anything too specific to his family, in that public context. His mother's reaction reminds us that methods have unintended (and sometimes painful) consequences too, to which we need to remain vigilant. In this chapter, we use the culinary metaphor to present the three methods employed in the project, offering these as 'recipes': revealing the resources necessary to use them (ingredients), the steps involved in preparation, data generation as well as data analysis and representation (cooking the data). The methodological innovation involved in this longitudinal project has been ground breaking yet each of these recipes has a particular lineage, having evolved in practice through experience and inspiration. Each recipe is contextualized with a backstory of how it came to us and how it sits within a wider methodological literature. Like all recipes, it is very difficult to do something entirely 'new', yet, each generation reinvents its dishes, giving the old recipes a contemporary twist while paying their dues to a tradition in which they stand. Read in conjunction with the story of the study (Appendix 1), this chapter both authorizes the methods through which the Everyday Childhoods data set was generated and demonstrates the potential of digital methodologies for the co-production of new kinds of knowledge.

The favourite things method

Practical ethical complexity: medium/low
Good for: documenting material culture, personal identity, parenting culture,
Temporal range: the past, biography and cumulative time as embodied in
    objects/ domestic interiors.

Origins and sources

As a discipline, anthropology has been most attuned to material culture and the ways in which 'things' and 'stuff' may express the organizing categories of our symbolic universe (Lévi-Strauss 1978), circulate as gifts or tokens of value (Mauss 1950), be recontextualized over time and space (Appadurai 1986) and act as the concrete sites of ordinary affects (Stewart 2007). In recent years, anthropologist Daniel Miller has popularized interest in domestic interiors and homes as a way of thinking about contemporary culture, and Sarah Pink has captured our enthusiasm for narrating our homes (Miller 2010; Pink 2012). Cultural studies has also been alert to the importance of objects as routes into our moral universes – such as Hoggart's (1957) meditation on the rag rugs of working class parlours – but also as carriers of dynamic social meaning that get redeployed over time, for example, the punk appropriation of the swastika described by Hebdige (1979). Cultural sociologists pioneered the practice of following the 'thing', connecting stages of production and consumption in the 'biography of the object' (du Gay & Hall 1996) – and drawing on post-humanist philosophies to provide concepts such as 'assemblage' and 'actant' that transcend the human-object divide (e.g. Mol & Law 2002).

Within gender studies, attention has been paid to the preservative practices of home-making. Iris Marion Young observes that 'women trace the family lines and keep safe the trinkets, china cups, jewellery, pins and photos of departed ancestors, ready to tell stories about them' (2005: 132). These stories have been collected by feminist researchers such as Annette Kuhn (2002), Jo Spence (1986), Susan Stewart (1984), Carol Smart (2007) and Rachel Hurdley (2013), who see photo albums, souvenirs, heirlooms and mantle-pieces as starting points for the study of intimacies and often unspoken stories of class, social mobility and gender trouble. The materialist turn of the new millennium has reenchanted the 'object' across the humanities and social sciences (Brown 2001), giving rise to ideas such as 'vibrant matter', an affective current that transcends the human/ non-human distinction (Bennett 2010), and 'technicity', which conceptualizes the human and their tool together (Stiegler 1998). Sherry Turkle suggests that 'things' are good to think with, operating as 'common and 'concrete' ground for interdisciplinary conversation between 'physicians and philosophers, psychologists and designers, artists and engineers' (Turkle 2007: 8). This is something recognized in a range of practice traditions were objects are understood to facilitate play and reflection, bringing into symbolization that which may not yet have been previously voiced (Vygotsky 1976; Bollas 1987; Lucas 1992). Echoes of such practices can be seen in research techniques that either combine doing and telling (such as the walk and talk) or use visual and material prompts within interview settings (see Rose 2011 for overview).

As a research team, we first experimented with using objects as a part of a 10-year study of young people's transitions to adulthood, where we built on methods used in social work and adoption practice to create a 'memory book' technique where participants gathered and shared mementos collected over a 6-month period and shared these in an interview (Thomson & Holland 2005). In a study of new motherhood, we invited grandmothers to choose objects that represented their past, present and futures as a basis for in-depth interviews – discovering that this approach resulted in emotionally rich encounters and narratives (Thomson 2012). In this study, we adapted the method for children and teenagers, inviting them to share some of their 'favourite things' from the past and present, documented their accounts using digital recorded sounds and images.

Ingredients

- Skilled researcher
- Digital recorder
- Digital camera
- 2 hours – 1 hour interview and 1 hour field notes

Preparation

From the outset, our intention was to create a multimedia output that brought to life the young people's favourite things. Based on a pilot interview and working in collaboration with our media consultants we identified the following as key goals for the fieldwork:

- Wide-angle 'canvas' photo with favourite things in shot
- Close-ups of each favourite thing
- Audio recording of interview
- Sounds of favourite things if relevant
- Audio 'atmos'

In advance of the favourite thing interview, we communicated with participants and parents for the younger group, asking that they 'choose two special objects to discuss (they could be real or digital), one that represents your past and one that represents the present/future. These will be a starter for conversation and the conversation will be recorded.'

Generating the data

Interviews generally were arranged to take place at the homes of participants for the sake of their convenience, as it was anticipated that the 'favourite things' were likely to be at home. With the younger children, our interview to discuss their favourite things turned into a guided tour of their bedroom, with special and favourite toys and objects explained. The focus on past and future tended to be understood in terms of toys they no longer play with and toys that are current favourites. The researchers quickly adapted to the broadening of focus and the way children appeared to interpret the task as an invitation to play. This was especially true of the time spent with 7-year old Tempest (see Chapter 6), during which she and the researcher work their way through a series of toys through which she communicates her preoccupations and pleasures in a vivid but indirect way. Others explain or narrate their belongings to researchers, noting salient points such as how they acquired the toy, what its functionality was/how it was played and whether it was a current favourite or how it had gone out of favour.

No matter how the children approached the task, the result was always illuminating, providing researchers with a window into their play worlds and a sense of the people and places of importance to them. The research team have worked with and through the category 'play' as a way of thinking about young people's expressive cultures and their participation in the research process. Piaget famously described play as 'the work of childhood', the practice through which development is secured, including the transition from freewheeling fantasy of early years where rules are self-imposed, to the conformist game playing of middle childhood and game making of adulthood (Piaget 1951). Play has also been understood as a window into children's inner worlds, operating as a therapeutic practice and a route to talk about trauma (Bettelheim 1987). Finally, play has been seem as providing insight into the collective cultures of children which constitute a dynamic yet preservative 'tradition' (Opie & Opie 1959; Burn & Richard 2014) and a space for creativity, adaptation and interpretation (Corsaro 1992; Marsh & Bishop 2014).

Through this method, we have also gained insights into the importance of the child's bedrooms as a site of collaborative identity making – ephemeral in character, remade over time yet memorialized through documentation (see also Lincoln 2012, Edwards & Weller 2010). Not all children invited us into their bedrooms, and for some, the bedroom was now considered redundant as a play space, filled as it was with the 'old', with the exciting new action being in shared spaces of the home. The invitation to share favourite things was received in quite a different way by our teenage participants, who were more focused on the significance of the distinction between past and present/future. The extent to which young people put thought and effort into their selection varied. Jasmine, for example, improvised with objects to hand – grabbing her latest favourite lipstick to represent 'now'. Others such as Aliyah had put much thought into the project of curating her own youth independently of our interest and shared with us a 'memory box' that she had prepared earlier (see Chapter 5 for a full discussion). Age made a difference to how young people responded to the invitation, but it was not the only, nor the most important, factor in play.

Cooking the data: Methods of analysis

The data generated through the favourite thing method includes photographs of the objects and their setting, audio recording of the interview, 'sound effects' from the object and researcher field notes reflecting on the encounter. All of this constitutes 'raw' data that is used for analysis and that is deposited in the archive. These are the ingredients that are drawn on for the 'cooked' multimedia documents that are made publically available. The process we followed in making these was as follows:

1   Transcribe the interviews and organize/label the audio and visual documents.

2   Convene an analysis workshop involving research team and advisors. Transcripts were read by participants in advance of the workshop. At the workshop, audio and visual material was screened and each case was discussed in turn, focusing first on younger, then older cohorts. Our focus was on sharing our affective and intellectual responses to the material, discussing similarities and differences between the cases and identifying emergent themes from the data.

3   Raw materials were then used to create favourite things multimedia documents, which were drafted and edited in consultation with researchers and participants and their families before being published. For the younger cohort, we worked in collaboration with professional media consultants who used Pano-2VR software and its panorama-style canvas to create the child's bedroom, within which were embedded short audio clips linked to images of favourite things. These documents were then integrated into a public website showcasing the Making Modern Mothers research project.[1] Documentation of teenagers' favourite things was integrated into DIY multimedia documents created by the research team using Prezi software. Both sets of documents were made available via the Everyday Childhoods website. Here, our professional media collaborator Susi Arnott comments on this process from her perspective:

'Meetings included some brief but enjoyable training sessions on digital photography and audio recording. Researchers then collected interviews with children describing their "favourite things" (almost always toys), along with sound effects, photographs of the individual items and a "wide angle" and/or "panoramic" photograph of the interview space containing them. There were unspoken assumptions in our "wish-list". First, that the "favourite things" would all be in one place, would be individual objects of a manageable size (rather than, say, a PowerPoint presentation, a concept like "getting up in the morning", a story or an entire playground) and available to photograph at the time of the visit. Secondly, that the researcher's interview with the child could be recorded without too much accompanying sound; radio and television/ video game noise, as well as other speakers' interjections sometimes confused the audio and made editing problematic. We also might not have communicated well enough with researchers about the desire for the "things" to occupy real or at least possible "places" in the wide angle or "panoramic" photograph. However, the end results – again using the Pano2VR interface – were

---

[1]See the 'Making Modern Mothers' website http://modernmothers.org/.

pleasing. It was a joy to hear these children speak! The interviews and sound effects were edited into short pieces to accompany the photos; as before, a mouse-click on a photo would "pop it up" larger, and play the sound file.' (Susi Arnott, 'Notes on method' 2014)

4   Raw and cooked data was then deposited at the Mass Observation Archive.

Reflections on the method

The favourite things method was the first in a sequence of methods to be employed in the study and proved to be an ideal way of establishing or renewing relationships with participants. Certainly, for the teenage group, it allowed a degree of control over the research agenda – enabling them to direct discussion. Moreover, talking about and through 'things' could provide a less intense way of talking about oneself. Younger participants also embraced the method; however, the invitation to narrate objects tended to be interpreted as an invitation to play, which was productive, and yet presented its own challenges for analysis and interpretation. In general terms, the notion that things can be 'favourites', and that this changes over time, resonated with our participants, who were able to discuss issues of obsolescence, personal identity and growth in relation to the material culture. Technology is one marker of change, and the method made explicit the significance of broken and obsolete objects, which became a focus for our analysis (see Chapter 5).

The favourite thing method captures how time is held in and through material objects (Hohti 2015) and the durational project of documenting material culture as bedrooms are reconfigured and toys adapted, disavowed or archived. The method is temporally sensitive, providing a route into the slow temporalities of family life carried by 'heirlooms' as well as the unfolding present that is made manifest in changing domestic interiors (Pink 2012). Objects could be forward facing providing a scaffold into the future, but could also operate as sites of revealing personal and technological change. We were fascinated by the ways in which the teenage cohort already expressed 'nostalgia' for their own childhoods, as well as the way in which objects passed between generations were treated with reverence by very young children, acutely aware that they were connecting with intimate traces of parents and grandparents. We can think of these research encounters as a three-way conversation in which the 'third thing' has an active part to play (Bollas 1987, Thomson 2014). Objects are emotionally 'evocative' in complex ways. Participants can exercise considerable control over what is discussed through the choice of the object. However, favourite things can also carry intense and unspoken feelings, which inevitably arise in the interview context, demanding respect and space within the research process. Our analytic process worked with the affective dimensions of the data, exploring these interviews as encounters and following the emotional responses of researchers as well as interviewees through the analysis and into our writing.

The 'day in a life' method

Practical ethical complexity: medium/ high
Good for: documenting mundane everyday practices, routines, atmospheres
Temporal range: the day

Origins and sources

A focus on ordinary and everyday practices has been a key element of ethnographic research traditions, with anthropologists and sociologists attempting to 'tag along' with informants as they go about their daily business. An assumption of this method is that researchers need to participate in many days in order to grasp meanings behind collective routines. The focus on a single day has a different genealogy, which we would trace back to the early Mass Observation project devised by anthropologist Tim Harrison, poet Charles Madge and filmmaker Humphrey Jennings – which, among other things, invited a panel of 200 untrained 'observers' to document the coronation of George VI and Queen Elizabeth on 12 May 1937. Together, these documentary fragments formed a polyvocal montage of a shared historical moment combining public and private sentiments. Since then, Mass Observation have regularly invited the public to contribute diaries documenting their activities on 12 May, contributing to a vast archive of 'the everyday' that has become a treasure trove for historians, artists, novelists and other secondary analysts. The original Mass Observation was arguably ahead of its time, foreseeing the participatory and documentary potential of what was 'mechanical' media.[2]

The 'day in a life' has also emerged as a key genre of self-documentary in digital popular culture, providing an accessible and cheap window into human commonalities and cultural differences. The genre is capacious, with the relationship between uniquely unfolding lives and our common implication in a shared calendar /clock time, digital platforms and other extensive systems. One life many days; one life one day; one life different days; many lives many

---

[2]As part of the Curating Childhoods stage of this project, we worked with the Mass Observation Archive to invite children and young people to contribute to the 12 May mass observation 'diary day' in 2014.

days[3] – each animates, juxtaposes and abstracts the everyday into public facing modes of display.

Our interest in this as a research method began with our research on motherhood and our wish to get beyond narratives of mothering to an engagement with the situated practices that mothering involves. In particular, we wanted to document the *work* of mothering which is so often implicit and invisible. Drawing on 'work shadowing' methods developed in organizational research, we spent a day with mothers asking them to describe and explain what might be taken for granted practices and routines (Thomson et al. 2012). Our approach was also influenced by the quality of observation and description developed within the tradition of psychoanalytic child observation and attempts to extend these from a training method to a tool for research (Urwin and Sternberg 2012, Thomson et al. 2012, Hollway 2015). Lessons were integrated into a reflexive and sensitive ethnographic mode, involving the production of detailed reflective field notes supported by the use of digital photographs taken as aide memoires throughout the day. The field notes were produced as 'thick descriptions' combining a moment-by-moment account with reflections on researchers' responses and tentative interpretations. Initially written for members of the research team, these accounts became increasingly public as we shared them with fellow researchers and with participants.

By the time we came to use the method with children and teenagers five years later, we were much more attuned to the affordances of digital media, the role of the archive and the relationship between research and popular practices of documentary. We also had the benefit of a burgeoning tradition of child led ethnographic methods (Johnson et al. 2014). From the outset, we invited participants to collaborate with us in the creation of public documents and a special collection within the Mass Observation Archive. By literally walking alongside participants, we hoped to understand how the digital infuses everyday practices including those that are face to face. As before, we generated researcher field notes and photographs, but this time with the knowledge that they would be shared. We also documented audio 'soundscapes' with the

---

[3] *One day many lives,* as exemplified by the 'Life in a Day' documentary shot by filmmakers all over the world 'that serves as a time capsule to show future generations what it was like to be alive on the twenty-fourth of July, 2010' (IMBD);

One life, one day: a common media genre portraying different jobs – for example, an interactive 'day in a life' of a social worker as created by the Open University http://www.open.edu/openlearn/body-mind/social-care/social-work/try-day-the-life-social-worker, or experiences, for example, a day in life with Downs Syndrome http://www.adayinthelifewithdownsyndrome.com/.

One life different days: repeating the methodology over time with same person – this might be a research approach or popular (e.g. vlogger).

Many days, many lives: using the format of the day as way to bring diverse situations into comparable view. For example, comparing the days of children around the world, for example, by contributors to imgur https://blog.imgur.com/2016/07/07/a-day-in-the-life/.

intention of integrating them into multimedia documents. Participants were encouraged to produce their own 'day in a life' documents, and we were able to explore the relationship between these and those led by researchers.

Our temporal focus throughout has continued to be the single day, capturing time related routines and practices, movements between spaces and changes in atmospheres. In practice, we found it impractical to negotiate access to the full 24 hours (though see Kousholt (2015) who included a sleep-over in her research with young children). Our observations were not synchronized, but were timed to fit with the schedules of families and researchers. In practice, they took place mostly during the winter, with rain and cold a common motif. Early and late morning starts gave rise to ethical and practical challenges as explored below.

Ingredients

- An experienced researcher, willing and available for a very long day
- A digital sound recorder
- A digital camera
- A packed lunch
- A note book

Preparation

This was the second method used in the study and we negotiated informed consent in advance, explaining in detail what the method involves and talking through issues of confidentiality and anonymity – both as it affects the participants and others who may unwittingly become part of the research – for example, teachers or other children at school. This is a method that involves a high level of trust, and the families with previous experience of the method were better able to make sense of what the request entailed.

Generating the data

We tried to arrive early and to show, explain and get to grips with the equipment involved. Our intention was to use photography and audio recordings to document settings and events as they happened. Along with jotted notes, these would operate as aide memoires for writing thick descriptions of the day. Here is an example of the 'beginning of a day in a life' from researcher Ester's account of her day with Jasmine:

> When I arrive the front door is slightly open. I knock anyway and Jasmine opens to door. I can see baby R in a baby seat in the living room crying and ahead there is a man in the kitchen cooking. Jasmine is in grey leggings and a vest top and after opening the door returns to the kitchen where she has been making up three bottles for R. As I walk through the hallway I see that Jasmine says something to the guy in the kitchen and he glances at me and nods. I get the impression he didn't know that I was coming. I say hi and introduce myself. He says hello but doesn't introduce himself in return.

We understood and communicated our role as 'shadowing'. Typically, this entailed travelling with our participant to school or college and then being there during lessons and breaks before travelling together back home and staying until our welcome expires. Each time a change in setting occurs, the researcher has to renegotiate their presence. Ester takes a taxi with Jasmine to school and records the conversation between them. In the following extract, the researcher Sara tries to keep up with Abi and her friend on their walk to school:

> They off at quite a pace, with me trailing behind trying to record the sound of their footsteps and worrying about my own being too loud until I remind myself that I don't actually have to be invisible and inaudible. They talk together in the low, intimate murmurs of female companionship, fragments floating towards me: 'did you see …? They were just like … She was like … That must be really annoying!'

The presence of the research within institutions such as schools had to be negotiated with the institutional gatekeepers, the in-situ professionals (class teachers), the young person who we were following and the rest of the class. Keeping the young person 'in view' and 'in focus' could be a struggle for the researcher, whose attention might be distracted by pupils and teachers. Here, researcher Rachel struggles to keep Lucien in view in a busy classroom.

> 9.50 'Year 3, you are being a little bit noisy now. Back to tables'. The main event is over, the children move back to their tables and the atmosphere relaxes. Mr B resolves a knotty moment 'lets not worry about rubbers today, cross it out'. Lots of counting on fingers and the children work through a series of problems. I notice that Lucien is physically tiny. A girl comes over to the table nearest me, K, 'am I invited to your party? 'Chatting and working away. Is anyone struggling Mr B asks. Hands shoot up, 'I'm struggling with 79 divided by 5' – ask your neighbour to help you, and the conversation

goes back to maths. 'K, you like to be given the answer without trying. You can do it!'.

The 'day in a life' method is demanding of researchers and of participants. It seems to have been perceived as more 'awkward' for teenagers, who tended to choose a non-school day to be observed. Younger children seemed more comfortable with the way that the methods made them the centre of attention, but arguably had less control over the schedule, as parents and researchers negotiated what was most interesting or convenient for them. The research gaze could generate a kind of temporary 'celebrity' within the context of the school, which may be both pleasurable and disruptive.

> Lucien wants to spend the last part of lunch in the book room, it is a classroom where they can spend time inside reading. He picks out a book, and the lunchtime organiser explains that Lucien is a regular visitor showing me a long row of ticks on his register. We sit down and I ask him some questions about school uniform [audio 28]. This is in a proper 'interview' style and is noticed by a classmate who says in a sing-song voice 'Lucien is a superstar'. He seems pleased. 1pm, times up, back to the class. [Researcher fieldnote RT]

Shadowing might also be experienced as a pressure, encouraging participants to fill their day with activity that might not be usual. While we recognize that activities like visiting the shopping centre were quite possibly staged for the research, they were the kind of special events that were nevertheless part of young people's routines. Our methods also enabled us to pick up the slow times of relaxing, hanging out and even sleeping, that filled young people's leisure time. Here, researcher Liam struggles to stay awake with Fumni:

> Funmi switches into a lying position on the sofa, propping the iPad up with her hand so that it's facing her. I realise up until now Funmi has been sitting upright the entire time, with her feet on the floor. I also realise that most of the day has been spent in just the living room and kitchen. Funmi continues to watch videos but I realise she looks like she's about to nod off.

The ending of the observation was something negotiated between the researcher, the young person and, to an extent, with parents/ carers. Rachel 'lost' Lucien immediately after school as he went off with a friend for a playdate to which she was not invited. In other situations, observations continued well into the evening, with researchers invited to eat with families and sometimes being drawn into bedtime routines – for example, as researcher

Sue was with Gabriel. The length of the observation depended on a range of factors including the access offered by the family and the endurance of the researcher themselves. Our approach was one of trying to spend as much of the day with participants as was feasible or comfortable. Where researchers had on-going relationships with families, this could make a difference to the duration and quality of the observation.

Cooking the data: Analysis and representation

Our approach to data analysis involved:

1   Production of reflective field notes that narrate the 'day in a life' and which contextualize the digital documents produced (for us, this was sound files and digital photographs)

2   These documents were then brought together and looked at comparatively across the sample in a data analysis workshop that included the full research team and project advisers. The aim of these workshops was to identify similarities and differences between the days and to capture what it was that the method made visible and what it eclipsed. Our discussions were guided by research questions.

3   Alongside this process, we worked with our media partners to both identify a method for representing the 'day in a life' cases in multimedia. This involved producing a pilot that was shared as part of the analysis workshop, highlighting synergies and tensions between social science analytic and documentary narrative approaches.

4   Draft 'day in a life' multimedia showcases were created for each case using the Prezi software, and these were shared with participants alongside a full 'day in a life' description. Changes were made to the multimedia showcase in line with participant comments in order that the documents could be made 'public' through the project archive.

5   Project members then worked with the 'raw' documents as well as the 'cooked' multimedia showcases in further analysis.

6   Project participants were invited to visit the Mass Observation archive to better understand the distinctions between 'raw' and 'cooked' data, to think through potential secondary analysis of the data set and to consider ethical key issues including confidentiality, anonymity, consent and the role of the archivist in acting as an agent for the original research team. The workshop was documented and short films created to share the learning.

7 Participants were invited to conduct their own' day in a life'
documentary and these were added to the multimedia showcase.

Reflections on the method

One of the strengths of this method was how it enabled us to capture movement between face-to-face and digital communication, revealing the layered
character of virtual and physical worlds. So, for example, researcher Liam sits
with Aliyah in her bedroom observing how she moves from doing her homework using online resources through checking Twitter and Facebook before
some light relief watching YouTube videos. His field notes record the interaction and the URLs, and reference the sound and visual documents that he is
making:

> 12:20 – Aliyah switches to YouTube and starts browsing through various
> channels and pages. She says she's going to watch some videos for a bit
> and asks if she should she put headphones on. I say she shouldn't for my
> sake, and that I'd quite like to hear them. She warns me before the first
> video starts that the girl on the video is 'probably going to scream'. As she
> starts to watch the video it gets stuck and Aliyah says 'oh no, it's going
> to buffer'. The video then starts playing again. Aliyah turns down the vol-
> ume a bit and remains seated on the floor by her bed watching the video
> (photos 13 & 14). The first YouTube video is of an American college girl
> discussing popularity at school – making various humorous observations
> that Aliyah occasionally laughs at (sound 8). The video is edited so that
> after each humorous comment the girl makes there is a sudden switch of
> camera angle and the colour of the video repeatedly switches between
> black & white and colour. I try to keep track of the videos that Aliyah
> is watching, but miss the first two. The second video Aliyah watches is
> of a pair of young American teens doing a series of comedy sketches
> showing how well known phrases might be taken literally such as 'spill-
> ing the beans' and 'breaking the ice' (sound 9). Occasionally Aliyah skips
> through bits of the video. I ask how she finds the YouTube videos that she
> wants to watch and she says mostly through subscriptions to particular
> channels.
> 12:30 – H comes into the room while Aliyah watches a third video. H sits
> on the edge of the double bed and ends up watching the video too. The
> video is of 'Nash Greer', a young American YouTuber, with his four-year-old
> sister. Greer asks his sister various questions for comic effect – such as
> what her favourite colour is and how many people she thinks will watch the
> video (sound 10, photo 14). Both H and Aliyah laugh at the video. Once the

video has finished H asks Aliyah whether she's still doing her homework. Aliyah says 'no', she's 'procrastinating'.

Later, we are able to 'reanimate' this material in such a way that we experience the felt interaction between online and offline activity.[4]

Our location in the offline world meant that participants could screen us out, for example, by use of headphones – a busy couple of hours online can from the 'outside' look like empty time on the sofa or at the screen. Nevertheless, using traditional ethnographic methods of participant observation facilitates an understanding of the digital as synthesized within routines. The 'day in a life' approach sensitized us to the part played by technologies at different times of day, with lulls during the school day and crescendos of intensity on return home and into bedtime. It also revealed the practices of multitasking that characterize the doing of homework, for example, where chat, news, research and play co-exist – as well as the ways in which everyday forms of documentation can be understood as techno-practices of care. Young people's self-documentaries also captured aspects of their online activity from the 'outside' in a similar way to our researcher observations, but using film and the standard features of fades and inter-titles that are part of iMovie and Moviemaker programmes.

The 'day in a life' is the epitome of a mobile method – building on ethnographic strategies such as 'walk and talk', it allows for the narration of practice and focuses attention on movement between the different spaces in young people's lives alerting researchers to changes in atmosphere and environment (Ross et al. 2009; Muir & Mason 2013). We can think of it as an experiential or sensory method, facilitating a sense of how the accumulation of the day may be experienced by the young person (Thompson et al. 2010). So, for example, it sensitized us to the relentless pedagogy in Saffron's day and of pain management in Sean's day – aspects that may have been difficult to grasp through other approaches. The priority given to description and researcher subjectivity in the production of reflective field notes also means that it can be a psycho-social method. So, for example, we have been able to think about the part played by the researcher in the production of the scene itself (Thomson & Baraitser 2017 forthcoming), and to work with researcher discomfort as a starting point for analysis – as, for example, in researcher Sara's strong responses to the school setting in Abi's day.

The teacher speeds up his rotation and a kind of banter: 'you've written the word Poetry Paul you are amazing', he says going over and patting

---

[4]See Aliyah's day in a life Prezi – 12:30pm 'Watching YouTube': http://prezi.com/_6xvsjgtncog/?utm_campaign=share&utm_medium=copy&rc=ex0share.

him on both shoulders in a mock-congratulatory way. Dark sarcasm in the classroom. A bit later: 'Paul you've drawn a – cow? Dog?'. The students (all boys) given detention seem resigned to it despite their mild (and to my mind, justified) protestations. I wonder if these are empty threats, not to be enforced? The teacher has a bluff, tough, macho manner – I imagine he's popular nonetheless?

As we go on to explore in the Chapter 3, the 'day in a life' method is ethically complicated, in terms of the trust and intimacy involved in data generation and in the kinds of decisions involved in creating and sharing and representations of these documents. It is a method that depends on co-production in order to be practically feasible and ethically acceptable – yet co-production itself does not solve or explicate the choices involved in building representations and interpretations from the data. Here, our professional media collaborator Susi Arnott opens up this space in her reflections on the decision involved in editing and compiling the multimedia showcases:

Quite often I'm employed to tell a story. Yet at the same time, early film-making experience in observational documentary (not to mention scientific training) discourages over-interpreting, or imposing narration that's too separate from the actual 'findings' or recordings. Even if all end-purposes were known in advance, over-interpretation would still be wrong. So the critique of 'injecting coherence' was taken seriously. The job seems to be to find a way to concentrate different-sized bundles of text, audio and photos (sometimes even video clips) into resources that are digestible and interesting enough for less academic visitors, and comparable to each other, but still open-ended and honest enough to invite deeper consideration. 'Boiling down' isn't the best metaphor.

Including some sentences/photos/ideas and excluding others means making choices; unless these are random, the process implies and almost demands 'interpretation'. Why is one moment to be included, and not another? Retrospective field-notes might fill the day with moments and meanings, but these notes stand alone in their own right; the job of the multimedia presentations seems slightly different. The 'first person narrative' of the field-notes often include a lot of reflection with no apparent direct bearing on the child's own day; the researcher's day or their relationships to the other participants are often outwith the child's own direct experience. And yet these might nonetheless be useful in understanding the researcher's own 'attention economy', their perspective and priorities. The multimedia presentations can only really 'pay attention' to moments and ideas the researcher has 'paid attention' to with their camera or recorder, at the time.

It can be so tempting to infer and construct, rather than record and re-present, and this is equally true at the fieldwork and editing stages. Especially while we were still considering linear narrative video as a medium. The fieldwork isn't what film-makers would expect or hope for TV researchers to bring back; but by the same token, there will be a sociologist's sensibility in the material to be somehow identified and reflected in the multimedia presentations And the film-maker's impulse to edit and sequence into narratives, explicit or implicit, could be made use of, or fought back against! So who is 'directing' the process, reflecting on the meanings conveyed by the 're-animations', and deciding on which are the 'final' versions to be shared and archived? [Susi Arnott, notes on methodology 2014]

The recursive workbook method

Practical ethical complexity: high
Good for: capturing continuity and change, negotiated time
Temporal range: the research period

Origins and sources

The recursive workbook is a method about mediation – it relies on an existing body of documents collected over time that can operate as provocations for understanding and discussion. In this sense, it is simultaneously a reflexive method (inviting reflections on the process and experience of being documented), a longitudinal method (reanimating a relationship between the various 'thens' and 'nows' captured in the research process), and an 'inventive method' (Lury & Wakeford 2012) in that it makes something happen that collapses the distinction between the research and the life that is documented.

For our research team, the origins of the method lie in our attempts to share the 'extraordinary perspective' that longitudinal methods generate. In earlier studies, we approached this by giving participants copies of their interviews and, eventually, copies of the published work arising from the research. The idea of presenting participants with a collection of edited highlights from the research process emerged as a research strategy within the decade-long Inventing Adulthoods study, when a collaboration with filmmakers faced the research team with the challenge of communicating the idea of a longitudinal study to a popular audience.[5] The research team selected

---

[5]A key inspiration for this longitudinal project was the Up! documentary series directed by Michael Apted, where a group of 7 year olds were revisited every 7 years to create a series of documentaries that were broadcast on national television. Each successive episode incorporated change since

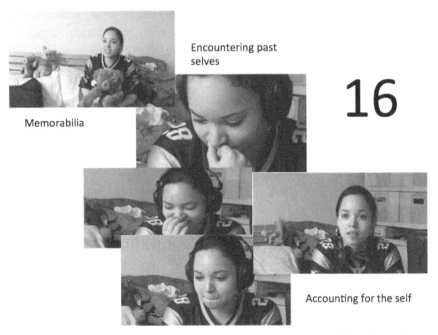

FIGURE 2.1 *Listening to past data in the Inventing Adulthoods study*

audio clips from interviews stretching back a decade, and the filmmakers invited participants to 'listen' to compilations of clips and then speak on camera about what they heard (see Figure 2.1). This 'montage method' was adapted in the Making Modern Mothers study into what we called the 'recursive workbook' method, involving the selection of quotations and images from previous interviews, which were organized under themes to create a book that could be worked through during a recorded interview. Like the 'memory books' we had used in earlier work, these 'workbooks' operated as a temporal collage, with earlier moments brought powerfully into play by 'quotation'. We repeated this method with the children in this study, in some cases tracing the research process back to a time before their birth as a way of explaining the involvement of mothers and grandmothers in the project antecedents. Looking together at the multimedia showcase and anticipating audiences and reactions to the material can be understood as part of this

---

the last round of filming, as well as the consequences for the participant of the previous broadcast. As the series developed, the relationship between the participants and the director moved to the centre of the exercise, as did contestations over the way in which individuals were portrayed, with some participants removing themselves from the frame. Seven Up has been considered a sociological study in its own right (Thorne 2009) and as a precursor to 'reality television' (Cousins 2006) and the development of intensive documentary tropes, such the technique of 'edited highlights'.

method, with the process of viewing and editing the animations producing new layers of reflection and insight.

The principle of recursivity revealed by this method involves a call and response dynamic where documentation, analysis and representation are deployed in cycles. This rhythm is familiar from action research, but also captures the 'time line' and 'watch again' tropes that are a familiar part of contemporary digital culture. Our experiments are mirrored by those of other researchers, including Staunæs and Kofoed (2014:1242) who write about a 'double loop' methodology where children watch videos of themselves collected as part of a study. Drawing on the work of Lisa Blackman, they write of the 'teleaffectivities' associated with the method which involve 'a revitalisation of a certain subjectivity that is not identical to the subjectivity in the "now" during which the recording is being (re)viewed', remarking, 'It is a curious situation indeed. It is intense, intimate and often intimidating'.

Ingredients

- Fragments of data selected and organized purposively into a physical and/or virtual format
- Audio recorder
- Experienced and confident researcher

Preparation

The preparation of the workbook is time consuming and constitutes a form of analysis in itself, with decisions as to what to include and what to omit and how to arrange these suggesting potential narratives and insights. The recursive workbook is likely to be one of the final methods in a series, drawing on material generated by previous waves of fieldwork. The method is flexible and can encompass a wide variety of data forms, including images, audio extracts, field notes, quotations etc. Workbooks may be created as part of a process of case study analysis as a strategy for trying out particular lines of interpretation with a participant – or it can be used in a more standardized way in order to generate comparative data across cases. In the Making Modern Mothers study, we produced workbooks as physical albums – including images and quotations – and these were given to participants at the end of the interview as a record of their participation. In this project, the recursive workbook was virtual, viewed on a tablet and involving audio as well as images and text.

The recursive workbook can be thought of as a meta-method that engages with the experience of being involved in research. Conducting a recursive workbook interview is a slippery endeavour. Things happen in these interviews, as material is staged and encountered. In the Making Modern Mothers study, researcher Rachel notes the following after conducting a recursive interview with Monica:

> She is taken aback by data that captures her son at different developmental stages, and discussion turns to the temporal unboundedness of the child, always changing, escaping definition and description … She complains of being unable to remember very much, and worries that they are not recording or documenting the child.

Five years later, during his own recursive workbook exercise, Monica's son Lucien engages with her in some of the same material. Here is an excerpt from the researcher Rachel's field note – importantly for this method, it is the same researcher who accompanies the family throughout.

> We set up the interview around the computer so that we can move between the screen and my tablet. The 3 of us are together […] We begin by 'going back' and I explain to Lucien that the research began with me talking with his mum when she was pregnant with him and that I spoke with Monica, his dad and his grandma. Lucien pats Monica's tummy and say 'ma ma' and stays in baby-talk for much of the interview. I show images of the car seat, birth pool, nappies and buggy from our first meeting on my tablet. Monica is surprised to see them. The birth pool has an ongoing story. She managed to freecycle it to a woman who succeeded in a natural birth and they remained in touch for a while. I look to Lucien, does he know about his birth? (no) – so not yet a family narrative. It is clearly strange for both of them to go back to this time. We then look at the two quotes I have brought from the M2 interviews, a year after birth: one with Monica and one with his Dad (who is at work). I ask Lucien to read some of his Dad's words out aloud which is about the thrill of your child looking like you and connecting three generations of men together. Lucien manages with the sophisticated language: 'nostalgia'; and seems to enjoy reading aloud. We also talk about the 2nd section in which his Dad talks of his hopes that Lucien will share his musical tastes and it transpires that this dream was abandoned as it became clear that Lucien had his own interests. [. . .] We then move to look at the day in a life conducted in 2008. Lucien has not seen this before and is very interested in the 'drawing' technique. We click on several of the images including the trains, the bus (that bus no longer runs he explains) and the blocks. Monica wants to know if he remembers the park (no) and she laughs at all the time she dedicated to this. He does however remember the runny ice cream – and I explain that that is the

bit that I recall best too. We go to that photograph and the image of the water fountain (no memory of the latter). This is an intense and fascinating experience. Lucien wants to see more and I explain that he can look at it whenever he wants. This is now a new resource for him.

Cooking the data: Analysis and interpretation

Where we had followed young people over a relatively short period of time, the recursive workbook doubled up as an opportunity to review and edit the multimedia resources in advance of publication and archiving. We showed young people a selection of documents that we had gathered with them over the project, and explored what it was like to see this material from the 'outside' and encouraged them to think through how they would like the material to be edited. In practice, they tended to make few changes, but often had interesting responses to the material, explaining how things may have changed or remained the same since that time of was captured and/ or responding to hearing their own voices or familiar environments in a new way.

It was among the extensive sample (the younger children), with whom we had a longer research relationship, that the opportunity to reflect on the passage of time within the research project became more powerful and provocative – that is, if the children were interested in the task, which was not always the case. David strolled back to his console once he had heard his voice and noticed his room was different, leaving his mother and researcher Sue to attend closely to the material. Sometimes, responses were oriented more to the form in which the material was presented – for example, the children's panoramic 'favourite things' displays generally produced a 'wow' response while the Prezi presentations were seen as more 'clunky'. Young people are experts in self-documentation, and so our research experiments are judged against exacting standards. But, however children engaged, their responses were productive in helping us think through the meaning of 'research' as part of a digital landscape (see Chapter 10).

Analysis of this material has also involved us working directly with sound rather than transcription, as both the soundscapes and the interviews become nonsensical when transcribed. We have also explored the ways in which animating sounds, images and writings in new moments can create critical spaces between 'then' and 'now' and between changing versions of the self. Working with ideas of 'temporal drag' and queer temporalities (Freeman 2010) has helped us think through examples such as that presented above, where Lucien revoices the words of the researcher, who in turn is paraphrasing the words of his father and his hopes about Lucien's future. These kinds of experiments are made accessible by digital methods and longitudinal designs, but depend on trust that has been earned over time. However, the possibilities revealed may have wider application, for example, working with actors and research participants to revoice material and understand the educational potential of the critical space opened up by dissonance between speaker and script (McGeeney et al. 2018).

Reflections on the method

The decision to create open access multimedia representations for each young person involved in this project provided a focus for working collaboratively with participants in order to think through questions of representation, audience, archiving and secondary analysis. The genre we settled on, composed of selected 'highlights', was realized through a combination of social science analysis and documentary storytelling. Children and young people were much more likely to engage with short multimedia documents rather than the 'raw' documentation of the research. Working with both professional and DIY production approaches helped us understand the importance of the media for the reception of the message. Staging this kind of recursive interview involves gathering temporally rich and heterogeneous material together, which also documents concrete moments and periods of time through images, speech and analytic reflections. This is then the epitome of the mobile research method that allows dynamism for both the research participant and the research subject, revealing an interweaving of research, biographical and historical time. The recursive interviews are however complicated in that they bring the front and backstage of the research together – sharing with participants and wider audiences – what the method has enabled us to see. Working with field notes means that researchers make themselves and the analytic process visible to participants. Looking at this material together gives rise to new analytic jumps that are co-produced between researcher and researched in an explicit way.

We can think of the method as utilizing *revelation* as a tool of knowledge production – with researchers showing field notes to participants, children showing hidden parts of their day to their parents, parents showing the past to their children. These exposures produce flashes of new knowledge for all those involved, creating encounters that require unpicking, events with uncertain consequences. Staunæs and Kofoed (2014) characterize these flashes in terms of 'wunder' with the 'capacity to precipitate a sort of self-shift or self-modification' (2014:18). These are the 'live methods' made possible by digital media, methods that both depend on and realize the value of times passing: with the quality of insight rising proportionately with the duration of the documentation process.

Conclusion

In this chapter, we have presented the three key methods that have been used in this study, tracing how they have evolved, how they can be operationalized, their affordances and the kinds of documentation and insight that they give rise to. Read alongside the story of the study in the appendix, this account authorizes the data set generated and the claims made in this book, but also makes an original contribution to methodological developments in the field of childhood studies and digital methods. In the next chapter, we explore in more depth the ethical dimensions involved in research such as this, showing how the imperatives of protection and participation are both in play in researching everyday childhoods in a digital age.

3

Protection, Participation and Ethical Labour

Rachel Thomson with Ester McGeeney[*]

[Monica] is taken aback by data that captures her son at a different developmental stage, and discussion turns to the temporal unboundedness of the child, always changing, escaping definition and description.'[…] She complains of being unable to remember very much, and worries that they are not recording or documenting the child. [Researcher fieldnote, RT]

Informed consent is a keystone of the ethical governance of research. Research with children places the responsibility on professionals to communicate effectively in order that the potential consequences of methods and participation are understood – by the young people themselves and by carers and parents. Yet, how do we draw boundaries around the consequences of our research? Preoccupied by the demands of innovative practice and co-production, we may not be able to foresee exactly what will take place in our research practice. An example of this is gestured to above and discussed in the previous chapter, where we reflect on how Rachel worked with 7-year-old Lucien and his mother Monica to explore and review

*We would like to thank Janet Boddy for her detailed comments and guidance on this chapter and for sharing her ethical expertise with the project more generally.

fragments of data collected with his family over the course of an 8-year research relationship. The 'recursive workbook' method was used as a strategy for showing what it might mean to be involved in research over time (informing) as well as constituting a method in its own right for which we might negotiate consent.

As a qualitative longitudinal study, this project operated as a laboratory for defining and exploring emergent ethical issues. It is now well established that studies that maintain research relationships with participants over time have the capacity to reveal, amplify and complicate ethical challenges that are common to all research encounters, yet which are either obscured or formalized by the fleeting nature of the research relationship.[1] The enduring nature of long term projects bring with them closer relationships, and increasingly profound yet personal insights enabled by the passage of time. One of the issues explored in this project was what happens to data *after* a study is completed, investigating with young people what it might mean to 'archive' data and to make data available for reuse. Under the umbrella of the 'Curating Childhoods' project, we invited our participants and their families into the Mass Observation Archive and helped them turn these abstract notions into concrete practices (see Chapter 8). We discovered that the ethical implications of data archiving and reuse are not self-evident, and demand exploration if consent is to be informed. Most participants (irrespective of age) had but a hazy sense of what an archive is, how it works, what secondary analysis might be and who might undertake it. Yet, we were also impressed that once participants had the opportunity to visit the archive, to see its practices and to imagine the kinds of reuse that were possible or likely, they were taken aback by the care that was taken of their personal documents. Given the opportunity to communicate by postcard with future data users, one parent sent the messages to 'treat this data with the trust and integrity with which it was given'; a researcher explained that 'the data is messy and imperfect, just like us' and a young person expressed the hope that 'the information based on me helps you with your research. I hope you can interpret it well. Please try to keep it as accurate as possible.'

So what does it mean to do ethical research with children in contemporary times, when digital culture and digital research methods make it so easy to create, copy and link data. In this chapter, we explore the ethical learning involved in this study – thinking through ideas of protection, participation and

---

[1]Key discussions of ethics in QLR include the issue of amplification (Thomson 2007), a shift from prospective ethical plans to more responsive situated ethics (Neale & Hanna 2012), and the ethics of archiving and secondary use (Neale & Bishop 2012). A data bank of ethical issues in QLR can be found at http://www.timescapes.leeds.ac.uk/resources/knowledge-bank-for-ethical-practice-in-qualitative-longitudinal-research.html. For a sensitive discussion of QLR with vulnerable young people, see Bengtsson and Mølholt (2016).

ethical labour. We begin with an overview of debates within the academic literature focusing on the ethics of research with children, the difference made by digital methods of data generation/management and by qualitative longitudinal modes of enquiry. We then explain the ethical thinking behind our research design before presenting a series of vignettes from the project capturing the ways in which ethics are 'situated' – shaped by local meanings and our reactions to these as well as proactive principles of good practice. These include reflections on surveillance ('watching the watched'), on methods that obscure children's identities ('the dis/appearing child') and boundaries between the front and backstage of research projects ('what we record and what we share'). Revisiting these fieldwork encounters in 'slow motion' allows us to think through ethical complexity, including the discomforts provoked. In this, we are inspired by Kofoed and Staunaes (2015: 37) who suggest that we mobilize hesitancy 'as an ethical act', holding back from immediate action as 'a strategy for intervening in the urge to intervene'.

Governing ethics

Prompted in part by unethical practice in medical research (see Boddy 2010 for a discussion), there has been a growth in attention to research ethics, through the guidelines of professional associations whose training and specialist audiences together provide safeguarding against the exploitation of research subjects. Professional associations such as the BSA and SRA (in the UK) effectively police its membership through guidelines supported by academic peer review of social research proposals and publications and through regulatory requirements for independent scrutiny of proposed practice. Some researchers have criticized this as 'ethical creep', arguing that it undermines the self-policing of academic communities, creating an emphasis on bureaucratic compliance that prefigures particular forms of research practice and hampers methodological innovation (e.g. Hammersley 2010; Stanley & Wise 2010). Safeguards against the exploitation or mistreatment of research 'subjects' were once assumed to arise from the professionalism of social researchers rather than requiring an external 'holding to account'. The result is an expansion of the ethical register, yet its association is with the definition and management of risk by institutions. A parallel tradition also informs thinking about research ethics – with feminist and other critical projects investigating how knowledge claims are made and how the appearance of scientific independence is produced (Maynard 1994, Erickson 2016). The embrace of 'standpoint' and materialist epistemologies that query the possibility of an independent observer have facilitated the deliberate co-production of knowledge as well as revealing painful and potentially productive gaps between researcher, researched and institutional regimes. Rather than seeing research ethics in terms of bureaucratic questions of consent, this approach engages with ethics as epistemology situating ethical labour through the different stages of a research project (Edwards & Mauthner 2002). From this perspective, ethical dilemmas are inevitable and productive and may be the starting point for intellectual discovery. Ideally, research ethics guidance in social and medical sciences is informed by both these traditions, highlighting the importance of reflexive ethical practice within the research relationship.[2] These guidelines increasingly argue for more situated approaches that are cognizant not only of risk and vulnerability, but also of power in the research relationship.

Not surprisingly, the ethics of research with children has been the focus of intense debate, with official guidelines still dominated by concerns around protection, emphasizing vulnerability and a lack of competence to understand research and the implications of participation (see Boddy & Oliver 2010 for a discussion). At the same time, childhood researchers have been at the forefront of imagining a very different kind of research subject who is a social actor in their own right. In a review of the field, Morrow and Richards (1996) challenged the way that the vulnerability of children is elided with assumptions of incompetence. For them, an ethically robust approach to research with children would engage with the particular competencies of the children being worked with, adapting and innovating methodologically, ensuring that the research itself had relevance to the children's standpoint and was conducted with sufficient care, time and support to ensure that the inevitable ethical challenges could be responded to. They argued that attention should be paid to the potential for participation, reporting findings back to participants and securing impact for research findings. Morrow and Richards also called on researchers to become equipped and confident in the practices and procedures of child protection (knowing when and how to refer concerns, being clear about the limits of confidentiality and allowing for dissent) so that they are able to 'take children seriously as social actors in their own right, as sources of valid sociological data' (1996: 98).

Spurred by the problematization of young people as a 'vulnerable' group, a rich body of writing has emerged on the ethics of research with children, closely aligned with the Article 12 of the UN Convention on the Rights of

[2]For a discussion of the ethics of research with children in clinical research, see Sammons et al. 2016 and http://nuffieldbioethics.org/project/children-research. Principles of good practice in the ethics of social research with children are provided in the UK by the Economic and Social Research Council (ESRC) which includes case studies and links to detailed guidance from organizations including the National Children's Bureau, Save the Children, the National Centre for Social Research, Young Lives, ERIC and the UK Data Archive http://www.esrc.ac.uk/funding/guidance-for-applicants/research-ethics/frequently-raised-topics/research-with-children-and-young-people/.

the Child.[3] In research terms, this has involved a focus on informed consent/assent/dissent) as well as the use of participatory methods to enable young people to express their views to stakeholders who shape their lives (Alderson & Morrow 2004; 2011). Reflecting on developments in the field ten years after her original intervention, Morrow (2005) welcomes a rapid rise in research and consultation with children over the period, yet notes ongoing tensions between the desire for clear technical guidance on the part of Research Ethics Committees and the inevitable fluidities associated with more situated and participatory approaches. One ongoing concern of the childhood studies community is that ethical anxieties inadvertently promote the kinds of research that can easily operationalize the advanced 'informed consent' required by research ethics committees – rather than more open-ended and collaborative approaches that characterize qualitative longitudinal studies and which involve situated ethics and renegotiations of consent over time.

The difference of the digital

The evolution of digital methods amplifies the concern to protect children as well as expanding the potential for children to participate in knowledge building enterprises. Digital technologies offer researchers the kinds of creative methods that resonate with the competencies of children. Not only do children often have relatively strong digital skills, but techniques such as digital photography, sound recording and GPS tracking provide a way to make malleable data out their everyday practices. As explored in the previous chapter, in a world of polymedia, it becomes possible to document on-line and off-line worlds in new ways and for young people to play an active part in researching themselves and each other. Yet these new modes of documentation have consequences. Most of the debates about children's online privacy and security have been conducted around their use of social media such as Facebook and Instagram or chat sites and online forums (Woodfield & Morrell 2013). The primary concerns relate to young people sharing personal details with unknown and potentially unsafe others, with losing control of documents (especially photographs that might come back to haunt) and with aggressive and bullying behaviours that may be enabled by the kinds of anonymity afforded by an online environment. New technologies invariably bring new concerns, and in some respects, these panics are the latest in a long line of worries associated with the arrival of new media that tend to focus on young people as a

---

[3]'Parties shall assure to the child who is capable of forming his or her own views the right to express those views freely in all matters affecting the child, the views of the child being given due weight in accordance with the age and maturity of the child'.

potentially vulnerable group yet also one prone to making trouble (Osgerby 1998). Yet, digital media also creates genuinely new possibilities which may demand new kinds of governance (Oswell 2006), opening up new areas of ethical enquiry.

As digital methods become mainstream, some of the ethical norms of social research begin to appear awkward, even anachronistic. Anonymity takes on a new guise as practices of trolling are recognized as a powerful cultural trend. The social researcher's 'promise' of anonymity may no longer make sense to research participants who are increasingly comfortable and practiced as public persons. Our *a priori* obligations to offer publicly funded data sets for archiving means that we think about the labour and costs of producing anonymity from the outset of the research process or go through a process of arguing against the appropriateness of archiving. What it takes to identify individual identities is also transformed by the digital,[4] and we are likely to engage in more complicated conversations with research participants about anonymity and its limits as well as extended negotiations about the kind of confidentiality that can be expected as the ethical responsibilities of a primary research team are delegated to an archive and secondary data users. Primary researchers need to be very careful that they do not make promises that they cannot keep (Mauthner & Parry 2013, Thomson 2014).

In a methodological project focusing on these questions, Wiles et al. (2006) concluded that 'perhaps it is time that we think through more clearly what confidentiality in research actually means in practice and what participants understand and expect from researchers' promises of confidentiality'. In particular, they identify a tension that may exist between 'data quality' and anonymity, especially from the perspective of archived data, where material could be used in completely new ways by secondary analysts, with relevant meaning arguably destroyed by anonymization practices (Crow & Wiles, 2008; Crow et al. 2006). Social researchers working with archived data sets have also encouraged us to think critically about what 'good ethical practice' means (Gillies & Edwards 2012), and the effects of practices that allow our traces to be covered (Savage 2010). Expectations as to what constitutes ethical practice are also shaped by discipline. The norm in oral history is to understand interviews as 'testimonies' which are authored and created in order to contribute to a public record. There is still a strong case to be made for anonymity in social research. For example, writing about a longitudinal study of voluntary organizations, Rebecca Taylor (2015) shows how anonymity may be a crucial component of academic independence in a context where research validity

---

[4]Thirty-three items of information to identify someone online: http://blogs.wsj.com/digits/2010/08/04/the-information-that-is-needed-to-identify-you-33-bits/).

could be compromised and incorporated into a form of public relations. What seems to be changing is the assumption that anonymity is automatically an ethical good.

What becomes very clear in discussions of research ethics is that time makes a difference. Material that seems very sensitive at one point may become much less problematic with the passage of time – a point recognized by time embargoes such as the 30-year rule on government papers and the kinds of embargoes commonly placed on access to un-anonymized archives. Time also brings the deaths of original participants and researchers, changing the relationship between the person and the archival trace. The passage of time may also create new dissonances with, for example, the marginal musings of researchers exposing casual snobbery to a modern eye (Gillies & Edwards 2012).By democratizing the project of documentation and publication, digital methods also compresses these timelines. We do not have to wait for archivists to decide what is worth preserving, or for collections to be opened to the public. In this project, we followed Niamh Moore's (2012) suggestion that we understand archiving as a form of publication, giving rise to questions concerning what archiving does and in whose interests it operates. Starting rather than ending with an archive reconfigures our moral compass, necessitating that ethical challenges relating to engagement, control and ownership are shared in the present, something we explore further in Chapter 8.

The commitment to archive can itself be seen in ethical terms as a duty placed upon researcher and participant alike by the use of public monies, or a claim to make public knowledge out of private problems. The role of the archive and archivists then comes into view as ethical responsibilities are delegated and trusted to the future with the care of documents closely entangled with the care of the many selves involved. As intimacies develop, care must be taken to respect boundaries and privacy, as the 'extraordinary perspective' facilitated by an iterative research design reveals more and more. As digital methods become the tools through which qualitative longitudinal research is done, so we become more aware of the complicated ways in which a new ethical landscape for research is emerging.

Starting with the archive: A new ethical approach

Embarking on this study, we sought to build on our previous learning of generating longitudinal data sets with a potential for archiving and reuse. These principles evolved in practice over the project.

A principle of possibility: One of the starting points for our project was the concern that research with children was seen as increasingly ethically challenging and high risk. We approached the research with a conviction that it should be possible for social researchers to document the everyday lives of children. This entailed us working with families and gatekeepers to establish ourselves as trustworthy and skilled researchers and working with research participants over time to explore the meaning of being involved in a research study. While this aspect of reflexivity may not be feasible for all kinds of research, we endeavored to map out the parameters of an ethically robust yet permissive approach.

A principle of shareability: from the outset we wanted to generate a data set that could be shared with others in a way that would not compromise the privacy of participants nor undermine the quality of the data set for secondary users. This included incorporating strategies for anonymity into data collection, for example, avoiding documenting faces in visual data and avoiding the use of real names and places in field notes. It also involved employing a range of digital methods and platforms that are freely available to researchers and the general public that form a wider culture of self-documentary. Although we are not driven by the norms of visibility associated with social media, we are concerned with staging a discussion about the ethics of social research, and those of personal and professional media practices.

A principle of co-production: An explicit aim of the first stage of the research was to create public documents based on individual data sets, and we worked closely with our young participants and their families to negotiate these public accounts. This involved us selecting extracts of visual, audio and field note data and working closely with participants to edit these in such a way that they were comfortable for their publication online. These 'public' documents expressed the kind of anonymity with which participants and researchers felt comfortable.

A principle of posterity: From the outset of the study, we explained to participants that we intended to archive the dataset and to make it available for reuse. All participants were asked to consent to having data archived both in a lightly anonymized form (available soon after the project end) and in a non-anonymized form at the end of a time embargo. As the project evolved, we were able to make this promise more meaningful by inviting the families to visit the archive, to see how it would be cared for and to imagine the kind of users who may be interested in the future.

These principles reflect the way that we imagined the ethical sensitivities of our project, and they shaped our approach to data generation and informed consent (for details on how we formulated this, see the appendix). In practice, a range of ethical challenges arose that continue to demand our attention. In the next section of this chapter, we share three vignettes from the research process, which in different ways reveal the ethical labours and insights involved in the study, moments when our proactive ethical principles came into collision with other situated values and practices. Each of the examples revolves around questions of visibility and its relationship with participation and protection. This is a theme that recurs throughout the book and which we argue is characteristic of this moment in the digital revolution. In thinking through our ethical challenges, we also develop insights for how we might respond to these challenges and for how research may continue to be a vehicle through which public knowledge is created.

Situating ethics – three examples

Watching the watched

Jasmine, one among our teenage panel, is 15 and a mother. Both she and her child are seen as potentially 'vulnerable' and both have been on the child protection register. Our initial contact with Jasmine was through her guardian rather than her parent or social worker. However, in order to establish a research relationship, Jasmine needed to talk to her social worker, foster carer and key worker at school (specialist provision that included childcare). Following Jasmine for a day was enormously productive for the research team because it showed us how practices of childhood and parenting can overlap, but also because it revealed the ways in which social media and documentation can become a focus for the institutional governance of risk. One issue that became immediately apparent was how photographs of children (which included both Jasmine and her child) were a focus of professional concern, as illustrated by the following example from researcher Ester's field note, soon after she arrives to meet Jasmine at her foster home on a school day:

> Baby R starts to get agitated again so Jasmine gets out her phone and goes on to her Netflix app. She puts on a programme called Bubble Guppies and shows it to Baby R. (http://www.nickjr.co.uk/shows/bubble-guppies/. R is instantly quiet and transfixed. I record the sound of bubble guppies and take photos of Jasmine holding the phone for Baby R (see Figure 3.1) I comment that Jasmine has a new phone and she tells me that the old one broke and her boyfriend bought her this one. When I ask her what she uses it for mainly she says WhatsApp, Snapchat and Instagram. She tells me she has lots of apps that she doesn't use and shows me them on her phone. I ask her what's the difference for her between Snapchat and Instagram – why would she use one and not the other. Jasmine tells

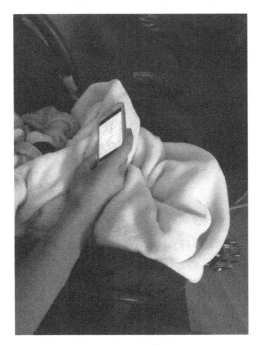

FIGURE 3.1 *Bubble guppies*

me that Snapchat is when she wants to 'write on a photo' and 'its quick' whereas Instagram 'you try and make it arty'. I ask if she takes photos of Baby R and she tells me that she used to but then social services told her she wasn't allowed to so she had to go through and take down all the pictures of her and she doesn't do it anymore. She said that she doesn't understand why, that they didn't really explain and that it doesn't make sense because all her settings are private anyway. I asked if they had safety concerns and she says yes but that R is not on child protection anymore and neither is she – as of last week. Jasmine tells me that Netflix is great for children's programmes. Baby R seems to like the colours and the sounds. She downloaded the app for free and then her carer has given her his log-on to use.

The problem of photographing children (as opposed to counting, audio recording or describing them) came up repeatedly in the research as soon as we entered the environs of the school. Interestingly, in Jasmine's special school setting where keyworkers sought to extend regulations around documenting children beyond the environs of the school gates, there appeared to be a deliberate attempt to create a safe space inside the institution, captured again in a field note:

> The nursery is a large bright room with windows all along one side, lots of cots, toys, mobiles, bright colours and a comfy area in the corner with lots of cushions and drapes. There is an outside space too full of brightly coloured materials and objects. It all feels very calm and welcoming. I ask if I can take a picture but the staff tell me no – there are too many pictures of the babies on the walls / displays / cots etc. They tell me that they take lots of pictures of the babies but that each mum has to sign a consent form first for me to do this.
>
> We leave the classroom and Jasmine comments 'I'm tired'. There is a display of photos on the wall from the year 11 leaving prom and Jasmine points herself out. She is wearing a black dress and has her hair straight and down. She looks happy and glamorous. (2.05 pm)

Yet inevitably, in practice, Jasmine and her friends are involved in intensive communicative work that includes the making and sharing of images – most of which went 'under the radar' of official safeguarding practices. As researchers, we become entangled in these relationships, gaining insights into how the young person is seen, as well as the ways in which the young person can be understood as thwarting practices of surveillance.

Here, we share a series of extracts from researcher Ester's day with Jasmine, moments when the researcher experiences an awkwardness. By revisiting these moments, we can observe Ester struggling to find a role that does not replicate the practices of surveillance that surround Jasmine and her child.

> We go into the nursery, taking our shoes off first. They are expecting me and I am introduced to baby R's key worker – a friendly, young white woman – who pulls the project information sheet out of baby R's box file and tells me that I can look inside at any of her observations and other documents if I want to. I smile but don't look – I feel like the child protection social worker all of a sudden, coming to check up on Baby and Jasmine's progress [9.40 at the nursery]
>
> I'm feeling odd and out of place. It's such a small group it feels impossible to be anonymous. I feel uncomfortable about the surveillance aspect of what I am doing. Sitting and scribbling notes. I keep thinking of Jasmine and baby being on the child protection register and the ways in which they must have been surveyed by a range of professionals wanting to assess Jasmine's parenting and both children's wellbeing … Jasmine is very involved in the activity. She answers all of the teacher's questions first, volunteers to take on tasks and seems to be a key player in the small group. The other 3 girls say very, very little. Jasmine comes across as the bright, popular and assertive member of the group and the person in the room with the most power. [10.15 business studies lesson]

Jasmine puts her hood up and rests her head on the table. I feel worried about her and unsure whether this is normal – does she usually feel like this? – or whether it is because I am there. Is it stressful / difficult to be observed and followed around all day? [11.20 English lesson]

We drift out of the ICT room and into the Art room next door. There is a bit of milling about and I hang, slightly awkwardly near the door. Jasmine sits down at a stool at a bench and rests her head. The teacher comes over and asks her if she needs a hug. She says yes and teacher hugs her. [11.50 Art class]

Several of the group, including Jasmine, are checking their phones. I ask whether they are allowed phones in the classroom and am told that they aren't and that some of the teachers confiscate them at the beginning of the lessons but that no-one has bothered today. One of the girls puts on a film of her little brother dancing. He has long dreads, is about 5 years old and is wearing a onesie. I record the music and L. laughing and commenting on it. She calls out 'He's so gay' and tells us that 'my mum doesn't know this is on YouTube'. Jasmine comments 'I love his onesie'. After this film has finished L asks 'what else is funny?' to no-one in particular. I ask how they choose what films to watch and for a brief moment, as everyone turns to look at me, it feels like I am facilitating a focus group on 'how you use YouTube'. [lunchtime]

Jasmine walks very slowly out of the common room looking exhausted. A sporty looking black teacher comments to her – 'you look dead' and Jasmine replies, 'that's how I feel'. I feel worried about her and say that she can go home if she doesn't feel good although I know this isn't my place to say so and that she doesn't need to stay at school just because I am there but she shakes her head' [1.20]

I chat to baby's key-worker who says how nice it is to have someone visit them. She says that they are really proud of what they do but because they 'are not meant to promote it' no-one really sees what they do. She is interested in the research and on whether I am researching Jasmine or her baby. The staff all look tired and the room has a Friday afternoon feeling. [15.21 the nursery]

In the car Jasmine and I chat and start to debrief the day. Jasmine seems relaxed and open again, much like she had in the favourite things interview. Throughout the day she had been short, almost irritable when I had asked her questions ... Jasmine comments on how she can't wait to have a shower when she gets in. I asks her what time she would like me to go and she seems unsure. I say that I can go straight away or wait around but she is unsure. [15.33 in cab on way home]

The carer asks Jasmine about her day and she shows her the origami box that she has made. When I ask she tells me that she works as a teaching assistant at a nearby all-girls school. She still has her staff badge round her neck. She says that work is alright but the girls are getting harder. She tells me that they have recently had an extension in the house which they need to do up so that Jasmine can use it and have her friend's or her sister round. She repeats this a few times – it seems like an important message for her to give to Jasmine. [4pm]

Its 16.52. I take a photo of the house from the outside and walk back to the train station. I feel really mixed as I leave – impressed by the bright, loved, loving, fit, capable and competent young woman I have just spent the day with and concerned for her with all her up and down energy levels, skinny body and feelings of exhaustion. I wonder how long she will be in this house.

These extracts capture the peculiar nature of the 'day in a life' methodology, where shadowing is intimate yet awkward. Carolyn Steedman (1995) uses the phrase 'watching the watched' to capture the new kinds of subjectivity that arose with a fascination with the plight of the street child in the nineteenth century – focusing on the fated figure of 'Mignon' a child-woman who combines experience and innocent, vitality and fatality. Steedman argues that the identification with Mignon for nineteenth-century gentlemen involved a romantic attachment with the child-within, an imaginative project that opened an interior space of reflection and empathy. In watching Mignon, they were also watching themselves. Can the same interpretation be made of this present day version of 'watching the watched' involving a turning of attention to the researcher and away from the researched?

Certainly this is an interpretation and a possibility that we need to keep in view. Yet, the example shared here involves a critical engagement with the consequences and accountabilities of surveillance. Ester draws attention to how Jasmine's and her child are being observed in a range of different ways, and that these modes of observation are partial, boundaried and easily subverted. The research gaze emerges as a distinctive mode of observation and one that has communicative potential – as well as the dangers and dead ends. The extracts also reveal the relations of care that can be involved in observing and documenting individuals and their environs, creating moment-by-moment descriptions as a starting point for knowledge building and action.[5] The ethical dilemma that first presents as 'what can be documented' soon transforms into questions about personal privacy and professional boundaries. What kinds of ethical obligations does this kind of noticing produce? Should the

---

[5]As noted in Chapter 2, our approach has also been enriched by psychoanalytically informed observation techniques, see Urwin and Sternberg (eds) 2012 and Jennifer Wakelyn's account of holding a child in mind through a research process https://www.google.co.uk/search?q=jennifer+wakelyn+&ie=utf-8&oe=utf-8&client=firefox-b&gfe_rd=cr&ei=5PWdWNayA-nR8geFrZ7IDA.

researcher accept the responsibility for the YouTube weblink of the 5-year-old brother dancing? For making sure people know about the hidden work of nursery workers or foster carers? Can we hold Jasmine and her baby in mind into an uncertain future? These are urgent questions for public services grappling with the challenges safeguarding in a digital age. Perhaps researchers can play a part in showing how documentation can be used in a way that recognizes, celebrates or honours participants without also engaging in practices of exploitation. We can begin a conversation about the kind of value and values that are generated through the exposure of that which has been hidden, including an understanding of how such value can be harnessed or harvested. These are important emergent debates within social research, that operate along the boundaries of ethics and aesthetics, demanding that we understand our practices of knowledge-making and representation within a wider frame of reference that includes both popular and scientific genres of documentary making.[6] Allowing hesitancy to open up a space before intervention, a space for thinking, feeling and discovering is an important part of the practice of situated ethics. However, a model that treats reflection as action can also be problematic, as 'watching the watched' turns into a self-contained loop: aesthetically satisfying, yet potentially voyeuristic.

The dis/appearing child?

In the early 1980s, Neil Postman lamented the disappearance of childhood – pointing to the erosion of clear divisions between childhood and adulthood. Central to his argument was that childhood was brought into being by the printing press and that the emerging new electronic media 'are "disappearing" it' (1982/1994: xii). Thirty years later, we are living in a complex media ecology characterized by electronic media that are instant, ubiquitous and unevenly governed. Childhood has not disappeared, in fact, the figure of the child looms ever larger in the public imaginary, but documenting the lives of children is complicated and contested. A theme that we return to several times in this book is the way that children come in and out of focus depending on settings, and the ways in which these settings (public, private, commercial, institutional) reconfigure the ways in which children can be represented. Visibility may be the cost of participation, and the arts of occlusion and disguise may be central to forging new ways of being in the digital age.

One of the ways in which we made our research project feasible was deciding to avoid the documentation of faces in the visual methodologies

---

[6]Key commentaries include Berlant and others on the 'case' (Berlant 2007), Les Back's writing on social representation (2007), Skeggs on reality television (2009), Warr et al. (2006) on ethics and visual research, and Reavey (2011) on visual methods in social psychology.

employed. While we did not promise absolute anonymity to our participants, we used a range of practices to obscure identity. This decision was rarely questioned by parents, institutional gatekeepers or teenagers – it seemed that the common-sense of avoiding or disguising faces fits easily into a set of accepted practices where faces have become imbued with a sense of risk (Gabb 2011). Younger children sometimes usurped our attempts to 'unpeople' the data. Lucien, for example, took a selfie as soon as he had control of the camera and insisted that the researcher took a picture of him and his best friend in their favourite spot in the playground. It was only once we started working with media professionals that we were challenged as to why we were avoiding faces and to account for how this practice might be making the research more 'ethical'. Schooled in the importance of collaborative working and the value of human interest in story-making, our media partners found our research norms to be bizarre, challenging us as to explicate what we imagined might be the negative consequences of allowing individuals to be seen and recognized within public documents. It is here that we become acutely aware of the disciplinary differences between media and research practice and how the production and management of 'data' rather than 'content' triggers different regimes of governance, and value, even if the methods of production are similar or even the same (Thomson and Arnott 2015).

During our analysis workshops, we shared the animated 'days in a life' that combined audio recordings and still photographs, and became acutely aware of the ways in which our methods gave rise to a particular genre of 'unpeopled' data. Colourful rooms full of objects, soundscapes of classrooms, numerous shots of feet and the backs of heads. A note of our discussion records our reflections as follows:

> Ethics as shaping the form, missing faces. 'Unpeopled' – lack of bodies also. Important to include the reflexive voice of the researcher that makes these omission explicit. The development of a new grammar of how the child is not represented. Why are we invested in anonymity? What kind of account do we get as a result of these ethics? Why can television companies film/show children's faces and we aren't able to? [Researcher Rachel's note of analysis group]

It was only in the researchers' ethnographic notes that it became possible to discern how our methodological choices became an intervention into the field of enquiry. Here, we share extracts of researcher Lucy's day with Saffron:

> 8.25 Leave Grandma's house: It is nearly time to go. We stand in the hallway and talk about Saffron's homework. She tells her grandma she did all her

research on the Internet. Saffron's grandmother laughs and says how funny that is, how different it is now. I ask Saffron if she does any research from books or in the library. Saffron is a bit confused, she thinks she does. She is reading the blue book at school. I take a few pictures of Saffron waving goodbye to her grandmother, one with faces showing and a couple without.

The classroom is small and the tables and seats are tightly packed. I don't know where to go. Feels too conspicuous to sit right next to Saffron, I don't want to make her feel self- conscious with her peers. The teacher is talking to another teacher. She nods her head at me but is not overly welcoming. Eventually I approach her and shake her hand and thank her for letting me observe Saffron. We chat about the day and she explains that all parents have given their permission for their children to be photographed apart from one child and she describes the girl I must avoid. I reassure that I will avoid photographing her and that I will not be photographing faces but rather focusing on activity or objects. Finally I settle on the edges but move around and visit Saffron's desk at times that feel appropriate. [8.50]

I go outside and find Saffron and her friends. Saffron comes running towards me smiling with one of her best friends. They have been skipping so I film them skipping (with faces and without focusing on the rope and feet hitting the ground) (see Figure 3.2). I make an audio of the sound of

FIGURE 3.2 *Skipping*

the skipping. They soon get an audience because I am recording. Children want to know who I am and why I am there because one of their teachers in the playground has asked. They ask to talk into the recorder and go daft making silly voices and noises. Then they want to see the photos. We find a shady area and I show them but we get told off for standing near a doorway. [10.30 break time]

In contemporary times, researchers have to fit themselves in and around a range of competing documentary cultures: the regulation of image making at school, familial practices of memory making and in situ practices of documentation and sharing. Our ambivalence regarding visual documentation was accompanied by a concomitant investment in audio – something about which our gate keepers were less sensitized. Already used to recording interviews, this project gave us the opportunity to expand our repertoire to include soundscapes – a form of documentation that was both indexical (capturing the specificity of the moment and the space),yet also expansive and ambient (providing an information rich sensation of 'being there' without exposing identities of people and places). Working with sound also engaged us with a new ethical vocabulary around the aural, including Bull and Back's (2003) discussions of 'deep listening' and Kate Lacey's (2013) 'listening relation', characterized by distinctive modes of *listening in* (a kind of eavesdropping that can make us part of a listening public) and *listening out* (an attentiveness and ethical concern for another). Tuning into sound felt like an escape from the traps of fixing and classifying associated with the history of visual methods in the social science (Reavey 2011). It also helped us notice the active manipulation of sound in the everyday and how sonic bridges are made and broken through the use of headphones, whiteboards, doors and speakers. As we have come to understand, digital methods allow us to play around with sound and vision, combining them deliberately in unusual ways that allow for the communication of voice while honouring confidentiality (McGeeney et al. 2018).

What we record/what we share?

Our broadly ethnographic research methods involved the creation of observational notes and decisions to record images and sounds. In the 'day in a life' method, these are then edited and reduced to a selection of images, sounds and descriptions that are animated and made public in consultation with participants. Although the final decision on what is made public lies with the participants, editorial control is in the hands of the research team and their media partners. Because we had made the decision to archive all project documents if possible, we also decided to make our observational records open to participants as part of the research process. This was something that we had done in an earlier project, and while the researchers experienced it as challenging, we had found it to be a productive process. In our view, nothing should be archived and made available for reuse that participants had not had the opportunity to see and to edit/redact material if they wished. In the project team, we described these edited versions from which material had been removed as the 'cooked' data. In creating the 'cooked' showcase, we imagined an audience that might be internal and/or external to the research – ranging from interested strangers through to friends and family. With the 'raw' data stored under embargo in the archive, we anticipated an 'expert' audience of academics and historians whose access would be vetted by the archivists.

One question that arose for us as a research team was whether these imagined audiences made a difference to how we wrote our research observations. The answer has to be yes. One aspect of this was how we wrote so that material did not need to be redacted (avoiding naming actual people, places, etc.) knowing that others would read them, even if only our immediate research colleagues. These were public accounts from the start. Yet we encouraged each other to make our observations as detailed as possible, with a view to cutting material that we chose not to share rather than not recording it in the first place. The analysis groups[7] through which we interrogated our data posed a different kind of challenge to us, as we were encouraged to reflect on what we had observed and why, treating our observational notes as partial and constructed texts. For example, in one analysis session, we noticed the way in which our attention was drawn to behaviour transgressions in the classroom and how researchers noted the ethnicity of certain children rather than others. We also noticed how our observations of a disabled child focused on his bodies in a way that other records of observations did not. As researchers, we felt vulnerable during these analysis sessions, feeling that our personal ethics as observers were at stake – what we noticed becoming evidence of who we were. However, opening our material to the minds of others was also a productive process, reminding us of how researchers are drawn into the social and psycho-dynamics of the settings, and how researcher subjectivity as captured in observational texts constitutes 'evidence' that demands interrogation (Elliott et al. 2012).

One of the most challenging aspects of our approach involved noticing and showing the vulnerabilities of the children in our study. Our concern was that by focusing attention on these moments, we would be 'fixing' children in unhelpful ways when, in practice, these moments of sensitivity may

[7]These groups involved the research team and a wider group of expert advisors to the project (David Buckingham, Ann Phoenix, Carey Jewitt).

pass – a form of what Pierre Bourdieu would call 'symbolic violence' (Bourdieu & Wacquant 1992). At the same time, if done well and with respect, the research has the potential to capture, share and celebrate moments in a series of young lives, conveying what Bourdieu calls the 'extraordinary discourse' that research has the potential to generate (Bourdieu 1999: 614). The extent to which we achieve this depends on the kinds of encounters that we have with our participants, the ethos of those relationships and the skills that we bring to the processes of listening, watching, writing, editing and storying. It is useful to reflect on the differences between the data account that we the researchers generate and those generated by the young people themselves. Aliyah's account of her own day makes no explicit reference to her religious affiliation as a Muslim, highlighting instead teenage practices of shopping, bedroom culture and homework, capturing favourite colours and images. In contrast, the researcher-lead account also notices when and where she and her sisters are veiled and how prayers are part of the temporality of the household. In our analysis for this book, we have tried to make these kinds of disjunctions between researcher and participant perspectives visible, using them as a way of enriching our analysis. By making our data sets open and our practices of documentation accountable, we hope to create a living archive that can be mined for meaning now and in the future.

The social relations of knowledge building

In setting out to create a live public archive about children's everyday lives, the research team took on a novel and challenging task. We wanted to conduct research to the highest ethical standards possible – demonstrating that it is possible for children to contribute to the public record without jeopardizing their safety or compromising their well-being. One of the drivers for this endeavour was our concern that a focus on child protection might be constraining or distorting publicly funded research with children, and that this is happening at the same time as an explosion in the harvesting of children's data in private and commercial spaces. We set out then to combine a commitment to participation with an awareness of children's particular competencies and vulnerabilities as research participants, as well as our competencies and vulnerabilities as researchers. In this chapter, we have moved between discussions of research governance and ethical reflections on how we to operationalized our ethical principles of possibility, shareability, co-production and posterity. A situated approach to ethics goes beyond a focus on protection and participation, pointing instead to challenges at every stage of the research process that demand the expenditure of ethical and analytic labour.

By offering three examples of situated ethics in this project, we have brought this process to life and contributed new thinking to debates around visibility in social research. Our commitment to start rather than end with the archive, we believe, has the potential to reframe the social relations of knowledge building in a digital age.

4

Spectacles of Intimacy: The Moral Landscape of Teenage Social Media

Liam Berriman and Rachel Thomson

For 15-year-old Jasmine, her Blackberry phone and messenger app were a source of intensely mixed feelings. In her first interview with researcher Ester, she described how her Blackberry messenger (BBM) app had become a site of on-going 'dramas' amongst school peers, with arguments quickly erupting and spiralling out of control due to miscommunications. For Jasmine, a key turning point came when her phone was irreparably damaged, leaving her 'cut off' from all social media discussions. During the three months it took to get a replacement phone, Jasmine described how life had been 'so much better' without having to constantly respond to 'everyone's dramas'. Returning to BBM on her new phone, Jasmine decided to limit the number of people who could contact her and to avoid being involuntarily drawn into peer arguments.

In this chapter, we map the contemporary landscape of teenage social media use, suggesting that this is a highly moralized terrain, bringing with it the potential for the spoiling of identities and reputations. Drawing on qualitative interviews with our panel of teenagers about the place of digital cultures in their everyday lives, we identify two underlying moral logics in young people's accounts of their practices: a concern with the imperatives of social media presence and participation, and a concern with the values, 'risks' and consequences of visibility. Using these two logics as axes, we present a heuristic model that captures the nuanced moral landscape of contemporary social media practices for young people, like Jasmine, including the dangers and potential rewards. Our use of the term 'moral' to describe this terrain refers to the way normative codes of acceptable and unacceptable conduct are challenged by participation on social media – with young people's moral codes sometimes at odds with attempts to govern these new spaces.

Media publics

Like media technologies before it, social media has played a key role in the shaping of publics and ideas of what it means to 'be public'. In the early modern era, the development of print brought into being a reading public that was both particular (the single reader) and collective (the literate) (Altick 1998). In the first half of the twentieth century, the emergence of radio and television in turn brought into being listening and viewing publics who tuned in at the same time each day as 'national audiences' (Lacey 2013; Oswell 2002). As we have moved from live to recorded modes of communication, so too has what it means to be heard/seen/read changed, with publics no longer dependent on synchronicity. Most recently, the internet and social media have been characterized as creating 'networked publics' (boyd 2007) that have collapsed traditional boundaries between public/private and author/reader. Theoretically, this process has been mapped as a shift from the idea of a singular public sphere (and its private corollary) towards ideas of contingent and emergent publics that can be called into being through moments of communicative action (Warner 2005). Alongside a proliferation of publics, Silverstone (2007) has described the increasingly globalized media landscape as shifting towards a convergent 'mediapolis', a single 'moral space ... of hospitality, responsibility, obligation and judgement'.

The idea of children's publics as outlined by Nolas (2015) builds on this body of work to explore how the possibilities of digital communication might inform and invigorate ideas about children's participation, which have been 'narrowly conceptualised as the right to be heard and to be consulted on decisions that affect the child as an interpersonal experience that may only occur at certain institutionally defined moments' (161). Drawing on the work of Mahoney et al. (2010), Nolas encourages us to think of publicness as a quality that cuts across and connects the public, the personal and political and which may be characterized by 'idioms' especially accessible to children such as humour. In contrast to the school councils that operate as a top down mode of institutional participation through which certain children are invite to speak for others within a constrained field of possibility, Nolas illustrates the idea of children's publics through the communicative actions of 9-year-old blogger Martha Payne's daily photographs of school dinners that caused a national scandal in 2012 (BBC News 2012). By focusing on 'claim making', the forging of new narratives and a reaching towards connection with audiences, it may be possible to think of young people's communicative action in terms of dialogue and debate in invigorating ways.

While digital media holds the offer of enabling the emergence of new kinds of publics, it is also implicated in the transgression of the private. Thompson draws attention to the way that emergent publics operate as 'spheres of information and symbolic content' which are 'detached from physical locales' creating 'territories of the self' which are 'constantly challenged' creating 'a new battleground' that is highly moralized and where 'established relations of power can be disrupted, lives damaged and reputations lost' (Thompson 2011, 64). Writing about the scandals of Victorian Britain associated with the rise of the popular novel, literary historians Chase and Levenson suggest that controversies can be understood as 'paradoxical spectacles of intimacy' where 'the stress of popular sensation' provides a mechanism through which 'private life' can be known and shared (Chase and Levenson 2000, 6). For the historian, it is evident that these scandals were 'energising … inciting insightful discussion of authority and sentiment'. Contemporary sociologists have pointed to reality television (Skeggs 2009; Tyler & Bennett 2010) and social media (Ringrose et al. 2013) as key spaces in which moral personhood is contested. Skirmishes on the borders of privacy are – by definition – spaces within which popular morality is contested and where identities can both be displayed and concealed (Miller 2011). These are the 'dramas' that Jasmine experiences through BBM.

Risking privacy and privatizing risk in an age of social media

The notion of 'risk' is a dominant theme in discussions of childhood and youth (James & James 2008; Thomson 2013), with young people simultane- ously constituted as a group 'at risk' *from* others, but also as a risk *to* others. James & James argue that this agenda has led to a closer alignment between notions of risk and protection, with children and young people increasingly framed as 'in need of protection *from* risk' (114: emphasis in original). In con- temporary public discourse, the internet emerges as a key site for discus- sions around risk and protection, with early concerns about grooming and paedophiles increasingly replaced with concerns over young people's capacity to sexualize themselves. The New Labour government-commissioned 'Byron Review' (2008) captures these doubled edge notions of youth 'at risk' and 'risky' youth, focusing on the promotion of digital literacies as a solution, including raising awareness of the unforeseen consequences of internet display for their future reputations. Young people's management of privacy has also emerged as a topic of concern in public (Valentino-Devries 2010) and academic discussions (Lincoln 2012; Marwick et al. 2010; Robards 2010), including the concern that the public display of personal data may risk both present and future reputations.

A key voice within these debates in the United States has been danah boyd (2014) who has published numerous accounts on young people's online privacy practices. In juxtaposition with research focused on safety and risk, boyd's work offers an account of how teenagers and young people make sense of privacy within an increasingly digitally mediated environment. boyd treats young people as experts of online privacy and as capable of developing sophisticated practices and techniques for managing digital content. Adopting a 'youth centred' approach, boyd has observed how the increasing regulation and surveillance of young people's 'offline' public spaces (see Valentine 1996) has led them to pursue social media as an 'alternative' public space to escape the intrusions of 'concerned' adults.

However, young people's 'networked publics' have emerged with their own sets of challenges for managing privacy. Boyd (2014) describes how the affordances of networked technologies, such as the persistence of online data, has meant that past conversations and content can resurface in later life with potentially negative consequences. The 'spreadability' of content has also made it difficult to maintain control of what is being shared and with whom. Perhaps of most immediate concern to young people is what boyd describes as 'context collapse' – where networked publics bring together people from different parts of their lives, including family, friends, co-workers etc. Boyd's account raises important questions as to how we conceptualize the meaning of 'privacy' and 'public-ness' for young people at a time of social and cultural transformation where social and digital media are increasingly ubiquitous and media landscapes are uneven and dynamic. For example, Marwick and boyd (2014) and Fisk (2016) observe that those interactions adults conceptualize as bullying may be reframed by young people as 'drama'. This more 'slippery' terminology, which echoes Jasmine's comments at the start of this chapter, allows for ambiguity of meaning and the kinds of complexities of agency impossible within the rubric of victim/perpetrator associated with a child protection approach.

Yet risk continues to shape public discourse on young people's use of social media in profound ways. Andrew Hope (2014) argues that our ability to have an informed debate about children online is subverted by four factors: the discursive construction of e-kids (as vulnerable); the muting of young people's voices (not asking about what happens in practice); the responsibilization of students (making the work of privacy a private business) and finally, a diagnostic inflation of risk through realist discourses – leading to a conflation of different kinds of risks – for example, those associated with content and contact. The EU Kids Online projects has been doing the painstaking work of mapping the digital lives of 25,000 children across twenty-five European countries, and confirms that many users are 'underage' for the platforms and apps that they are using and lack the skills to control privacy settings (Livingstone & Helsper 2013). Yet, among 9–16-year olds, self-reported harm is low (12% reported being 'bothered' by something online) and although exposure to mild risk is common (e.g. mean comments on Facebook), severe risk (e.g. grooming) is rare. This research reveals a complex picture of risk with 'some aspects of the online world draw in certain groups of young people that would normally be less at risk offline. Girls and those who are digitally but not socially confident are likely to migrate to cyberbullying, and those who are either digitally confident or sensation-seekers are more likely to take contact risks' (Livingstone & Helsper 2013: 6).

Studies such as EU Kids Online suggest a highly dynamic picture, where the affordances of new technologies are enacted by young people as intensive users within an uneven landscape of access and support. Livingstone and colleagues note that high digital literacy does not protect against risk in a simple way. 'Risk' is higher in wealthier countries with greater press freedom, more broadband, more computers and longer schooling, and children who are vulnerable offline are also vulnerable online (Livingstone & Helsper 2013). The EU Kids Online study also found that most young people stick to parental rules, but that the nature of parent-child relationships depended on many things, including the speed at which online access was taken up. Patterns of parental-child interaction are shaped by these synchronicities, enabling researchers to distinguish a typology that characterizes families' situations within differing national contexts and socioeconomic and technological landscapes.

The aim of this chapter is, following Hope (2014), to contribute to a research agenda that goes beyond 'the promotion of personalized responsibility for e-safety for all' to one that 'engages more positively with digital rights'. Our starting point for this research is an account of everyday rather than problematic social media use, which is focused on young people's reports of their own practice. As such, this work sits alongside a growing body of research that suggests teenagers are concerned about privacy and are actively involved in negotiating the affordances of a rapidly evolving social media environment (Livingstone 2008; Marwick et al. 2010). In the rest of the chapter, we explore the privacy concerns expressed by young people as they move between

face-to-face and online communications, including their underlying moral logics. Drawing on a cultural studies model, we seek to understand young people
within and beyond a rubric of cultural and political production, engaged in making and responding to audiences. Following Carpentier (2011), we are attentive
to the operations of access, interaction and participation, using a focus on
'spectacles of intimacy' to provide clues as to what is at stake and how new
forms of value are being generated and exploited.

Mapping the moral landscape of teenage social media use

In our initial pilot work with teenagers, we explored key questions relevant to
the study, including outlining typical daily routines, enquiring how they would
feel about sharing online and offline activity with a researcher and exploring
the kinds of self-documentation that they may already engage in. These pilot
interviews, proposed as a way of us feeling our way into fieldwork, were
highly generative and revealed elaborative ethical codes and language for
thinking about privacy and mediating personal boundaries. The model presented in this chapter is informed by analysis of interviews with teenagers,
and seeks to make sense of the diversity of their practices and emotional
investments in social media as well as how they spoke about this practice,
revealing distinct moral discourses linked to peer negotiations and parental/
institutional governance.

Similar to Ito et al.'s work of identifying 'genres of participation' in young
people's media use (2010, 14), we have mapped a landscape of media practices along different axes of participation and value. However, in contrast
with Ito et al.'s more descriptive typology of young people's media practices, we have sought to elaborate an analytic model that explores both
the different kinds of reported *practices* that young people engage in as
well as the *emotional investments* associated with this activity. This enabled us to pay attention to some of the underlying issues that gave rise to
worry, pleasure, excitement and dread. In attempting to make sense of
what we heard from a small, diverse, and far from representative group,
we have created an analytic model that plots practices and feelings along
two axes, representing on the one hand a continuum of participation and,
on the other, a continuum of in/visibility. We have characterized the map
as 'moral', suggesting that these practices are contested because they are
mechanisms through which private life can be known, giving rise to debate
about appropriate and inappropriate conduct and revealing broader formations of authority and sentiment.

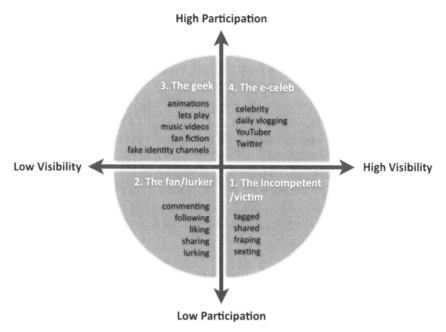

FIGURE 4.1 *Moral map of teenage social media use*

Here, we introduce the model (see Figure 4.1), mapping within it a set of practices and characterizing four quadrants, distinguished by the kinds of 'spectacles of intimacy' that are realized or imagined in the accounts of different young people interviewed, and which may themselves represent different cultural positions that young people may inhabit or move between over time. The quadrants include (in clockwise order) high participation/low visibility (personified by the figure of 'the geek'), high participation/high visibility (personified by 'the internet celeb'), low participation/high visibility (personified by 'the victim/incompetent'), and low participation/low visibility (personified by 'the fan/lurker'). Like young people's media worlds, the model is highly contingent and 'works' for a moment in time and within a particular social and geographical location – yet, we hope, provides a way into thinking through the spectacles of intimacy involved.

Visibility Axis: The horizontal axis of this diagram relates to a young person's *degree* of visibility via digital media. In a recent paper on the transformation of online/offline identities, Miller (2013) describes how we have witnessed a shift from mediated environments where anonymity was the norm (e.g. chat rooms), to one in which we are increasingly expected to share and display information about ourselves (e.g. Facebook). Though by no means a hard and fast rule, *opacity* and 'presentation of the self' are emerging as new norms for mediated social interactions. The latest social media trends adopted by young people have also increasingly placed 'visibility of the self' as their central logic. From Instagram and the 'selfie', to the ephemeral Snapchat and YouTube vlogging – young people's media practices are increasingly visually orientated, with 'the self' and the body framed firmly at their centre. Consequently, this axis of the diagram explores how young people's media practices shape the degree of a young person's visibility (or invisibility). The axis of visibility also ties into debates around privacy, with increased visibility leading to fresh concerns around young people's online exposure and concerns that they are 'broadcasting' themselves. Our discussion focuses on how and in what ways young people reflect on their own visibility and the significance of local and more abstract or imagined audiences, including how they weigh the risks and opportunities of increased visibility, and how visibility and invisibility may not always be voluntary choices.

Participation Axis: The vertical axis of this diagram relates to the *forms* of media participation undertaken by young people. This axis does not separate between 'more' or 'less' active forms of participation, but rather, delineates between different participatory modes of 'production' and 'consumption', treating both as implicated in the creation and generation of value. At the top of the end of the scale, we have those young people who seek to position themselves as producers of content or attempt to harness the value of themselves *as content* (e.g. vloggers). At this end of the scale, value and success are defined through the cultivation of audiences and the measurement of viewing figures. The pinnacle of this scale is characterized by young people as a form of celebrity status, such as YouTube stars. At the reverse end of the scale, we have those young people who primarily identify as content consumers and who largely participate in the tagging, curating, sharing, following and liking of content created by others (both media corporations and other young people). Though these young people are not directly involved in the *production of content*, they are still heavily implicated in the *production of value* – circulating and sharing, and ranking and arranging, content generated by others. These are by no means exclusive categories, but rather, serve as an indicative scale of how young people's participation can variously be involved in the creation of value through different modes of production and consumption.

In the rest of this chapter, we introduce each domain, explaining the practices involved and illustrating with examples drawn from interviews. All these examples are taken from our teenage sample (ages ranging from 10–15), capturing an age-sensitive set of cultural practices. While our sample was highly heterogeneous, the media resources and practices were common across the sample (if expressed in idiosyncratic ways) and firmly distinct from the media practices of our panel of 7–8-year olds.

Low participation/ High visibility: 'The incompetent/ victim'

This domain embodies the alarming side of social media – the creation and display of intimate material and the loss of control of this material resulting in personal exposure and shame. Examples within this domain make up the very spectacles of intimacy that characterize much public debate in this area, such as sexting and cyberbullying – with material shared in moments of intimacy then revealed to wider, unsympathetic audiences. A key issue arising from this domain is the absence of consent, with material extracted and exchanged under false premises, epitomized by 'fraping', where a person's online identity is hijacked without their permission. Less extreme but also frustrating is the experience of being tagged in photographs and the creation of a digital footprint through the activities of others. This domain reveals the impossibility of non-participation – that one does not have to create an online persona, it is something that can be created by others. Activity in this domain also reveals the creation or extraction of value within the overall 'attention economy' of participation/visibility. The self and the body are sources of value, which in turn can be objectified and circulated by others. In research on sexting, Ringrose et al. (2013: 312) write about the affordances of 'persistence, manipulation and uncertain audiences' associated with the combination of camera and social media technologies. When circulated in a peer group, a sexualized image becomes a cipher for sexual reputation – potentially, an intimate gesture consensually shared, but also potentially dangerous, exposing them to judgement and ridicule through practices of rating and boasting – giving rise to questions such as 'why are the images valuable, who can they create value for and who can they devalue?' (2013: 309).

The imaginary occupant of this quadrant is an abject figure: incompetent – a digital media user without the knowledge to make themselves safe – and a victim of those who persuade or trick them into sharing intimate information. This is the territory imagined by e-safety logics (grooming, bullying and exploitation), with young people encouraged to be wary about sharing information and incited to be vigilant about privacy settings and circumspect about digital footprints. As Marwick and boyd (2014) observe, young people avoid locating themselves within such discourse of victimhood, eliding the significance of painful encounters with cautionary tales of others. In our project, 13-year-old Claire voiced some of these concerns in response to a question as to whether she posted any material on the social media platform 'Vine':

No, I just watch, because … I think. I usually do something and I think I'm really cool, and then I'll look back and think 'that's really stupid'. So I try not to post too much online, in case I regret it. We always get shown that cyberbullying stuff can affect you later in life – if you bully or get bullied […] They showed this job interview where a person went for a job, and they looked them up online and found all these things about them, that they'd done to this person who was really innocent. And they said 'you're not getting the job because you're a really horrible person, and you have bad people skills'. So I try not to post too much.

Claire distinguishes herself from others who 'tend to put themselves out there'. She explains:

'I don't post much. I'm mainly tagged in things. I think it would be a bit embarrassing, because there are things like, where my friends … well not my friends, but people … they swear or whatever. It's mainly ok, but there's just … some embarrassing photos of me that I've been tagged in. Nothing too bad. If it was just my wall. If it was my news feed there would be a lot of stuff, but that's not to do with me.'

So although Claire is neither an 'incompetent' nor a 'victim' her overall social media profile is informed by the dangers of being visible, encouraging a circumspect relationship with social media.

Low visibility and low participation: The fan or 'lurker'

This quadrant is largely characterized by more cautious practices of limiting online visibility and avoiding uninvited and unwanted public attention. This can be an active choice, with some young people expressing a desire to avoid the potential risks of a more public online presence and audience. However, young people might seek wider audiences and publics, but find that their online presence draws little attention and remains largely unnoticed. In this latter case, invisibility is not a voluntary choice, but signifies the inability to secure and cultivate a public audience. For the most part, media participation in this group consists of activities that deliberately avoid exposure to wider public attention. By commenting, following, liking and reposting, these young people consume content posted by others, but rarely contribute any substantial content about themselves. This is not to say that they do not participate in the creation and production of value. On the contrary, their attention and promotion of content is highly valued and sought after by both corporate and amateur media producers.

During our discussions with young people, we met many who might be located within this category. In the following example, we focus on just one person. Aliyah, a 14-year-old girl from a Muslim background, is largely a cautious social media user. She tends to avoid using her Facebook account and characterizes her social media practices as follows:

> Facebook is for school [...] I don't really go on it 'cos it's really boring now [...] usually school fights happen through Facebook and stuff like that.

Instead, she opts for more private forms of mediated communication with her close group of school friends – using the phone messenger application 'WhatsApp' to arrange meet-ups and to share news and gossip. Over the past year, she has also increasingly used Twitter as one of her main social media platforms, using it to keep up-to-date with news about celebrities and popular music artists. As massive fans of the boy band Union J, Aliyah and her friends keenly follow the band members' various social media accounts. Aliyah watches out for breaking updates from the band so that she can either be the first to share it with her friends via WhatsApp or to retweet it to her Twitter followers.

Aliyah's media practices attempt to avoid making herself too publicly visible. By maintaining a cautious distance from Facebook, she seeks to avoid becoming embroiled in public conflicts amongst her school peers. The more private channel of WhatsApp provides an intimate and secure space amongst trusted peers between whom there is an implicit trust that conversations are private and are not for wider circulation. On the social network Twitter, Aliyah is largely a 'lurker' – primarily recirculating Tweets shared by others, rather than posting her own. Within her group of friends, Twitter also provides an important means of 'stalking' celebrities. As Aliyah describes:

Aliyah: This new British Band came out, and we all kind of stalked them.
Researcher Liam: What does stalk mean?
Aliyah: Like look at what they Tweet, so my friends are going to [airport] today 'cos they found out the band are coming home, they're coming back from some other country they went to. So they're coming back and they're going to stalk them.

For Aliyah and her friends, being a successful researcher, or 'stalker', of other people's digital footprints is a highly valued skill and practice. Stalking offers a playful means of keeping track of their favourite band and occasionally provides the opportunity to engineer face-to-face encounters in offline public spaces. Aliyah has yet to join her friends on one of these trips, but eventually hopes to do so. For now, she derives pleasure from the anonymity afforded by Twitter whilst 'stalking' her favourite bands, maintaining a wary distance from the more public visibility courted by those e-celebs that she devotedly follows.

Low visibility and high participation: 'The geek'

This quadrant is configured by the coincidence of low visibility and high participation, characterized by practices that involve the creation and sharing of original content that do not rely on or reveal the identity of the creator. Examples reported to us include a range of strategies for narrating or voicing over extant material including 'let's play' short films that capture live gameplay and the narration of the players; animations that are played over audio recordings; homemade music and accompanying videos. Although closely associated with a boy subculture of gaming, we found girls were also engaged in these kinds of practices, creating YouTube content, animations and fan fiction. What is distinctive about these active social media users was the entrepreneurial character of their practice, with 'play' reenvisaged as a form of economically rewarding work. By gaining an audience, young people are aware that they *could* capture advertising and corporate sponsorship. The dream is to 'go viral', establishing a career as a cultural creator. In the face of a need to build a credible professional identity, as well as the necessity of taking risks in the kinds of content created, young people are aware of the need to make careful decisions as to how much they reveal about themselves and seek comfort in forms of display that maintain anonymity. This is performed at many levels, but includes the use of ambiguous screen names, a shying away from photographs of the self, and pleasure in the creation and exploration of false identities and disguise. Andrew, a 15-year-old white middle-class boy explains that he communicates with friends via Facebook, but by posting content on his own YouTube channel, he can 'communicate with people I don't personally know [...] Some friends subscribe, others are from forums I use, some are just random people with the same interest in games'. When asked whether he ever records himself he replies:

> Not so much myself. Haven't ever recorded myself and posted it on YouTube. I'm a little shy and have confidence issues – I don't think I'd be good talking to a camera [...] Some YouTubers can talk off the top of their head. Mainly I do videos on games, animations, music. I make some music for YouTube. It's just public, unlike Facebook with privacy settings. [...] It depends how much content you put with yourself in it. If you do a lot of videos recording yourself and your face, people would recognise you in the street. That's if you have a big enough following. If, like me, you have about 86 subscribers, and without your face in videos, it's unlikely many people would know who you are. So you can take some precautions to keep private on YouTube, even though it's public.

As a serious gamer and a would-be musician and video maker, Andrew feels he must try and be noticed by making his content visible to the corporate players of the internet. For example, he tells us that he posts pictures to a company's profile page who might 'respond if it gets enough interest. People can like comments and those with the most go to the top of the page. It's a good way to ask big companies a question'. Making your content open to evaluation is also risky, as negative comments are visible and permanent records of failure. Added to this, the difficulty of distinguishing local and abstract audiences creates the potential for a 'spectacle of intimacy' in which schoolboy and professional identities spoil each other:

> YouTube is public, but I get embarrassed showing people stuff I'd made. You create content which you're happy for people you don't know seeing. They come up to you and say 'why did you do this' and criticise what you've posted. But it's different with people you know. They can say 'I don't like this, it isn't good'. I try to post quality stuff, but people might not see it that way. With people I don't know I think 'are they being serious?' You can get the type of person who says 'this is terrible' but not say why. […] More often people are rude, especially if it's serious stuff. If you're not careful you can get negative comments. If it's bad enough, you can get their YouTube account suspended. Or people can down vote it and mark it as spam. So technically it's public, anyone can see your YouTube.

The logics associated with this quadrant are of the cultural entrepreneur: creating content and carefully building audience and reputation. There is a high level of control attempted, yet the problems of 'context collapse' (boyd 2007) associated with public platforms such as YouTube create many challenges and ethical complexities. The adoption of alter egos and pseudonyms appears to be a protective strategy, allowing the risk-taking that is necessary for creativity while also developing a recognizable brand and audience. We found young people operating within the quadrant could experience high levels of anxiety and fear of ridicule as well as spending enormous amounts of time cultivating their online projects to the extent that local and face-to-face worlds could suffer and parents might step in to limit what was framed as obsessive or addictive behaviour. Indeed, such intensive investments of time and labour might already begin to mirror the precarious conditions faced by those media professionals seeking to make a living in the creative economy (see Campbell 2013; Gill & Pratt 2008; McRobbie 2011). Nevertheless, despite the costs involved, young people seriously engaged as producers of popular content were admired by others suggesting the ascendency of the producer identity over that of consumer in young people's values.

High visibility and high participation: The internet celeb

The fourth quadrant is characterized by activities that demand high levels of visibility and participation. The quintessential member of this category at present is the 'YouTuber', who gains a degree of e-celebrity status through their video blogging activities. In the case of YouTube, high visibility is realized through visual exposure in front of a camera (Miller & Sinanan 2014). In contrast with the media producers described above, the young people in this group seek to gain notoriety through the cultivation of 'self as content'. Whether describing their daily lives and relationships, performing sketches or pranks, or reviewing media and products, vloggers aspire towards the generation and cultivation of a loyal audience. To achieve fame, a trade-off must be made in which the security of anonymity is surrendered for the opportunity to be seen and heard by others. For this group, the value of their activities emerges not at the moment of production but rather accumulates through the attention of their audience.

Though none of the young people in our study could be regarded as achieving high levels of attention in their content production, many of them discussed and idolized those YouTubers and Tweeters who had achieved e-celebrity. Fourteen-year-old Abi, an avid YouTuber viewer, has started to run her own channel with a friend, and spoke knowledgably and enthusiastically about the world of YouTubers:

> There's this thing on YouTube, like YouTubers, there's loads of them and *that's their job, they just get paid to make videos*, all these skits and things … some do pranks, some do advice, some do things about their life.

For Abi, the potential to transform a hobby or interest into a viable 'career' is the ultimate reward of being a successful YouTuber. Here the term 'playbour' (an amalgamation of play and labour) (Kücklich 2005) seems particularly apt as a way of describing the transformation of something that starts out as 'just for fun' into something that can generate economic value. For many, however, this remains a pipe dream and the likelihood of attracting the attention of a wider audience remains slim. As such, this group of young media users also represents an aspirational category in which becoming a successful YouTuber is the new dream profession of working/not working. As Abi describes of one YouTuber:

> he is like a professional so they're really lucky because they don't have to get up and go to work […] So now everybody wants to be a YouTuber because it's a super easy job, but you get paid really well.

Though Abi reveres the success of certain YouTubers, she also remains cautious of the potential risk arising from greater audience exposure. When asked about potential negative comments and 'trolling' from viewers, Abi presented a blunt ethical position that to upload a video is to invite all types of audience exposure:

> I think when people are being mean on YouTube it's kind of like, you shouldn't have uploaded the video then.

In regards to her own channel, set up with her friend, she describes how 'no one watches it, which I don't mind because then no one's being mean!'

Although we find celebration of the possible benefits that might arise from becoming a famed YouTuber, there is little sympathy for the forms of negative exposure to which you might expose yourself. The decision to trade in anonymity for public recognition must be carefully weighed, with the onus for weighing risk placed firmly on the individual.

A cultural economy of spectacle

Touring these four quadrants of our model captures a moment in time of the UK teenage media landscape, a common culture, where the affordances and logics associated with different applications are realized in different ways, yet fall into recognizable patterns when mapped against axes of visibility and participation. Our choice of these axes was informed by the emotional investments of our young informants – these were the themes that they stressed upon in their accounts and which made sense of their practices. Yet, in mapping practices against these axes, we were struck by the relative (un)inhabitability of the different quadrants and the kinds of reputational and physical risks associated with them. Many of these figures form part of a cultural imaginary embedded with distinct modes of value that label them as either figures to be celebrated or derided. Similarities may be drawn here with Tyler and Bennett's (2010) discussions of the productivity of 'celebrity chavs', moral figures operating as 'a key vehicle through which value is distributed in public culture, and ... instrumental in practices of distinction-making between individuals and groups in everyday life' (389).

In our model, quadrant 1 is, in identity terms, uninhabitable: a space of bullying, exploitation and humiliation. It is also an implicitly gendered space, showcasing the extraction of value from the circulation of sexualized images, and a space into which the unsuccessful would-be e-celebrity can fall in the face of failure to establish an audience beyond the local network of those who control sexual reputations. If we reflect on why so much attention is given to this space and the consequences of this, we can understand it as a site of moral warnings for new players or for 'fallen' e-celebs. In a twenty-first-century 'moral map', this is the land of the lost that is a warning to all, but especially perilous to young women who not only risk professional reputations in the future, but also sexual reputations in the here and now. Many of the practices of invisibility adopted in quadrant 2 can be understood as responses to the dangerous spectacles of intimacy represented by quadrant 1 and amplified in the popular media and e-safety discourses. Yet, interestingly, we also learn how young people are experimenting with and enjoying invisibility – something striking in a commercial context where personalization and revelation are incited. Practices such as the 'stalking' of e-celebrities involve realizing the potential of group identities such as the 'fan' and the 'swarm', while connecting offline adventure (meeting with other fans, travelling to 'witness' celebrity), with the development of online community and the power of collaborative research. Quadrant 3 represents a moral high ground – defined by controlled display and public creative risk-taking, anticipating the future while attempting to enjoy the present. This may be a destination point in a developmental journey or an aspirational figure facilitating induction into a new economy of content creation and circulation. Unlike the celebrity of quadrant 4, the geek does not risk a public downfall into the land of the lost, but rather, the kinds of risk that Livingstone et al. associate with the 'digitally confident or sensation-seeker'. In terms of their practice, most of the young people we spoke to were on the left-hand side of the figure, and moved between quadrants 2 and 3. Yet all knew about quadrants 1 and 4 with the dream job of e-celeb and the perils of a spoiled identity powerfully linked in the cultural imaginary.

The moral space represented by the model has been monopolized by e-safety discourses that have sought to define and govern acceptable models of young people's public participation and visibility on social media. In *Framing Internet Safety* (2016), Nathan Fisk illustrates how this moral economy has been dominated by adult (policy makers, parents, journalists, law enforcers) attempts to frame themselves as knowing best how young people should inhabit media publics. He suggests that a focus on risks to future reputation has served to inflate concerns about what gets posted online and has largely been used to justify greater surveillance of young people's online activities by adults. In addition to inflating certain concerns and risks, e-safety discourses have also led to some aspects of young people's social media participation becoming hidden from view and left un-interrogated. As observed in our moral map, social media is also a public space whose architecture is owned by commercial giants (Facebook, Google etc.) who encourage young people to imagine themselves as cultural entrepreneurs (Instagrammers and YouTubers) investing in their own future economic value. However, the primary economic benefactors of this media landscape are the commercial firms who profit from the content hosted on their sites by harvesting user data to generate targeted advertising. As Fisk argues, e-safety discourses 'largely eschew any critical discussion of mass data collection, advertising practices, digital labour or alternatives to Western concepts of intellectual property' (2016: 188) – instead focusing on the moral responsibility of the individual to cultivate good models of citizenry for their future employability.

Our model is a heuristic device that captures the moral landscape of contemporary teenagers in a tradition of moral maps that encapsulate, represent and mediate moral uncertainty in changing times. It may be best understood as outlining a developmental journey, from the dangers of entry into social media through to strategies for making social media work for you (Robards 2012). Within this landscape, young people are driven by a dual emotional imperative: seeking to navigate between the potential emotional pleasures derived through praise and recognition, whilst simultaneously attempting to avoid the anxiety and distress of being exposed to criticism and derision. The map has an underlying political economy, sorting and distinguishing the ways in which value is extracted, circulated and harvested. Content created through intensive media practices (e.g. taking and sharing a photograph) are absorbed into extensive systems of value judgement and appraisal (e.g. 'likes' and resharing). Exclusion also plays an important role in this moral imaginary, through figures of ridicule and pity. However, there are also hints of how these forms of abjection may be 'resisted and recuperated in forms of counter-political speech' (Tyler, 2013: 5). Perhaps most clearly, the map shows the analytic salience of the axes of visibility and participation – both deeply ambiguous terms in their own right – giving rise to contested hierarchies and new analytic strategies for moving beyond binaries of active production and passive consumption (Carpentier 2011). That 'spectacles of intimacy' can be generative gives insight into the tangled relationship between publicity and the generation and destruction of value. Our analysis suggests we are inevitably required to risk our privacy, yet this risk need not be privatized, nor must it rely on or trade in abjection. Young people are constantly experimenting and realizing the affordances of social media, combining these creatively with face-to-face socialities, and trading off visibility and participation. This is an arena that deserves attention and critical reflection as a site of politics as well as play, and as a starting point for a new kind of public engagement beyond 'e-safety'.

5

Materializing Time: Toys, Memory and Nostalgia

Liam Berriman

Fourteen-year-old Abi describes how her room used to be 'cluttered' with items from her past. Recently, she has turned to eBay and has sold a lot of the items that were just 'shoved' in her wardrobe to help 'make space'. When researcher Sara asks which items she has decided to keep, Abi describes 'stuff that has memories attached and stuff that my mum wanted me to keep as well'. Whilst her mum 'wouldn't force me to keep anything', she has encouraged Abi to keep 'baby stuff' that she 'might not ... be that bothered about' right now. For Abi and her mother, the process of sorting through childhood belongings has prompted reflection on the changing value of material objects over time and their significance as sites for creating and curating memories of childhood.

This chapter reflects on the significance of time and memory in children's material worlds. It is inspired by recent iterations of practice theory (Shove et al. 2009) and studies of material culture (Miller 2009) which have provided ways of observing the 'materialization' of time and memory in everyday life. From birth and throughout childhood, material objects act as important markers of change and continuity (Clarke 2004). A soft toy kept from birth can be a source of continuity and comfort, whilst an out-grown childhood toy can herald change and transition. In this chapter, we explore how the children in our study engaged with toys and material objects, allowing us to think of these as sites of temporal imagination and practice. As museum curators and historians of childhood have long known,[1] toys are objects marked in and by time, and their material design provides insights into the popular imaginings of children's play at different historical moments (Brookshaw 2009). This has become increasingly evident in a fast moving technological culture where toys have become markers of subtle generational divides.[2] Toys have increasingly become sites of 'retro' nostalgia for past childhoods;[3] however, the historical and generational marking of toys is not an exclusively adult pastime. When we invited children and young people to share their favourite things from the present and past, we also encounter objects marked in and by time. Toys from the 1990s and 2000s already provoked nostalgia for many of the young people we interviewed, providing anchors for the navigation of a changing sense of self and values over time.

Drawing on two of the key themes of this book – time and documentary – we explore how children's toys and other personal belongings operate as 'sites of memory' within children's everyday lives (Nora 1989). This chapter draws on interviews conducted during the first phase of the Face 2 Face project, where children were asked to show and tell us about 'favourite things' (see Chapter 2 for more on this method). This approach enabled children of different ages to imagine their biographies as stretching both 'backwards' in time – reflecting the significant memories attached to toys – and 'forwards' in time – reflecting on what toys they might wish to keep for the future. As discussed towards the end of this chapter, decisions about what to keep or to throw away, and whether broken and obsolete toys still had value, are highly significant in shaping the value of toys as objects beyond play. This chapter proposes that children can be nostalgic for their own recent pasts and engage in everyday curatorial practices which assign value and meaning to favourite toys and objects over time. The chapter pays close attention to the practices through which time is materialized in children's toys and objects – first, in terms of the 'storying' of time and memory, and second, through the 'sorting' and curating of material pasts.

Throughout our study, we observed how toys and other material objects were a constant presence in the everyday lives of our research participants, acting as playthings, comforters, gifts, collectables, hand-me-downs,

---

[1]During our research, we encountered an oral history project led by the Brighton Toy and Model museum that recorded adults' accounts of their favourite childhood toys. The interviews from this project offered insights into many of the different temporal markings of toys as historical and generational artefacts that live on in adults' memories of childhood. Its online archive of oral histories can be found at: http://www.toysinthecommunity.org.
[2]For example, the film *Boyhood* directed by Richard Linklater features several toys as generational markers for different moments in time (e.g. Nintendo's Gameboy).
[3]For example, television programmes such as Channel 4's *100 Greatest Toys* and the BBC's *The Toys That Made Christmas*, which invite adults to recall their favourite childhood possessions.

keepsakes and decorations. Here, we consider the 'temporal affordances' of children's material cultures. Affordances is a concept originating in design studies, where it is used to describe the multiple ways an object might invite action (Gaver 1991). We use it more narrowly to describe how children's objects may invite temporal purpose, for example, as sites of memory or nostalgia. We begin by considering different ways of approaching the relationships between time and material culture in children's everyday lives. We then explore how children 'story' their pasts and biographical narratives through material objects, and how, through practices of 'sorting' and curation, children assess the changing meaning and value of objects in their lives.

Childhood, time and materiality

Discussions of the materiality and temporality of childhood have grown in prominence over recent decades. Time has been an ever-present backdrop to the study of childhood as a period of biological and biographical transition (James & Prout 1997; Neale & Flowerdew 2003; Nielsen 2016). In particular, debates in the late 1980s and early 1990s about childhood as a state of being vs. becoming generated a conceptual 'crisis of time' that was caught between temporal immediacy and future potentiality. More recent contributions to this debate have taken a more nuanced approach to the temporality of childhood (Uprichard 2008), with researchers critically exploring children's experiences of time and memory in their everyday lives (Christensen 2002; Hohti 2016b; Moss 2010). This in turn has been supported by theoretical developments that encourage us to understand how the figure of the child is tied into normative biographical tropes connecting historical and biographical notions of progress (Steedman 1995; Stockton 2009). Attempts to queer time and to locate us within queer times move our attention away from universalist developmental temporalities towards the recursive, layered and contested temporalities of lived childhoods (Freeman 2010; Castañeda 2010). This chapter draws on these latter developments by approaching children as agentic in their practices of memory making, acknowledging how memories are created and located in broader sites of shared, communal and hybrid memory, such as family narratives.

Children's material cultures have become a prominent focus for childhood studies (Buckingham 2011; Gutman & Coninck-Smith 2008). Research in this area ranges across children's toys and play cultures (Sutton-Smith 1986; Woodyer 2013) to marketing and consumer culture (Cook 2004; Seiter 1993). A shared theme across these studies has been recognition of material culture as a space of agency, play and meaning making for children. Time and memory have not featured prominently in these studies, though many have featured historical accounts of how particular material cultures of childhood have evolved over time, focussing, for example, on books (Rudd, 2010), clothing (Cook 2004) and toys (Brookshaw 2009). In contrast, youth studies has a strong orientation towards the temporality of young people's material cultures. In particular, research into 'self-documentary' practices examines the materialization of time through diaries, scrapbooks and photo albums (Day-Good 2013; Himmesoete 2011; Tinkler 2008) and, more recently, social media practices of curating 'timelines' and 'news feeds' (Lincoln & Robards 2014). Though diaries have long been a source of historical interest for understanding the construction of childhood and youth at certain moments time (see Ariés 1962), we are only now beginning to consider how these practices contribute to the *materialization of time* in children and young people's everyday lives.

Storying objects

During the 'favourite things' interviews, we invited children to share the objects that were most important in their lives, telling us how they came to own them, what memories they associated with them and how the objects were important to their past, present or future. Across these interviews, the children shared a wide assortment of treasured items with us, along with the stories and memories they evoked. In this section, we explore some of the common ways that children 'storied' their objects, and through this, gain insights into how childhood becomes a focus for the making of memory and nostalgic investment for individuals and for families (in Chapter 6 we discuss more specifically how these objects relate to the work of gender). The following section suggests that objects enable children to tell stories about mundane and momentous times in their lives – anchoring and materializing particular memories. We also consider how absent objects could be highly significant, representing moments of separation and loss in children's symbolic universe.

Across the interviews, favourite toys and objects occupy a space of both mundane and momentous significance in the lives of participants. Some of the objects we were introduced to had very mundane existences, either in common use as everyday playthings, or residing in drawers, on shelves or in boxes where they are displayed or stowed away. As objects for discussion, however, they evoke 'momentous' stories relating to significant people, places and events within the children's lives. These stories are rarely told in a linear fashion (e.g. from earlier to more recent memories), but are reported in a patchwork arrangement involving multiple layers of time. Through their objects, children weave together different strands of time, focusing our attention on particular relationships and events with meaning for them at the time of the interview. For those children who had been followed since birth, we experienced resonances with conversations that took place in their babyhood where presents bought for them were prized by parents for their connections to particular gift givers (e.g. parents or close friends). Eight years on, we understood ourselves as engaging with an unfolding and materializing symbolic universe of significant relationships, yet one in which the children are increasingly in the driving seat as collectors and narrators.

Fourteen-year-old Nathan has been accumulating a collection of teddy bears since he was born, and the bears provide a site through which he is able to talk about his relationships over time and can reflect back on a range of childhood memories. One of his first bears was inherited from his older brother and formed the basis of a collection that has gradually grown over time. Nathan explains:

> I used to play with them a lot and [...] (they were) the first thing I thought of, like straight to the head because I can't really think of anything else that would be, that will be important from the past.

Nathan's description of where and when he had got the bears enables him to name important relationships and to communicate a sense of continuity and stability over time. Whilst the bear he inherited from his brother is particularly special ('I had it since I was a baby'), each of his other bears is also an important site of memory. The way that the bears are narrated draws attention to what Nathan values, including a special holiday ('I got this one couple of years ago in America') and a theme park trip ('I got this from Chessington'), as well as important relationships with family members whose affection is materialized in the object ('My auntie made this for me') and friends whose agency is affirmed in their ability to contribute to his collection ('my best friend bought it for me'). While each bear is singularly important for its connection to a specific person or event, the bears also existed as an interconnected set of objects collectively representing Nathan's evolving relationships and investments.

At the time of the interview, Nathan's bedroom is being renovated as part of a wider house extension, and so most of his belongings have been displaced from their normal home and packed away in boxes in the family's living room. The bears are amongst those belongings packed away, and Nathan retrieves them especially for the interview. At a later point in the study, after the renovations had been completed, Nathan gives a tour of his bedroom to show some of the items he hadn't been able to find for the favourite things interview. During this, he highlights many of the changes to his room, which include a new dark grey colour-scheme, self-drawn art-work on the walls, and a new computer desk. Over the course of our study, a number of the children's bedrooms changed or were redecorated. At these moments of transition, it is interesting to note which objects have remained, been moved, or been displaced entirely. For Nathan, the bears maintain a highly visible place in his room – on a bench below his window – remaining a significant point of material continuity. It is unclear whether Nathan's sharing of the bears and their stories during the study is influen-tial in his decision to place them back into the room. Whilst many objects may already act as 'sites of memory' for children, it may also be possible that our request for them to story significant objects in turn generates new value for those possessions.

The invitation to share something from the past could also be interpreted in a much more casual manner. For example, 15-year-old Funmi chose a pink door sign embossed with the word 'Princess', hastily selected in the last min-utes before the interview. During the interview, it became clear that the act of selecting the object had prompted Funmi to reflect on why she had kept it, and what memories were attached to it:

> I got it for Christmas from my uncle. It's pink because, because it was my favourite colour. It says princess because, I guess that's how he thought of me. So I really cherish it, I think it's really special.

Over the course of the discussion, Funmi describes how she has now grown out of the colour pink – rejecting it as 'too girly' – and has instead started to cultivate a purple colour scheme in her bedroom that the door sign no longer matched. In contrast with Nathan's bears, Funmi's object has been displaced within her room and instead resides inside a drawer. The object's obsolesce is undercut by important family memories and so the sign is 'kept' rather than disposed of, memorializing her relationships with her uncle and a past 'pink' version of self.

Though objects could evoke stories of important relationships and events in children's lives, they also serve as reminders of significant moments of change and transition – such as Funmi's transition from pink to purple. One commonly recurring narrative involved objects marking 'agentic change', where children described a broadening of choice, freedom or responsibility in their lives. These stories share parallels with the notion of 'critical moments' (Thomson 2002) – where a particular moment or event is narratively constructed as a critical biographical turning point. In this instance, objects are described by the children as closely involved in shaping or marking a critical moment of change. Whether these moments will find their way into well-worn stories of self is another matter, and one that only a longitudinal research design can capture.

For David, the occasion of choosing or purchasing a favourite item stood out as a moment of newfound agency. In the following extract, he narrates how he came to possess his soft toy dog 'Bernard':

> I was walking in Morrisons (a UK supermarket chain), I was in a trolley, well I wasn't walking, I was in a pram, maybe, I don't know. I was in the trolley and, when you walk in, the first thing on like your left and right was one of these doggies. He's really soft, and I wanted to get it, so I grabbed it out of the shelf and I was like hugging it really tight. And when we got to the checkout I didn't want to let go of him, didn't put it on the conveyor belt, so my mum had to rip the label out and give it to the lady and she scanned it.

Children's relationships with soft toys have often been a focus of childhood research – particularly in psychoanalytical theories of attachment. Winnicott's work initially highlighted the significant role of the teddy as a 'transitional object' for young children exploring the world beyond the familiarity of their mother's body. He suggested that soft toys could provide a stable presence during periods of transition – offering a constant comforting presence in the mother's absence. David's narrative of meeting Bernard almost has a fairy tale (or romantic) quality to it as he describes them forming an almost instant attachment. The soft dog is represented as an important 'companion' object (Turkle 2011) and source of comfort for David. Alongside reflecting on the important emotional bond that David describes with the soft toy, it's also important to consider the significant role of the narrative of 'finding' Bernard. For David, the story marks a significant moment when – possibly for the first time – he could exercise physical and emotional agency to obtain a toy of his own choosing. David represents himself as a persuasive figure who can successfully convince his mother to buy Bernard for him by combining affectionate display for the soft toy with a firm refusal to let it go. Looking at the narrative enables us to see how David uses Bernard to tell a story about his growing abilities to 'get' what he wants.

In a similar series of stories, 14-year-old Abi describes how several of her favourite possessions reflected her on-going 'obsessions' with different animals. During the interview, Abi describes how efforts to persuade her mother to let her own different animals had mixed results. During a phase where she was particularly keen on horses, Abi manages to accumulate a full set of horse riding equipment, but had been unsuccessful in persuading her mother to let her take up riding lessons:

> **Abi:** I used to be obsessed with horses and I didn't have a horse, but I had like everything else, the saddle and all the equipment (laughs).

Researcher Sara: Oh really? But you didn't go horse riding?

Abi: (Laughs) No! And then I just like really didn't know what to do with the saddle, so it was just shoved in my wardrobe.

Although Abi was not eventually successful in taking up riding lessons, persuading her mum to get her the riding gear had taken her one step closer to her dream. Abi's greatest success came in persuading her mum to let her have a pet rabbit. She explains:

I wanted a dog for quite a long time. So because my mum wouldn't let me have a dog she felt kind of bad so she easily let me have a rabbit.

In the lead up to buying the rabbit, Abi describes how she spent her 'whole time reading about rabbits' and researching the best cage and equipment. In these stories, Abi illustrates how her persistence eventually paid off as she gradually persuaded her mother to let her adopt a pet rabbit. Her eventual success also marks a moment of increased responsibility. The rabbit is kept in Abi's room and her mother makes it clear that it is Abi's duty to ensure it is fed, cleaned and exercised. Like David's story, Abi's emphasizes her ability to attain something much sought after, however, it also narratively traces her transition to being recognized by her mother as 'responsible' enough to care for an animal. In both cases, the objects play a key role in helping the children 'to grow' by materially scaffolding their transition to new forms of agency and responsibility.

In the case of 14-year-old Aliyah, one relatively mundane object was evocative of an important new period of developing friendships and spending time outside of home and school. Initially, Aliyah shared her mobile phone as a highly significant object in her life, particularly for keeping in touch with her closest group of school friends. However, during the interview, it was a small plastic Starbucks 'anti-dust plug' shaped like a Frappuccino and a plastic phone shell with the Starbucks logo that promoted the most discussion about spending time with her friendship group. Together, the phone accessories were relatively mundane items, however the Starbucks brand associated with the objects became an important emblem for experiences she shared with friends away from home and school:

Researcher Liam: Why do you like Starbucks?

Aliyah: Basically there's a Starbucks that we, my friends, always go to. We always end up going Starbucks, they went there yesterday. Everyone likes Starbucks [...] I like everything in Starbucks, apart from some of their drinks, but I like everything else.

Liam: What kinds of things do you order when you go?

Aliyah: Hot chocolate or Frappuccinos, something like that. Usually Frappuccinos.

Liam: And then you all sit there and –

Aliyah: Yeah and then we come back home, so it's weird but

Liam: No, it sounds good.

Aliyah: Basically it happens if my friend Lisa, she always goes, she's like the Starbucks queen, she knows everything about Starbucks. So sometimes after school she wants to go Starbucks and if anyone wants to go with her then yeah. I didn't go yesterday, but yesterday they went Starbucks and bowling, so we always end up going Starbucks.

For Aliyah, Starbucks epitomized a social space that was independent from school and family. Carrying the branded accessories on her phone provided an ever-present reminder of that experience, but also visually displayed the brand as a shared site of value and meaning within the friendship group. The significance of the Starbucks brand also exceeded the objects – signifying the intensive experience (Lash & Lury 2007) shared by Aliyah and her friends of meeting and hanging out together at the coffee shop. For Aliyah, Starbucks represented a newfound sense of independence that was realized through the 'mature' consumption practice of meeting for coffee. However, later in the interview, Aliyah describes how time meeting with friends outside of school also provides a licence to 'act weird' and to have fun in a way that isn't possible whilst at school. This subversiveness is also made possible by Starbucks as a transitional space between home and school where the group can act and talk in ways not possible under adult scrutiny. In this instance, the immaterial and intensive experience of the brand plays a highly significant role in marking a key period of transition in her life.

So far, we have considered the significant role objects play in materializing and memorializing important memories and relationships in young people's lives; however, objects could also stand in for and mark absences in their narratives about themselves. For 15-year-old Jasmine, everyday life is marked by regular domestic upheaval. On each of our research visits, she is living at a new address, moving between different family members and temporary foster carers. Jasmine chooses a soft unicorn that had been left behind at her mother's house as her favourite thing. Physical and emotional distances converge as Jasmine expresses sadness at not being able to pass on her unicorn to her 2-month-old daughter. She has, however, begun to accumulate a collection of soft toys for her daughter to treasure in the future. In Jasmine's words, 'she's got like loads of rabbits, and she's got like two little cats [...] I just want her to have a lot'. Toys are important as comforters and playthings, but they also hold value as a way of materializing love and care and both making and holding onto childhood memories in the future (see also Pugh 2004 and Ponsford 2002).

Curation: Object pasts and futures

By inviting participants to choose and narrate objects, we were also inviting them to act as curators of their lives – something that connected the research to the everyday practices of sorting, valuing, and caring for objects that young people were already engaged in. We can understand curation as taking many forms, including the assembling of collections in digital photo albums, memory boxes and on shelves, as well as single objects stashed, storied or cared for with a future purpose in mind. The etymological root of curation is 'to care', and in our research, we were particularly interested to explore how children cared for objects, and the forms of curation this entailed. Discussion of children's curation practices was most commonly prompted by researchers asking which objects children felt would remain important to them in the future. Though not all objects were deliberately kept or preserved by children with a view to having future value (e.g. as a keepsake), we did find that it was common to value certain objects as having significance beyond its everyday 'use value'. It is in these instances that we might think of young people as 'curating' their own pasts. In the following examples, we consider a variety of different curation practices encountered in the research. We initially explore curation as a 'site of care' for the material past, where children begin to reflect on the evolving value of objects and the memories they evoke. These are ideas also explored in Chapter 10, where we use the term 'votive epistemology' to capture something of the way in which the materialization of time gains value within the wider culture. Here, we then explore instances where the value of objects becomes explicitly future orientated as children weigh tensions between obsolesce, nostalgia, sentimentality and economic value – shaping choices about what to keep and what to shed.

Curating pasts: Making and editing memories

One of the teenagers most visibly engaged in curating her material past was Aliyah. As one of the older members of the research panel, Aliyah had grown out of most of her childhood toys and had begun to sort through and reassess the value of her childhood possessions. She described passing on her collection of Barbie dolls to her younger sister, but was unable to recall exactly what had happened to the toys:

> I don't know what happened to my old toys. Oh, I think I handed them down to my little sister, and then she probably lost them or something, 'cos she always loses, she has nothing from her past, so yeah she probably lost it or something, I don't know.

Aliyah's sister is described as lacking sentimentality about past possessions, and as failing to keep safe objects that had been passed on to her. This is held in contrast with Aliyah, who describes herself as treasuring certain special items from the past. One favourite object shared by Aliyah was a Tamagotchi that she has held onto despite it having been broken a number of years. The toy evokes pleasurable memories of primary school for Aliyah and, during the interview, she recalls how she and her friends would all sneak their Tamagotchis into school to surreptitiously play with during lunch and break times. When asked where she keeps the Tamagotchi, Aliyah shares a shoebox (see Figure 5.1) containing a variety of possessions from her past:

> **Researcher Liam:** What other sort of things have you kept in the box?
> **Aliyah:** My old school tie, and badge from the blazer [...] And I have this handbag, that was my first handbag. yeah I've got some other stuff.

Aliyah describes how she has retrieved the shoebox especially for the interview, and that it is normally stored in her dad's garden shed and that she doesn't have space to store it in her bedroom. Along with the Tamagotchi, Aliyah's shoebox also contains memorabilia from Disney's *High School Musical* (she was a fan, but has now grown out of it), her first purse and an old school tie and badge. These latter school items hold particular significance for Aliyah, and although she had not originally intended to share them in the interview, she is happy to discuss them. Over the past year, Aliyah's secondary school has undergone a great deal of upheaval – with an 'inadequate' Ofsted inspection result leading to a new head teacher and a high turnover of teaching staff. As part of an overhaul by the new head teacher, the school uniform has been replaced with different logos and colours. This has been a period of difficult change for Aliyah, affecting her schoolwork and grades. Aliyah has positive memories of how the school used to be, and holding on to the tie and badge provide her with a means of preserving that past identity of the school in her memory.

When asked how she chooses what to keep in her shoebox, Aliyah struggles to articulate a logic for her choices:

> **Liam:** How do you choose what to keep in there?
> **Aliyah:** If something really like, if something happened, I don't know (.) it just, I don't know.

Whilst the interview prompts Aliyah to consider what items of value she has kept from her past, the act of curation itself has not been informed by any explicit or previously articulated logic. Nonetheless, Aliyah's decision to curate a shoebox has been a conscious choice. Her original inspiration came from YouTuber 'Jack's Gap', who posted a popular video sharing the contents of his own memory box. As we describe in Chapter 4, YouTubers, were

FIGURE 5.1 *Aliyah's memory box*

often an important inspiration for many practices of self-documentation that we observed. After seeing the video, Aliyah felt inspired to create her own memory box:

> I was telling myself to make one for ages and then I watched their video and I was like I should, I should maybe do it now.

For Aliyah, the practice of curation is one simultaneously inspired by popular culture and marks her practice as typical of the times within which she lives. Though Aliyah couldn't articulate an overarching logic for selecting items to keep in her box, the decision to curate a memory box is nonetheless an explicit choice and what she saves and why has unique biographical significance.

Thirteen-year-old Sean is similarly invested in materially curating past memories. Using a tablet and a digital picture frame, Sean captures and stores large numbers of photos depicting important people and events in his life. These photo collections take on heightened value for Sean in recent years. In his final primary school years, Sean was diagnosed with a muscular degenerative disorder that saw him gradually lose movement across nearly his entire body. Adjusting to the rapid pace of his body's deterioration has been both a painful and deeply frustrating experience for Sean, leading to him attending a school specifically designed for children with complex physical disabilities and health needs. Through support from charities and other organizations, Sean is able to take part in a number of experiences that are held especially for him, including visiting his favourite football team's stadium and riding at high speeds around a race car circuit. These experiences are all documented in Sean's photo album, either recorded by himself or family members. Curated in his digital photo albums, the documented experiences form a treasured collection for Sean that play on constant rotation on a picture frame in his room.

Sean's photo albums are also marked by absences – particularly from his early childhood and prior to his diagnosis. One of Sean's carers at his school explains that he no longer looks at photographs from before his condition, as this has become too distressing. Instead, the digital picture frame in his room has been carefully curated to show images of significant memories during the advanced stages of his condition, with earlier photos filtered out. Through the exclusion of certain photographs, Sean has made an explicit break with part of his past – avoiding the memories evoked by those affectively charged visual traces of his earlier life. For Sean, curation provides the ability to selectively sort and bring to the fore those memories which have provided moments of joy and pleasure during a difficult biographical period of physical and emotional transition.

Curating futures: Value and obsolescence

Researcher Sue: How do you think the things you play with have changed as you have got a bit older?
David: Get a bit dusty.

In our discussions with younger children, we often asked them to reflect on how their relationship to particular toys or objects might change as they got older. For some, attachment to early childhood toys had already begun to wane and some unused objects were gradually slipping into obsolescence. As David describes above, these toys and objects are often left collecting 'dust' under beds or in the back of cupboards. Obsolescence has a twin meaning in this context – representing a cultural shift towards products designed with shorter material life cycles that rapidly grow out of date and are consumed by 'dust' (Gabrys 2011; Parikka 2013), but also a revaluing of objects over time as children decide which objects to keep and care for *despite* their breaking or falling out of everyday use.[4] Seven-year-old Lucien, for example, describes how his

---

[4]The film *Toy Story 3* captures both of these trends, as Andy grows out of his toys and younger children see the toys as dated and defunct.

interest in motor vehicles changed as he got older. A previously prized Lego camper van[5] is no longer considered 'fast enough' and, instead, he wants to collect models of motor cars that are similar to those he watches on the television programme *Top Gear*. For Lucien and other children, a challenge of 'growing older' is deciding which toys matter enough to be kept, and which can be given away. In some instances, these decisions become a source of debate between children and parents about the sentimental value of early childhood objects. For 10-year-old Megan and her brothers (a set of triplets), this debate arose when they decided to sell some of their soft toys at a local jumble sale. The children were prompted to sort through old toys after seeing an advert for the jumble sale posted through their letterbox. On learning of their plan to sell one particular set of soft toys from when they were born, Megan's mother felt that they might regret giving them away later. The children were eventually persuaded when their mother explained how the soft toys had been embroidered with their initials when they born, and placed in their cots to help differentiate them. For Megan and her brothers this vicarious memory adds new sentimental value to toys they had been willing to part with. Decisions about what to keep or discard become political within the context of collective family memory, with parents and children debating the sentimental significance of childhood objects.

Seven-year-old Nkosi similarly found that his parents weren't prepared for him to part with certain childhood objects yet:

> **Nkosi:** One time I put [the toys] in a box and I wanted to tell my mum and dad I am going to sell them tomorrow. I am going to sell them for £2.50.
> **Researcher Sue:** Wow that is very good. Did you get £2.50?
> **Nkosi:** No. Mummy and daddy said no.

Though Nkosi is disappointed that he can't sell his old unused toys, he also acknowledges that certain toys can be too special to give away. He describes his plan to hold onto one prized remote controlled racing car to pass on to his own children in the future:

> **Sue:** So that is like a real favourite. And do you think you will ever get fed up with it?
> **Nkosi:** No. I think I will have it when I am a man.
> **Sue:** Yeah, why not.
> **Nkosi:** I might keep it for my son or daughter-
> **Sue:** Ah that is nice.

---

[5]This Lego camper van was given to Lucien by his parents because of its similarity to the family's own holiday camper van. During the Making Modern Motherhood study, Lucien's grandmother had described the significance of the camper van for enabling the family to make annual trips to relatives in Germany.

Nkosi: And if I have a daughter I am going to sprayed it pink or purple.

Sue: Well it is rather nice orange. She might like it orange.

Nkosi: And if the son doesn't want it orange I am going to spray it red.

Sue: Right, do you like red?

Nkosi: Red is my favourite and my dad's.

Nkosi's favourite toy car is described as having value and life beyond the present – a souvenir from his childhood to be passed on to a future generation. Nkosi also expresses willingness to customize the colour of the car for his future offspring. For his son, Nkosi suggests he would be prepared to spray the car 'red' – identifying, it as a favourite colour of both himself and his father. Nkosi thus not only proposes to share his much-loved toy with his future son, but also a (male) family preference for the colour red. The toy in this instance becomes a medium through which Nkosi curates his own childhood tastes and values for the future, as we discuss further in the next chapter.

A few exceptional objects have inter-generational histories that stretch back one or more generations. During one of our pilot interviews, 7-year-old Emily shares a collection of dolls that had originally been her mother's childhood possessions, and which she has since inherited ('my mum got me loads from her past'). Emily is fascinated by their worn fabrics and curiously vintage designs:

> Emily: It's great because they don't actually break because they've got stuff inside. Not like you know those plastic ones that the arms come off that are not actually huggable. But these are huggable.

For Emily there is something uniquely comforting about these dolls that had once been her mother's companions and playthings, and she emphasizes their durability and hug-ability compared to modern 'plastic' dolls. The dolls are also a site of care for Emily and, during the interview, she affectionately buttons their clothes and plaits their hair. Curation in this instance becomes a very literal form of care. By being passed down from mother to daughter, the dolls had become a material point of inter-generational connection interweaving memories and histories across two different childhoods.

Curating childhoods: The materiality and temporality of the research archive

Although our focus in this study was on children's everyday cultures we became aware that the research process itself was playing a role in documenting and memorializing a particular period in the lives of the participants.

FIGURE 5.2 *Megan's changing bedroom*

Our research activities captured brief snapshots of the children's lives that often rapidly become outdated as representations. A year on from the favourite things interviews, we returned to participants to carry out 'recursive interviews' where we looked back with them (and sometimes their parents) at the archive of research records we had collated (see Chapters 2 and 10). These interviews highlighted the rapid pace of change in different aspects of the children's lives over the course of the project.

Of all the data, records of the 'favourite things' tended to signal the most significant changes. In some cases, children described how the objects previously identified as most important to them in the present had changed. Aliyah's Starbucks adorned phone was replaced with a new iPhone brought as a birthday present by her brother, just as Abi's iPad was displaced by a new iPhone. Lucien's interests had expanded to include Minecraft – marking a new foray into social and online gaming with friends and associated commentaries on YouTube. Objects materially embodied continuity and change in the children's lives, with bedrooms – the home of many of the children's material possessions – providing a key indicator of shifting values and interests (Lincoln 2012). When we first met Megan, her bedroom wall was adorned with Moshi Monsters, only to be replaced for a short time by One Direction posters, which were in turn consigned to the bin (see Figure 5.2). David's bedroom had also undergone significant change, with toys cleared away and a hanging basket of soft bears emptied. Potentially, to signal his transition to becoming an 'older boy', David described how Bernard was no longer a bedtime companion. Returning to the favourite things data provided an opportunity for us to reflect with the children on the evolving value of their material objects over time.

Preparing to archive the research data also brought to the fore how families perceived our research as records of the children's lives. In Sean's case, our favourite things interview became an event photographed and archived in his digital album. In this instance, the research event overlapped with Sean's personal curation practices. The idea of a period of the children's lives being 'immortalized' in an archive and becoming a 'part of history', as one parent described, appealed to many of the families. Megan and her mother described how they liked the idea of revisiting the archive with future generations to show them what Megan's childhood was like. Sean's mother also described how pleased she was for Sean to have a part of his life archived alongside other 'everyday childhoods' – commenting 'Oh fancy them picking you!' For some of the families then, our research record was an important 'archive' that might have value for them over time as a site of memory or 'time capsule' to which they could return. In some instances, however, children and parents voiced uncertainties about how the archived research record might be (mis)read or (mis)interpreted by others at a future point in time (see Chapter 8). In this case, the archive was regarded as 'locked' in time as the world changed around it. Whilst the meaning and value of children's own archives remained under their careful custodianship, the public research archive would be subject to the interpretation of others.

This chapter has explored how children's material worlds are infused with time, nostalgia and memory from an early age. During our 'favourite thing' interviews, we were struck by the significant role material objects played in shaping children's sense of their past, presents and futures. Rather than simply being the 'material backdrop' to children's lives, toys and other treasured objects were central to the practices by which the children explored biographical storytelling and narrative, nostalgia and aging, memory and forgetting, and sentimentality and obsolesce. We also observed through these interviews how children begin the work of 'sorting' and 'curating' their material pasts – selecting which objects to keep as important markers of time and sites of memory for the future. The overall aim of the chapter has been to contribute new child-centred perspectives on the significance of time, memory and nostalgia in material cultures. Moving between childhood studies literatures and the accounts of children in this study enables a sense of childhood as a self-conscious period of becoming, enjoyed by parents, monitored by markets and enacted by children in distributed networks of agency within which time is materialized. Some of the themes introduced in this chapter will be revisited in the final chapter of the book, reflecting on how time, technology and documentation may be coming into a new configuration in digitally saturated time, associated with a heightened sensitivity to the passage of time and new forms of value thereby made available.

6

The Work of Gender for Children: Now You See It, Now You Don't

Rachel Thomson, Sara Bragg and Mary Jane Kehily

As part of her 'day in a life' study of eight-year-old Nkosi, researcher Sue walks for half an hour with him, his sister and his mother Lorraine through the rain and London housing estates to reach his Catholic primary school. On the way, Sue and Lorraine chat about Nkosi's recent, costly, birthday party, and how his father is returning to the Caribbean soon. They pass the local, more convenient, primary school that his cousins attend, and a police stop-and-search, which Lorraine comments has been happening regularly for months. Before entering the school, Nkosi changes his rain boots for shiny black shoes.

In this chapter, we explore the work of gender that we find in the everyday lives of children, but also the work of gender that characterizes the analytic labours of the feminist researcher – reflecting on both these aspects and the

FIGURE 6.1 *Nkosi's shiny black shoes*

connections between them that we encounter through a reflexive and materi-alist orientation to methodology.[1] Our approach involves theoretically focused understandings of gender, which in turn inform our orientation towards empir-ical material and empirically grounded research practices, asking how these categories are created and experienced in everyday life. These are not distinct approaches, instead marking the directions of traffic that are always involved in the back-and-forth processes of knowledge construction that characterize social research. Yet, a lack of awareness about the categories that we impose on the world through our research may not only impoverish our analysis, but also diminish the lives we seek to know. The lens that we adopt has conse-quences for what and how we see it. Our subtitle 'now you see it now you don't' refers to a series of questions including the part played by the research-er's gaze in producing accounts of gender, how gender differences are more or less explicit and marked in different spaces, and how we might make sense of why, when and how gender does (and perhaps does not) matter in children and young people's everyday lives.

---

[1]An early version of this paper was presented in March 2015 at the Arctic University of Norway at an international research symposium called 'The work of gender in the lives of children and young people'.

Nkosi's walk to school might be taken as telling a powerful story about growing up as a young black boy in London, in post-colonial contexts marked by fluid migrations; about the futures that beckon or threaten, the ambitions and fears that his family has for him. In wondering whether his school can appreciate the significance of those shiny black shoes (see Figure 6.1), carefully preserved from the rain, we ask ourselves too what a feminist gender lens enables us to see, but also what might be missed, and how we can honour the complexities of the lives we glimpse.

Operationalizing and assembling sex/gender

The approach we take in this chapter follows Nayak and Kehily's 2008 project, which pinpoints three analytic foci for empirical research into gender. First, it adopts a *situated frame*: asking what does it mean to be a 'proper' girl/boy in this precise time and place? What are the costs of failing to inhabit this identity? What are the possibilities for doing things differently? The 'situation' may be very precise, going beyond the usual dimensions of class, race and sexuality to include more precise contingencies such as what it means in *this* family, as perhaps a first child in a new generation, in a certain neighbourhood of a particular town. Working with longitudinal case studies, we are attuned to the importance of these questions of timing and positionality, while also understanding them as part of and contributing to wider patterns and formations. Secondly, we adopt an *observational approach*, to document how gender is experienced, enacted and embodied in everyday life. Thirdly, we work with a *performative theory* that draws attention to how gender is produced (what is the work children do); how it is regulated (noticing the role of schooling/state) and how it is consumed (in/by popular culture, the 'market').

Our analysis makes no distinction between on and off line environments, and we explore how bodies and the non-human material world are implicated, assembled and entangled in sex/gender and family projects (Fox & Alldred 2013; Barad 2007; Blaise 2005; Castañeda 2002). We think about sex/gender as operating simultaneously at different scales – extensive and intensive. We zoom in for the close-up of a moment of interaction and zoom out to think about gender regimes and normativities that are part of the apparatus of governance. These scales are also temporal and involve the long slow timescapes of intergenerational family transmissions as well as the intensive temporalities associated with mastering a new toy or classroom technique (cf. Castañeda 2002).

In analysing our data through a post-empirical but materialist lens, we set out to recognize the intra-action between bodies, identities and material /

cultural resources, showing both what young people do *with* these resources and what these materials might do *to* them. Arguably, debates about the commercialization and sexualization of childhood have made this more difficult to do outside a moralistic framework or a determinist bias. These debates have captured popular and political attention across the developed western world in recent years, with a range of anxieties and constituencies circulating around the supposedly dangerous shaping of modes of sex/gender by consumer products and by digital lives and play.[2] This agenda has reinforced polarized assumptions about girls as victims (objectified and undermined by popular culture) and boys as boosted by the same material (learning problematically sexist but dominant attitudes and behaviours). A focus on the material and commercial practices of parenting and children's own consumption, exemplified for instance in boycotts of pink and blue ('Pink Stinks' or 'Let Girls be Girls'), has (in the UK at least) resulted in a situation where children's gender performances and practices have become markers for social class, ethnicity and social exclusion, effectively stigmatizing or marginalizing working class or non-western cultural values (Bragg 2014; Kehily 2012; Egan 2013; Renold et al. 2015). We aim to resist these shifts and preserve the gains made through the key analytic idea of sex/gender as performative effect – gaining the *appearance* of being natural through repetition over time. This changed the political project from earlier liberal modes of anti-sexism, towards strategies of disruption and the celebration of diversity and non-conformity where the very categories male and female and the assumptions that lead from them are open to contestation.[3]

Although gender is one (important) analytic lens and a difference that matters, we acknowledge that it is how it works in combination with other differences (such as social class, sexuality and ethnicity, in particular times and places) that gives it meaning and power. Gender can have an authorizing or 'fixing' role so that terms such as 'good boy/girl' can eclipse the significance of other differences. We attempt to maintain a 'queer eye' on our research data, meaning that we are sensitized not only to the intersections of gender with sexuality, but also to the performativities of our own analysis – how far we focus on and thus bring into view the non-normative alongside the normative. Finally, we contend that gender is simultaneously part of our inner and

---

[2]In the United Kingdom, various policy reviews were commissioned by both New Labour (1997–2010) and Coalition (2010–2015) UK governments. Some of these had little academic credibility, such as a 2010 review of 'the sexualisation of young people' led by psychologist Linda Papadopoulos for the Home Office and, in 2011, a further review of the commercialization and sexualization of childhood for the Department of Education led by Reg Bailey, CEO of a Christian charity. A key policy and academic document was a 2009 review of children and the commercial world (Buckingham 2009a).

[3]Although present within radical feminist theory from the 1970s, these ideas gained popularity through the writings of Judith Butler from the early 1990s.

outer worlds. Analysing gender should be able to connect the social and the psychic without collapsing into the 'mythic' and losing a connection to the significance of time, place and power. This requires a way of thinking about dependency and development as well as the psychodynamic processes of everyday relationships that involve 'family dialogues' (Rosenthal 2002), 'repudiations' (Nayak & Kehily 2013), 'investments' and 'unconscious defences' (Frosh et al. 2002) and what Reay (2002) calls the 'psychic costs of class, gender and ethic identifications'.

The collaborative work of gender at home: Younger participants' objects, histories and selves

The invitation to 7 and 8-year-olds to share their 'favourite things' generally took us into domestic spaces: bedrooms and living rooms and the diverse material environments of children's homes that reveal gender as a situational negotiation between parents, children and siblings.

Gabriel's home environment is powerfully structured by parental decisions about play: the absence of the digital and of explicitly gendered toys (coded by colour), a focus on games and practices that are pedagogical in character and open to adult participation and view (board games, make and do), and toys that memorialize people, places and moments in their lives (Minty the cuddly sheep from a family holiday). As his favourite thing, Gabriel chooses a bicycle which he describes in ways that emphasize his physicality and skills and perhaps his superiority to his younger brother. Growing up as two boys in a middle-class household with two mothers provides a particular quality to the project of gender making for Gabriel and his brother. He presents himself as a clever and active boy who is skilled in music, maths and games, but in a school context, he may struggle a little to display the kinds of qualities that make him a popular boy with other children.

Nkosi also draws our attention to a wheeled vehicle in his choice of favourite things, in his case, a plastic toy motorbike (see Figure 6.2). How he shares it with us reveals an understanding of loss and attachment and the sense that this is a sphere of urgent labour: he has imagined himself as an adult man, a father, giving this toy to his own children. If he has a daughter, he will spray it pink or purple. If his son doesn't like orange he will spray it red. Nkosi's position as the only boy-child in a family where his father is an inconstant yet enduring presence shaped by transnational migration practices suggests that he is taking up his affective work within the family. This includes bridging time, place and attachment through the careful curation of precious objects.

FIGURE 6.2 *Imagined masculinities: Nkosi's motorbike*

Because we have backstory about Nkosi's family from our earlier study, we notice echoes with his grandmother's choice of a box of personal belongings from her deceased father that she shared with researchers in her 'favourite things' interview seven years earlier (see Figure 6.3) – captured here in the researcher Sue's fieldnote:

> For her past object, Beverley had chosen a set of things that remind her of her father, who 'was quite a focal point in our family' and 'has a special place in my heart'. He was 70 years old when he died. These were things she 'will never do away with, ever', and she had them all together in a shoe-box. She had always been much closer to her father than her mother. The first thing she showed me was the wire chain that her father used to make up, recycling old coat hangers that she had obtained from her workplace, and explained how it was made and used to tie up animals without choking them. Then she produced her father's birth and death certificates, divorce papers, bank book, passport and NI card, that she had carefully kept. The items were all in the shoebox belonging to the trainers she had bought him, which he had only worn once. Finally, she produced his glasses, and his hat, and told me the story of her wearing his hat to go somewhere,

FIGURE 6.3 *Imagined masculinities: Beverley's mementos from her dad*

shortly after he'd been buried, and leaving the hat in a taxi. Greatly upset, she had thankfully managed to track it down.

David is an only child, providing a guided tour to his bedroom and toys that reveals him at the centre of a world of adult attention. When asked about how he has changed, he mentions the accumulation of dust on neglected toys and the difficulties he has with remembering. His favourite thing is his mum's old phone, through which he can Skype or WhatsApp the important people in his life, distinguishing knowledgeably between those who are online and offline. Games and toys are explained to the researcher according to what they *do*, how they fit into cross-media franchises, as well as with whom he plays them (and whether he wins) and in the case of his cuddly toy and guitar, how they facilitate his connection to places other than his home. He is attentive to the cost of things, noting that this is a concern within the household. Elsewhere, we have written about this case as illustrating 'relationship in context, that asks what we might understand if we just keep looking', noticing how material culture is caught up in ongoing processes of 'weaning', mediating attachment and separation for all parties (Thomson & Baraitser 2017). Six months later, we find David's room transformed, the cherished collection of his childhood universe radically edited, usurped by the PlayStation and a friend, marking a new moment and a more peer-based gender project.

Also an only child, Saffron narrates her various collections to researcher Lucy, paying attention to temporality (when they were acquired, and how different collections and associated play superseded each other). Fragments of this description can be heard on the audio recordings on our website, and her low, quiet voice, contrasted to Lucien's or Gabriel's emphatic tones, tells something of gender in their respective families. She explains that before she began collecting Moshi Monsters, she collected Barbie dolls, which are rendered into the past tense by her. She also shares her almost-forgotten 'Leapfrog' computer, surpassed by the iPad through which she accesses music, videos and a range of games such as the 'Cake pop' cooking app. The iPad is also used to interact with her Furby, which can be fed and nurtured in interaction with an app. She explains that you can 'make it sick if you give it food it doesn't like', noting that her Dad once made the mistake of feeding it virtual fish. Saffron's collection of Moshi Monsters is a particular focus of attention, and she describes their different characteristics, and tells of how she can share them with her cousin and friends who also collect. Saffron likes to organize her Moshi Monsters into colours while her cousin organizes them according to whether they are 'good or bad'. Saffron prefers not to bring her Moshi Monsters to school in case she loses them, and we are left with a sense of a contained play world within her own home, connected strategically to friends and family, yet also private and interior. Researcher Lucy observes:

> Collecting (and display) seems to be a bit of a theme – collecting dolls and soft toys past and present, collecting Moshi Monsters (MMs) and then collecting tracks on the iPad. All of these forms of collecting involve adults – buying, passing on, approving, displaying etc but as far as I could gather only the MMs involved interaction with other children (swapping). The type of play Saffron engages in with these MMs are about rescuing and adventures. Some of the MMs are duplicates so she has made them into siblings. Siblings argue together (said with a smile).

Saffron's media worlds appear to be surveilled in a way that we did not notice among the boy children: she asks her mother if she can look up particular (controversial) women performers such as Lady Gaga or Katy Perry online. Saffron's mother is aware that she needs to monitor and denies her request at that moment, but in practice, misses the fast-moving content that Saffron accesses by following all things Katy Perry. Debates about so-called 'sexualization', with

FIGURE 6.4 *Barbie dolls and their dramas*

their emphasis on the spectacular aspects of media consumption, and the threat to girls in particular, hover over such requests and their refusal.

The boundary between the everyday life of the household and fantasy/play seems more porous for Tempest, whose account of her favourite things takes the form of a vivid acting-out of the characters of her Barbie dolls. Tempest brings in a large crate full of Barbie dolls, too numerous to count and too heavy to carry, with the help of her mother, Kim (see Figure 6.4). Rifling through it looking for her favourite favourites, Tempest pulls out a few dolls and begins arranging them on the floor and dressing them up. Her 'very favourite' is a Barbie around which she builds a play scenario. The doll has a job looking after other people's babies, and sometimes has so many babies to look after that she has to organize helpers to assist her. The doll and looked-after-babies area grows as the play develops into a pyramid system of shared day-care. Tempest arranges and rearranges them, changing their clothes, brushing their hair and sometimes scolding them. 'I might as well talk to a brick wall!' she exclaims, quickly adding that Kim says that to her. Later, the looked-after-babies area breaks up and a group of other Barbie dolls prepare to go to a party. They are assigned their own car and a motorbike to take them there. Tempest gets them ready, asking for help in choosing shoes and accessories for the party posse. Should she wear the light pink or dark pink high heels? Off they go to another space by the door, in front of the cat-flap. The dolls are in an excitable mood, tossing heads and hands in the air as they arrive at the party. Different toys are animated at different points. Tempest negotiates with them, whispering in their ear to ask if they are happy to have their photograph taken: 'Yes, but no flash-lights'. Tempest's imaginative play combines the familiar and domestic with the mediated. The looking-after-babies play script can be seen as an enactment of the child-minding arrangement in place for her until she began full-time school. Organizing and taking care of the dolls captures something of the texture of family life as Tempest mimics the morning routines and forms of admonishment experienced within her own home. In contrast, the excitement of party-going, glamour, dressing-up and flash photography appears to be drawn from the world of celebrity culture and effortlessly blended into her Barbie playtime activities. Tempest's play operates as a parallel space from which she can engage with and sometimes make raids on the interactions around her. Gender is clearly central to these interactions – coded within the toys as well as the focal point of a predominantly matriarchal household.

Gender projects beyond 'childhood': Fluid self-shaping

As the one daughter and only girl of triplets, and also as the youngest of our intensive one-year panel members, Megan (aged 10 at the start of the research) has a particularly charged relationship to gender difference. She has a very pink room, and proudly shows the rosettes that she has won in the most feminine practice of majoretting. She also shares her fluffy teddy, which has her initial embroidered to its chest in order to distinguish it from those that her brothers were given. Similarly, the three were all bought tablets for their recent birthdays, in response to their insistence that they no longer share. In our first interview, Megan's has a pink case, although she spends much of her time playing the (relatively) gender-neutral games of Minecraft and The Simpsons with her brothers. By the time of our day in a life meeting, her tablet is white, and by the final interview, it has become an iPad of the model approved by her new secondary school. Meanwhile, her room decoration moves from Moshi Monsters, to One Direction posters supplied by her uncle. Researcher Liam notes that this 'seems like a significant transition for her', and how she appears 'quite embarrassed' about it in the interview. They have gone by the end of the study. Meanwhile, her mother proudly recounts how at school Megan campaigned for – and achieved – a weekly girls' only day on the football pitch. Megan also describes spending time with her brothers, watching the Disney series Liv &

Maddie (about identical twins) and the Simpsons. In other words, our research charted an array of identity shifts in the time span of her involvement.

In comparison to the younger panel, some of our teenage participants had a nonchalant response to the favourite things task, appearing to improvise in the moment. Fifteen-year-old Jasmine looks around her room and chooses a lipstick to show researcher Ester; Funmi (aged 15) shows Liam the book she always 'carries around'. Yet, their expositions of these to-hand items are nonetheless fascinating. Jasmine explains how time can be marked through make-up, looking back at the eyeliner she felt naked without just a year ago. Funmi explains how she rereads her book, going 'deeper into it' to 'understand what actually was going on'. Her description emphasizes the storyline's themes of grief, loss and relationships (the character's mother drowns in a tragic accident, leaving her 'torn up' inside but unable to cry, and she encounters a 'mysterious boy who she feels like she knows . . . I guess she's kind of learning more about herself as a person . . . ').

Others such as Aliyah (aged 14) take the task of memory-making seriously, sharing a box of objects including a dead Tamagotchi and an old school tie, which she has compiled to memorialize her childhood. Nathan (aged 13) has also retained a set of tiny trainers from his childhood, one of his oldest personal possessions. He un-self-consciously shares his collection of soft bears as his favourite thing from his past, reminiscing about the male friend from primary school who gave him one (see also Chapter 5). Several of the teenagers express nostalgia as they look back at favourite things that capture their lives at the age of seven or eight, as if this marked the end of a particular stage of enchanted or 'cute' childhood; an exception being Sean, who keeps few mementoes from before the onset of his degenerative illness. Teenage choices of favourite things of the moment tend to capture the here and now of their lives, whether intense internal worlds represented through music or books, or digital and connective media in the form of laptops, tablets and phones that connect them to peers and online culture, facilitating privacy from parents and the transcendence of home spaces. Teenagers reflecting back on their collections of toys and objects appear both to recognize and distance themselves from the gendered-ness of their histories. For example, bedrooms are often refurbished at this age (Abi at 15 and Nathan at 13 had already done this and Funmi, who apologises for the pinkness of her room, was planning to), with gender-coded colour schemes of pink and blue replaced by neutral grays, red and purple. Aliyah displays an amnesia about her Barbie dolls – indicating vaguely that she gave them to her younger sister who lost them – despite being reminded by her older sisters of their importance in her recent past. The adoption of androgynous and flexible favourites such as anime and Minecraft by tween-agers may suggest a new kind of self-conscious gender project, as we explore further below.

Materializing and situating gender: What the 'favourite things' method enables us to see

While much work on children's material cultures emphasizes normativity (how toys are coded as girl and boy, inciting, inflating and eroticizing gender difference (Buckingham 2011)), the invitation to children to talk us through their favourite things reveals the specificity and situated nature of their particular gender projects. The 'work' that our methods capture is defined by the immediate situation, but also the underlying family dialogue. Change can happen suddenly, as revealed by switches between backwards facing nostalgia and forward facing developmental spurts. The urgency and uneven intensity of this work suggests that we need theoretical tools that allow for a balancing of individual/biographical logics in interaction with wider social, cultural processes and material conditions. Toys can operate as scaffolds as children explore and master their affordances. Whether this process maps onto the progressive and (hetero)normative narratives of developmental stages is another matter, begging the question of the various push and pull factors or logics of practice that might be in operation – including the production of class, race and sexual cultures and the negotiation of local family dynamics. By thinking about the 'technicity' (Stiegler 1998) of toys such as the Furby and Tamagotchi, we can enrich our understanding of the work of gender; such toys operate as goads – demanding attention yet necessarily doomed to die proving impossible to care for.

The method also reveals how far early childhood gender projects are collaborations with parents and other significant adults who choose the toys and shape the environments within which children operate. Evidence in this data of active practices of identification and dis-identification through processes of growing up suggests that there is constant conversation with adult gender formations as apprehended in everyday interactions and within popular culture. The gender assumptions that are written into toys (Furby or Barbie) may come in and out of focus and be used strategically and creatively by children, but this is very different from the imposition of meanings assumed within the 'sexualization' debate. Key questions relate to *how* they are played with, with whom and for what ends/pleasures.

The work of gender at school: Where formal and informal gender regimes collide

The invitation to spend a day with the researcher resulted in us following a school day with all but one of the 8-year olds and four of the older panel (two in a special school, one primary, one secondary). Chapter 7 discusses schooling more generally; here, we focus specifically on gender. The distinctive contribution of our methods here is how, unlike much other research which looks at gender in one or other but not both locations, they enable us to explore the links and discontinuities between the respective gender projects of home and school.

When we look for evidence of gender in our field notes, we begin to understand how far the official curriculum deliberately elides gender while also embedding it. All the primary schools have simple uniforms which take the form of a standardized and badged coloured sweatshirt. The pre-eminent identifications offered by teachers are learning identities. For example, Lucien's Spanish teacher asks the class to articulate their 'learning intention' at the start of the class and congratulates them for their 'excellent learning behaviours'. Gabriel's class teacher uses circle time to invite the children to identify and name their learning styles (he opts for being a mathematical and musical learner, categories that he shares with his mothers at the end of the day). In Abi's secondary school, the formal curriculum and identities on offer relate primarily to learning and exam performance.

We note the traditionally gendered nature of some problematizations of behaviour. In Saffron's school, researcher Lucy observes how 'The teacher comes over and pretends to be cross about wasting school resources. She says she expected better of such *"good girls"*. One particularly shy girl looks ready to cry. I feel for her' (Lucy's notes, our emphasis). Saffron is seen by her teacher as 'too shy to ask for help', and we observe her tidying her table, writing quietly and neatly – but later, Lucy agrees with Saffron: 'she is right, she is not shy in school'. Gabriel's teacher talks to Sue about 'what a lovely chap Gabriel is, and particularly that he seems more in touch with feelings', which feels, on rereading, to be a covert comment on his family context. In Abi's school, girls entertain themselves by distracting and engaging teachers while boys pick up the lion's share of detentions, which are publicly posted for all to see. School uniform becomes the front line of gender trouble, with boys flouting requirements to tuck in shirts and Abi defying the regulation of footwear and ripping holes in her black tights (see Figure 6.5).

There is a sense that teachers must work hard to hold at bay practices that, in their effects, are gendering or sexualizing. Gabriel's teacher uses lollypop sticks as a way of disrupting the patterning of children's choices when he wants them to work in pairs or groups. Seating is controlled and calibrated for each lesson, with children moving without comment into different groups, reflecting an obscure personalized learning grid beneath the surface. Yet, there are moments beyond the system, and these are occupied immediately by the children to express other aspects of the informal pupil culture. David is always first and in front if he can be. In Nkosi's school, the boys rush to the climbing frame at break time; this masculine monopolizing of space is only indirectly

FIGURE 6.5 *Abi's tights and officially forbidden*
Doc Marten boots and mobile phone

tackled when adults intervene by asking the girls to leave first to give them a head start. Nkosi seems to fall easily into the embodied practices of being one of the boys; we do not notice a desire to be different, but rather, practices of connection and sameness with boys like him.

Wet play (which happens in many of the schools given the time of year we were researching) is an interregnum in which gendered behaviour was observable, with boys clustered around the cartoons and the front of the class and girls occupying the margins. Book time is also a moment of gendered 'self-making', with Saffron choosing *Princess Fairies*, Lucien *Matilda*, and Nkosi and his friend reading identical copies of *Football Crazy* (see Figures 7.2 and 7.3). It is as if the practices of neutralizing gender that have become part and parcel of (at least some) early years settings unintentionally enchant gendered play as a space of informality and intensity (Holland 2003). In Abi's school, the informal spaces between and sometimes within lessons are quickly occupied by young people, used for learning as well as consumption, solidarity and solitary pleasures. Sara observes 'intimate murmurs of female companionship' as girls chat on their way to school, is impressed by the 'pleasure' they take 'in each other's company', and the 'mundane eroticisms' of school friends as they plait each others' hair and trace patterns on their backs outside at lunch time.

It is girls who move in to 'annex' the researcher, engaging in feminine ban-ter about rings, husbands, mothers and hair accessories. Lucy is reminded of the fraught politics of 'sitting next to' rather than 'opposite' others during her observation of Saffron, and is drawn into the attention economy of her friendship group, noting 'Saffron goes straight back to her desk but her friend remains and asks me if I will be going back to Saffron's house afterwards. I say I will be and I look across at Saffron. She looks a bit upset (cross) I pre-sume, because her friend is still sitting with me and she is not'.

In our observations, researchers notice gender around seating and behav-iour. Whenever a child is called out by a teacher for bad behaviour, the researcher records their gender and usually too their ethnicity. It seems that this is a latent discourse that touches children too, despite being unmarked in the educational talk of levels and learning: when Rachel 'lets slip' that she saw a child in Lucien's class 'pinching' a 'good behaviour' house token, they imme-diately grill her: 'was the person black?' and encourage her to 'tell the teacher'. Researchers also observe the gender composition of the tables, attempting to work out when these are patterned by the choices of children (e.g. both Gabriel and Lucien appear to prefer the company of girls) and when they are shaped by deliberate selection – to differentiate by ability (the top set) or to harmonize behaviour (splitting friends apart). Certain children appear to be kept on a very short leash, with their seating and movement surveilled at all times, while others move freely around the classroom. We assume that the teach-er's choice of Lucien to fetch and distribute laptops is a sign of favour (this is explored fully in Chapter 10, where we consider how 'researching' operates as a practice that can transcend home and school producing valuable cultural cap-ital). Gender is part of these systems yet, as researchers, we were often left guessing how these systems worked. The times when children can make their own choices about where they were and with whom (playtime and lunch) are especially interesting for us. These might be moments when children effect-ively disappear from our gaze as, for instance, is the case with Nkosi, who runs off with his two best friends, or when David and his friend go into their own play-world. Or we may be invited to join their free time, as is the case with Lucien, who lets Rachel sit with him and Milly at lunch as they 'pick like hum-ming birds on the sweet bits' of their lunches, or when Gabriel waits for Sue in order to take her into the lunch hall. We are left pondering how far comfort with adult company and attention may be part of a gendered middle-class habitus.

Gender is also visible and noted by researchers in relation to the adults of the school. Descriptions of teachers invariably include age (generally 'young'), gender and ethnicity/ nationality. Researchers comment also on the profile of the teachers in comparison to the support staff, and how they fit within the gender/class/ethnic profile of the school community. Support staff are fre-quently identified as mothers of children who have passed through the school and appear to have a connection with the school history that goes beyond the time frame of most teachers and recent processes of gentrification. Rachel reports that she is called 'Miss' in the staff room by teaching assistants who are predominantly mature black working class women. In Gabriel's school, Sue comments on how young, fashionable and white the teachers all seem to be, but that this is 'no surprise'. In Abi's school, Sara observes how teachers all develop their own gendered styles, which range from the 'bluff, tough, macho' to the 'sharp/acerbic'.

We sometimes notice connections between the formal and informal gender regimes. For example, David's class are working with the myth of the Minotaur as a project that bridges different lessons and extends into homework. In an impromptu drama lesson, pupils are invited to imagine and sense the spaces through which the Minotaur moves, an invitation that is taken up by David and friends to imagine a cave full of 'lumps of lava, dead people, blood dripping' – echoing the violent motifs of their break-time games which revolve around a running boy who we are told is 'a bomb about to go off'. Classwork on Ted Hughes's book *The Iron Man*, discussed in Chapter 7, might be read as engaging with the vulnerability of masculinity as well as of the school system as a whole, as we read it there.

The particular character of the school setting is always significant. Researcher Sue's description of a religious education class at Nkosi's inner city Catholic primary school captures a sense of the dense interaction of formal and informal school cultures, official and unofficial knowledges, and behavioural and pedagogic techniques. The class begins with the (white Irish woman) teacher quizzing the pupils (who are predominantly male and non-white) about 'the kind of people God wants us to be'. Sue observes that 'The children quite like this and there are several hands up to contribute. For example, T talks about Nelson Mandela and how he got white and black together, another mentions the 10 commandments'. During the lesson, the children are invited to talk about this question and about 'the creation story' in pairs; later, they all move to different tables for this lesson in another configuration whose logic is obscure to the researcher. Some children get to put their names up on the circles for 'sitting and listening well'; two others (including T) are punished for allegedly fighting and have to sit on the carpet facing the board. Their work on the Beatitudes involves using the interactive board as well as worksheets to link the first ('Blessed are … ') and last ('for they shall … ') parts correctly, drawing pictures relating to the Beatitudes that they are told will be going into 'God's Garden'. Nkosi, for his part, seems a little distracted – 'I notice Nkosi is fiddling with a small tin of Vaseline, which he occasionally uses on his nose' – and when he and another boy are given a picture of a (white) woman weeping and a (black) woman comforting her to illustrate the Beatitude 'Blessed are those that mourn, for they shall be comforted', they 'trace the picture onto a blank sheet instead of doing their own interpretations'. At midday, 'They all line up for lunch and Miss M gives a religious blessing' (Sue's notes). We are struck by the saturation of this educational scene by raced and classed as well as gendered signifiers and meanings.

Schools outside the mainstream appear to work along different lines. Researcher Liam notes the following revealing moment as part of Sean's day:

> J spots that Sean is looking intently at the Teaching Assistant (TA) and points out that his eyes are fixed on her cleavage. The TAs joke a little about this and Sean doesn't seem to mind or notice. J tells me that he is just a normal thirteen-year-old boy.

Fabricating 'ordinary' childhoods at school is a visible part of the gender work taking place around Sean, and involves constructing and permitting the expression of (normative) gender and sexuality that, in mainstream schools, is both warded off and institutionalized. His school uses popular culture deliberately in order to connect to and construct a sense of ordinary teenage experience for children whose disabilities and communication problems may isolate them within families and institutions. Music videos and YouTube material are actively used as a tool of connection and communication with the young people, as adults seek to connect the young people with a common culture of 'teenagehood', marked heavily by heterosexual identifications.

Fifteen-year-old Jasmine's specialist unit for teenage mothers with babies provides a different kind of example of the fissures and fault lines between gender, sexuality, formal and informal curricula. Students openly watch and laugh at Vines such as 'don't look at my girlfriend'. Although not officially permitted, this content provokes neither comment nor intervention on the part of teachers. In fact, these signifiers of a gendered and sexualized teenage culture seem to be positively welcomed in a space where what is marginalized is the young women's status as mothers. Dropping their babies at the nursery first thing, the young women move into a space in which they are constructed as teenagers and as learners rather than mothers, and popular culture appears to be a key resource in this process (for a full discussion of this, see Chapter 3).

Days in a life outside school: Gender cultures beyond categories?

Nathan, Aliyah and Funmi opted to be followed on non-school days. As we explore in Chapters 2 and 10, as a genre 'day in a life' was not unfamiliar to teenage participants, being a popular YouTube form (235 million returns for 'day in a life' on YouTube at the time of writing). Those young people, who shared a day outside of school time, could be expected to offer a much more crafted version of themselves to the researcher, but this did not necessarily seem to be the case: Nathan invites Liam to join him at his Saturday morning football game, but rather than this being a demonstration of 'hegemonic' masculine physical prowess, Liam observes him enjoying the game without being particularly fit or athletic. In Liam's observation of Aliyah's day, questions of ethnicity and religion are foregrounded in his descriptions of headscarves and prayer time alongside Aliyah's interest in YouTube, Twitter and popular music cultures; and this contrasts with her own 'day in a life' (as we discuss in Chapter 3), where she downplays difference in favour of a version of herself more aligned with a globalized teen culture.

However, Funmi's day is fascinating in this respect as it appears to showcase her current interest in all things Japanese. Spent largely sitting on her sofa, plugged into her iPad by earphone, Liam the researcher observes Funmi move from a homework task for her Japanese language GCSE that involves watching and practising Japanese grammar; watching a behind the scenes documentary about the creation and timelines of the complex Zelda series of games; listening to a Korean pop star whose music is used in anime; and then catching up on her latest anime series Naruto. Funmi explains that she is seen as a 'geek' by her friends, an identity that seems to be associated with a tendency towards collecting and esoteric knowledge about her specialist subject. However, knowing a lot about anime seems to be very different to knowing a lot about One Direction or Union J, offering up an apparently androgynous and prosocial geek identity rather than the perversity of the fangirl. Nathan also shares his interest in anime as part of his 'day in a life' observation, including a sketch book in which he draws characters and a slideshow animation of a fight scene that he is constructing on his iPad. This is just one of a wide range of cultural interests he shares – others include loom band making (he insists Liam takes a photo of the one he made from the kit his mum gave him), boxing, kickboxing, trombone playing, graffiti art. In an overview of the Otaku culture that includes anime, Mizuko Ito reveals the complexity and capacious character of this transnational peer-to-peer fan culture, arguing that it shows a 'dynamic tension between democratic inclusiveness and highly specialised distinction' (Ito 2012: xvii). In contrast to more everyday and embodied forms of gender available to both Funmi and Nathan (including knitting, sport and family practices and roles), connecting to 'Japanese Cool' provides a parallel universe of meaning that is both easily accessed (and shared), comfortably alien and socially valued by others.

Temporalizing gender: What the 'day in a life' method enables us to see

What does the 'day in a life' method make visible in terms of gender? Perhaps most dramatically, at school it enables us to see how a 'son' or a 'daughter' becomes a pupil, a friend, a learner, part of extensive systems which make it harder for us to hold them in view – the child is eclipsed by a foregrounding of behaviour management techniques and assessment frameworks. In that respect, the method reveals something of how we are incorporated differ-ently into distinctive spaces, technologies and pedagogies between which we move over the course of a day. Some of these travel with us, some are con-text-specific, while others operate to connect or divide. This certainly pushes back against the essentializing or 'fixing' tendencies of some single-sited research into boys' and girls' lives.

As researchers, we are overwhelmed by the intensity of the primary school classroom, criss-crossed by personalized learning grids and behavioural peda-gogies which seem to both obscure and incite performances of gender, class and race (see Renold 2005, also Kirby, 2018 forthcoming). We gain a sense of the gender regime as layered, with each stratum requiring decoding, and of eruptions emerging at the fissures between formal and informal curriculum and all around the researcher as she moves disruptively through the space.

The 'day in a life' method also helps us gain a sense of home and school as relational spaces, which may be bridged by practices and pedagogies (as explored by Walkerdine and Lucey 1989) or by opposition, providing spaces for recovery or exile (see Gillies 2016). We understand ourselves as implicated in this relationship, adults without a clear role, comprehending the children in our view both as individuals, but also as categories, instances of something more general (like gender, class, race). We wonder how teachers who are also parents straddle these two ways of understanding the child (Thomson & Kehily 2011).

The 'day in a life' method involves a negotiation between researcher and researched as to what is observed and noted. With teenage participants, this is more anxiously negotiated than with our younger panellists, and where young people have documented their own days, we are able to gain a sense of what they choose to show to a wider gaze. Comparing these accounts con-veys a sense of how gender and other structural categories may come in and out of view depending on whose gaze is privileged – the idea captured in our title 'now you see it, now you don't'.

Now you see it, now you don't?

Sex/gender is a category that is both analytic and everyday, taken for granted and contested, abstract and concrete, extensive and intensive, intimate and institutionalized. As feminist researchers, we are invested in gender, in reveal-ing/creating as well as documenting and celebrating the creativity and beauty that can surround the work of gender (Nkosi and his friend reading their iden-tical football books together, see Figure 7.2). We are also positioned in and complicit with times and places, refreshing our perspectives with the latest theories or accepting the problems that policies define for unpicking.

We have tried to bring this methodological and conceptual reflexivity into how we think about data such as these. Methodologies are tools with material affordances. Interviews incite narrative. Observations privilege practices. Psychosocial methods elevate emotions and our reactions if we choose to record them. Multimedia approaches can alert us to sounds and the physical environment. Methods also centre and displace actors as we are asked to show or tell how we see the world.

The two methods outlined in this chapter made gender visible in quite different ways. The 'favourite things' method drew us into domestic spaces and object worlds. By asking about special objects, we were also told about the special people and places to which the objects connected them, and about the complicated relationalities that they materialized and evoked. We were shown what you could do with objects: playing, collecting, treasuring, mastering, forgetting. This method drew us into the world of commercial toys and markets, yet also demonstrated how market relations are quickly displaced by personal relations. The gendered play to which the method gave us access spoke more about the deployment of cultural resources into personal and familial projects than the commodification or sexualization of childhood. So too, Megan's swift cycling through gender identity projects (from Moshi to One Direction and away again) and participating simultaneously in what might be seen contradictory ones (majoretting and football), was able to suggest how 'sexualized' practices do not necessarily or permanently mark those who engage in them.

Gender (including the body) is a situation that is dynamic, that has reflexivity; the child is entangled, part of relational webs (families, peers, neighbourhoods, institutional systems, pedagogies, markets). But there are also disconnects, disassociations and misrecognitions rather than the certainties of linear connections assumed by popular discourse. Gender was present and contested within domestic spaces as part of a family culture, situated parenting projects, sibling negotiations and friendship gambits. By following children from home to school and back again, the 'day in a life' method enabled us to make sense of the different spaces of children's lives relationally – understanding them as dynamic beings positioned differently in changing environments, moving in and out of our focus, through different institutional frames. This alerted us to the question of when and where gender becomes visible, when it is named, by whom and to what effect. For example, we were able to see how the school simultaneously evokes and obscures gender, with children asserting gendered difference and solidarity in response. Equally, when participants resist conventionally gendered projects through their more self-consciously 'gender fluid' ones, we could identify how these evoke classed differences too. Our two approaches produce mundane accounts of the work of gender in everyday lives. These are not the spectacles of sexualization that dominate public discourse, but rather, small examples of gender coming into and out of view. They do so in ways that raise questions about the temporalities and spatialities shaping the environments within which children live, and how digital cultures saturate and structure these in new ways, giving rise to extensities as children become part of wider data grids, but also to intensities as the affordances of new digital devices are incorporated into play, growth and connection.

7

Understanding the Affects and Technologies of Contemporary Schooling

Sara Bragg

Towards the end of following eight-year-old Saffron's day at school, and scanning the 'wan faces' of the class she is observing, researcher Lucy comments on her own longing for the lesson to finish. 'School is tiring', she writes in her fieldnotes.

Members of the research team undertaking 'day in a life' studies expressed similar affective responses – of weariness, impatience and ennui – at points during their days in school. Trying to account for these experiences is a key focus of this chapter and is both a methodological issue of how (far) one mobilises researcher subjectivity, and a substantive one that relates our analytic language of intensity and extensity to the context of school. Bringing the affects of contemporary schooling to the foreground is also a way to trouble current rhetoric, in which tropes about the moral purpose of education, its role as the 'engine of social mobility', the need for discipline to enable children to achieve, and so on, may serve in our view to eclipse attention to some disturbing directions of travel for actual classroom practices. In the process, we aim to encourage a broader view of what might be meant by 'technologies' in school and to go beyond conventional thinking about 'the digital'.

We spent a day in nine schools, in different parts of England, in 2014. Five of these visits involved Year 3 primary children, aged seven or eight, who were part of our extensive longitudinal study (Gabriel, Lucien, Saffron, David, Nkosi). From our one-year intensive study, one participant, Megan, was 10 and in Year 6, although her small rural class included children from Years 4 through 6. Abi, aged 15, was in Year 10 of a secondary school, Jasmine, aged 15, attending a unit for young mothers within a Pupil Referral Unit (PRU), and Sean, aged 13, was observed at a special school for young people with complex physical disabilities. We describe the method in more detail in Chapter 2. Along with our visits to homes for interviews, and the outside-school day in a life studies of participants with whom we could not negotiate access to schools (7-year-old Tempest and teenagers Funmi, Aliyah and Nathan), we gained insight into the boundaries between home and school and digital practices therein. We thought with the (everyday) terms 'school' and 'schooling' rather than the more abstract and overly virtuous ones 'education' or 'learning', to focus attention on the 'doing' of school, the work that goes into achieving it, in line with Ian Hunter's suggestion that we move away from 'educational principles' to 'school premises' (Hunter 1994, 1996).

The meaningfulness and contribution of 'small-number' studies of this type lie, as Yates (2003) has argued, in multiple acts of design, comparison,

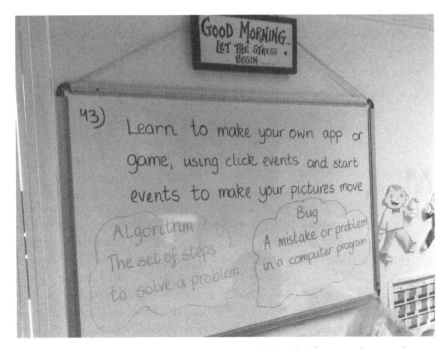

FIGURE 7.1 *'Let the stress begin': an off-the-shelf sign indexing the affective experience of contemporary schooling*

reflexive interpretation and dialogue with the broader field. We read our data diffractively and recursively through and against each other, in the light of our own investments or entanglements (as former schoolchildren ourselves, or as parents), our (generally feminist and sociological) backgrounds as researchers, and in relation to research and theorizing by others. The varied modalities of our data sources drew our attention in different ways: while the work of gender is relatively invisible in Lucy's written description of Saffron's reading time, for instance, it is more evident in the photographs showing Saffron's reading choice, a 'Pocket Money Princess' book (see Figure 7.3). It becomes more visible still linked to the photos taken in her home that morning, the spread of pink-themed birthday cards along her mantelpiece, or placed against researcher Sue's description and photo of Nkosi and his friend reading an identical football book (see Figure 7.2). Many photographs communicated feelings and experiences in powerful ways, such as one showing children's body language as they struggle to pay attention to the teacher at the front of the class, or another, a whiteboard in Saffron's school, above which a commercially produced wooden sign declares 'Good morning. Let the stress begin' (see Figure 7.1). A photo of Nkosi's school mural depicting children, flowers, skipping, football and books captures the pastoral or romantic ideal of childhood to which so many schools subscribe in principle but which felt sidelined in practice. As already noted, we worked from the subjectivity and embodied readings of the researcher, taking our own experience as clues to stimulate further thought about our participants' lives. Practices that travelled across sites (such as patterned clapping, or register-taking) constitute interpretive threads whose possible meanings we unravelled in dialogue with wider literatures attempting to account for contemporary education landscapes; while even isolated examples – such as the attention paid by Sean's special school to communicating with parents – made us question the relative absence of such connections from other sites, despite the obvious differences in context. Our aim is to present accounts that might be 'inventive provocations' or 'good to think with' (Karen Barad in Dolphijn & Tuin 2012: 50) about larger education issues and debates about what schools and young people are and should be like.

Boundaries – the closed book of schooling

A key part of our methods involves connecting together aspects of children and young people's lives that are normally hidden from each other. Parents express intense curiosity about their children's days in school, which appear to them confusing from the outside and impossible to access directly. Saffron's

mother Tina comments that you 'never see that' and how even accompanying Saffron on school trips does not give the same insights. We are asked
about whether their children are alone at lunchtime, if they have been 'good',
and realize that, like homework books and packed lunches, we too bridge the
spaces of the children's worlds. We hesitate to share some of our findings –
for instance, Sue's insights that Gabriel is often left until last or on his own
when groups were picked, or Liam's observation of how staff position Sean as
a 'normal' 13-year-old boy by claiming that he is gazing at an assistant's cleav-
age (see Chapter 6). Lucien's mother Monica notes how confused they are by
the school rewards policy, which has recently changed such that Lucien has
gone from 'often' to 'never' getting awards. She continues:

> **Monica:** I would love to do what you have done and just spend a day ...
> But obviously, they don't want us hanging around you know- [...] We don't
> know what goes on at school and that is really strange isn't it? ... You
> send your children off to school and you don't know what is happening
> there . . .
> **Researcher Rachel:** Though our parents didn't know and they didn't see it
> as strange.
> **Monica:** Really?
> **Rachel:** Well, did your parents know what you did at school?
> **Monica:** No I suppose not. I did find it very odd you know because, you
> spend every day with him
> ... And suddenly you are handing him over to someone ... What are they
> telling him, what are they teaching him? You have no idea.
> **Lucien:** I know. I am not telling you though.

Rachel historicizes Monica's concern, suggesting that parents are now being
pedagogized – addressed as those who should be concerned about the technical details of their children's learning and educational development –to a
greater extent than previous generations. Her remark also refers to what is
often identified as an earlier stage of teacher professionalism, where parents were expected to trust teachers to know what was best for children,
and teachers had autonomy to decide both what and how to teach (Whitty &
Wisby 2006).

Parents also vary in their reactions to our accounts. For Monica, learning
about the fast pace of children's days vindicates her less 'pushy' approach to
parenting. David's mother Anastasia is shocked by the school's refusal to give
Sue lunch. Gabriel's mother Nadia is critical of the school's wet play activity
of watching cartoons, a concern which speaks to a much longer history of
debates over television as inimical to learning, and as something that has to
be carefully managed by mothers today (Briggs 2009). Only in Sean's case
is our study of value not so much for his mother (who knows his day already

from the home books and photographs the school sends) than an audience for whom she hopes it might give 'normalizing' insights into her son's 'everyday childhood'. Researcher Sue is drawn unwittingly into conflictual family dynamics when Nkosi's mother Lorraine tells him 'that I was going into the school next week to read out all the things I'd written and did he want his friends to hear all about what he did? I felt appalled as it was so not true and Nkosi cast a hostile and miserable glance at me'.

Although we might be in a privileged position compared to parents, we also at points find ourselves struggling to make sense of school routines that the children and adults in school nonetheless inhabit as commonplace and intelligible. Researcher Lucy notes: 'Saffron does not move into a different class but moves to a different table. I assume this is streaming according to ability ... [...] It is ERIC time. (I forgot to ask what it stands for)'. As Livingstone and Sefton-Green (2016) have observed, schools have developed relatively arcane systems and vocabularies that can have the effect of excluding the uninitiated. Our aim here is to use our externality to good effect: accounting for schooling practices, as Biesta (2010) has argued, requires attention to the ideology that makes the incorporation of practices into particular networks invisible.

One school, many days? Encountering the atmosphere of primary education

Primary schools generally prove more accessible than secondary schools, which itself may reflect the different pressures to which the sectors are subject. Only in Tempest's case are we unsuccessful, for reasons that reveal institutional powers of classification: the head declines our request on the grounds that Tempest is new, has not settled in and is two years behind. This interpretation differs from Tempest's family's, who explain her getting into trouble as lack of stimulation (her previous school designated her a 'clever' child), or as the school's failure to offer the continuity and stability she needs.

Following children from their homes into school and back again is a fascinating experience, capturing the changing atmospheres through which they move and the particular rhythms of lesson-time, playtime and home-time. The journey to school reveals something of the material circumstances of children's lives, as we note of Nkosi's walk to school in Chapter 6. We are struck by the continuities between the schools (in contrast to the homes) and, in particular, the use of a range of teaching and behavioural techniques that appear to form a common culture of contemporary teaching, alongside a shared set of texts and techniques linked to the national curriculum. Our methods and recording devices focus us on the detailed organization and practical functioning of the school as a built environment that combines both physical and moral elements in its architecture, devices, body techniques, practices of surveillance and supervision. Placed alongside each other, photographs from the different schools all showing the trolleys on which children place their lunch boxes, the pegs on which they learn to hang their coats, the 'rules of our playground' with their irresistibly exhortatory tone ('We are kind, we play together ... we always tell an adult if we feel frightened or sad ...') and the 'rules of the classroom' ('walk sensibly, ask the teacher, be kind and thought-ful, don't interrupt, try your best, sit still, listen ...') accumulate significance as small enactments of moral invigilation for children. Our practice of collecting soundscapes inevitably sensitizes us to the aural, yet we are also struck by the extent to which teaching and behaviour techniques involve the control of sound. Some sounds about the school may also have been heard at points throughout the last century or more, revealing long established practices of productive care for, and moral training of, the learner as a 'good citizen'. Bells marking time; classes or whole schools singing, praying, or counting in a for-eign language; blessings; demands for silence; answering the register; 'circle time': these are all means by which children are subjected to general norms of development, what Goddard (2009: 184) describes as 'an individualizing moral formation within a social space'. Such long-established 'psy' disciplines (Rose 1999) encourage children to take responsibility for themselves by overseeing them in specific ways. Hunter's Foucauldian genealogy of the school (1994) encourages us to see these as productive rather than simply oppressive or repressive. And meanwhile, schools are also distinctive, sometimes because religious affiliation means that curriculum time is given over to prayer and reli-gious instruction (for example Nkosi's school), or because of an ethos that, as in Saffron's school, is self-consciously entrepreneurial.

We generally see dominant modes of age-, classroom- and subject-based, teacher-directed schooling. Despite our commitment to a child-centred per-spective, it often proves hard to maintain a focus on the individual child in school, and we wonder whether this is a consequence of schools feeling they need to perform for us; of a standard pattern of adults being 'captured' by other adults; of our own attention to the wider structures of school; or perhaps a clue to children's own experiences. We oscillate between noticing the teaching and noticing the child, discovering that some big personalities such as Lucien and David can become very small in school. Children have to work hard to be seen, and some appear unsure as to whether to hide in the group or stand out. Lucien, for instance, achieves being visible and spe-cial through the PowerPoint about cars he emails to his teacher, which we discuss in Chapter 10. Researcher Rachel notes how he 'glows' when the teacher shares an in-joke with him across the room. We also have to contend with the other children who take interest in us, our recording equipment,

FIGURE 7.2 *Nkosi and his friend's football books*

FIGURE 7.3 *Saffron's reading choice*
One of many acronyms we encounter in schools is ERIC – 'Enjoy Reading In Class'.
Reading is also a time for claiming gendered spaces, as figures 7.1 and 7.2 suggest

and the research process. While we are not the only adults floating around the school, observing or helping, we are unusual in our adhesive connection with a single child, something that probably makes that child more visible than usual.

We are struck by the 'power geometries' (Massey 1993) of time and space as we witness children in fast-paced, constant motion, orchestrated by adults. They change between 'home' and 'ability' tables or rooms ('for each different lesson, they sit at a different table' (Nkosi); 'The children are sitting at five different tables. They all know where to go and what to do and the class seamlessly moves into activity which is different at each table [...] the kids know the drill' (Lucien)), to and from (assigned) places 'on the carpet'; they talk to 'talk partners' allotted by lollipop sticks, fall silent at the shake of a tambourine or clapping pattern; they put up their hands ('show five'), thumbs or mini-whiteboards on request to show answers to problems, understanding or agreement ('we're good at maths'); show 'excellent learning behaviours' by sitting up straight with arms folded; they negotiate congested corridors, queue and eat in the din of a dining room, line up to enter or leave rooms and buildings, move from one regimented Physical Education activity to another. Often, activities are referred to by acronyms (WALT, 'We Are Learning To', ERIC, 'Enjoy Reading In Class') or other designations ('dominoes', involving each child choosing the next to line up; 'Stop Look Listen' to control restlessness).

Sets of behavioural techniques ricochet between our geographically distant sites. A device compelling silence and attention through a distinctive pattern of clapping ('clap, clap, clap-clap clap' or 'don't clap this-one back', QQEEQ) is a practice that has migrated to all our primary school research sites. It may have travelled in part because it is a repurposing of already-familiar approaches – clapping hands to keep rhythm, to call for silence – and combines features of both. On teaching websites, the exercise is sometimes construed as one simply of recognizing rhythms (teachingideas.co.uk), but elsewhere, the stakes are higher: on 'themusicjungle.co.uk' it is described as a 'listening game that ... quickly sorts out the classes that have learned focus and self discipline from those that have no idea! ... winning this game isn't about a *team effort*; it is about each *individual* being totally focussed and responsible for playing their part, by themselves' (emphasis in original). In a couple of instances, we observe girls usurping teacherly roles by instigating the clapping to quieten a noisy class, only to be promptly put back in their place: 'As [the teacher] is doing this, one girl starts doing the clapping method that the other schools used a lot, and he stops her saying "I don't need that." Later teacher and child reach a compromise: "she can do the clapping, as long as she asks permission first" ' [Researcher Sue's field notes]. On two occasions, we observe a formalization of a similar line of desire, with children conducting the afternoon register upon their teachers' requests. Student choice seems to be a danger spot, seen as problematic and requiring control.

Time is a topic focus of some Year 3 lessons, children learning to switch between digital and analogue time telling. Time is also made to count, insistently, relentlessly, by bells, by minutes and seconds – 'Five more minutes', 'One minute left', '20 seconds to clear up!' (Nkosi) – by 'countdowns' from 20 or five. Its significance is marked formally even if ineffectively: 'There is a strong awareness of time here in Miss M's countdown to finishing things, not always with success. "If it's not finished you can do it after the break" ' [Researcher Sue's field notes]. Time figures as anticipation – 'When the big hand reaches 12 we're doing handwriting' – as reward ('golden time' at the end of the week), as threat – 'The teacher is getting impatient and says: "before I start using my stopwatch I suggest you do things quicker" ' – as punishment (collective loss of play time, individual loss of golden time) and as longueur (as the researchers remark on their own boredom or fatigue). Researcher Lucy observes: '10.28am: Time to tidy up the clocks and pencils. I notice how efficient the teacher is at time keeping, two minutes to prepare before break time. Chairs are pushed in, children stand behind chairs. I wonder if she ever loses track of time when teaching a subject'. David's school stands out, by contrast, as not ruled by time in the same way: in the absence of the usual class teacher, the children engage in drama, music and Physical Education, a relaxed approach echoed by the more variable iterations of school uniform observed amongst children. Saffron's Information and Communication Technologies class is (narrated as) one where 'time just flies'. Wet play is a real disruption of routine in several schools, with classrooms left in chaos and only a cartoon to keep order.

Behaviour as well as time is constantly monitored. Children move their names up and down systems of traffic lights prominently displayed next to the whiteboard ('gold – is the best and gets you a "prize" '), are issued with warnings ('at this point, someone did get a yellow card, and were warned that they didn't want to get an orange card'), loss of golden time, lunch or break time, or threats of missing special school trips, 'timeout' sheets, sitting facing outwards (' "I'm the teacher, you don't talk back to me" '), rewards such as being in charge of handing out laptops, 'stars' given out to tables, or green plastic tokens for 'sitting well'. Indeed, these tokens become the focus of attention and drama, when researcher Rachel observes a boy 'stealing' them, or when 'T is heard saying "who cares about the stars" ' when the teacher is talking about earning stars for their table to contribute to getting a prize at the end. Researcher Sue notes that 'Miss M says she is "very disappointed" in him'. It doesn't take researchers long to work out who the 'naughty' children are in each class, that is, who are deemed to have strayed from normative school conduct by not listening or talking back to teachers, swinging on chairs, carrying on playing when told to stop, fidgeting, not investing in the collective. Although 'naughty' is our own researcher short-hand rather than school discourse, it highlights also the sociologically famil-iar patterning of 'deviance' – 'one black girl who is the naughtiest in the class'; 'a boy with Rasta hair won't pick up his ruler so he's told to go and "put his name down" ... as the class goes on it's clear he's a naughty one' (researcher Sue's field notes). Children too are adept at understanding this implicit patterning, as we noted in Chapter 6, where they ask Rachel the ethnicity of the token-thief.

Family life before and after school has been 'curricularized' too (Buckingham and Scanlon, 2003). Even Tempest's home has a behaviour chart – a list of things she has to do each day – suggesting continuities between school and home pedagogic practices. Saffron's step-grandfather spends the drive to school testing her and her cousin on their spelling. In many cases, the move-ment is relentless and pressurized: in the morning, Saffron moves from her home, to her grandmother's, to the car, and then, after school, to the sweet shop, to home, to swimming, then home again; Gabriel goes from school to piano lessons, then home for tea and educational games. Unstructured time appears to provoke anxiety that it may be unproductive time. It is perhaps little wonder that spaces in-between feel like 'release' – such as playtime, in the car on the way home for Saffron, and for many, time spent with screens as we explore below.

Performance anxiety permeates our visits (cf. Jackson 2010). Researcher Lucy notes that her visit seems to have been organized to include both ele-ments of time and ICT to chime with our research focus, and how the school seems to be trying to present itself in the best light: 'Sometimes felt like I was in an advert for the school (this school encourages competition, a good Ofsted, the software we may invest in) but that I was also complicit in this – praising the lessons, commenting on the children's confidence etc.'. Lucien's teacher apologizes for not offering a 'fun and zinging lesson'. The notion of 'zing' in lessons perhaps goes beyond the performativity of accountability, touching also on the contemporary performance of affective labour: work *and* play are now required from teachers, at least when in front of an 'audi-ence' (Ngai, 2007).

We came to think of schooling processes as being 'techniquified', con-nected by a set of practices to extensive networks through which the day, and bodies, are micro-managed to extract value from every moment. The dominance of extrinsic behaviourist approaches can be seen as evidence of the (neoliberal) commodification of intensive moments of learning. Targets, goals, outcomes, measurement, accountability and assessment represent the vocabulary of the marketplace; behavioural 'fixes' such as 'don't clap this-one back', ERIC, WALT, Stop Look Listen and the rest represent commodities or products that are packaged, disseminated and in many cases literally sold as solutions to educational problems. While behaviourism is by no means new, we wondered whether more and more of the school day was being worked on and managed in this way, filling up its time and space, with less available for openness, meanderings, or child-directed activities. Certainly, children have little say or control over the criteria by which they are judged. The strain is omnipresent if implicit, for instance, carried by the 'Let the stress begin' sign mentioned above. During a reading of Ted Hughes's *The Iron Man*, researcher Rachel notes 'The story is heart breaking. The giant has fallen over the cliff, and is smashed into pieces: eyeless, headless, an iron ear … ' The fact that several teachers around the country are reading the same book with their classes might indicate either a loss of autonomy or (more desirably) a convergence around 'quality' literature brought about by a national curriculum. Irresistibly, however, we wonder what unspoken emotions might be held by this tale of collapse, dismemberment and disintegration.

Evacuating the space of secondary schooling

Our observations in secondary schools yield some continuities with our experience of primary schools, although as we have noted it is more complicated to access them, and indeed for participants to contemplate being a focus of attention there in the way the method suggests. Where we recruit participants through school in the first place (Sean through his special educational unit), we tend to be invited in with the support of both school and parents. By contrast, Aliyah spends a long time thinking through whether she wants us to follow her at school, eventually deciding against it, in part, because of the school's turbulence following a period in 'special measures'. One of our participants withdraws from the project altogether at the prospect.

Both Abi and her school are eventually receptive to our visit, perhaps from the school's perspective, because the connotations of research are high status enough to seem worth the risk for a school graded 'outstanding' by the school inspection body Ofsted. Even so, the head takes the time to appear during a lesson to shake researcher Sara's hand and ask somewhat anxiously if she is 'getting the information you needed'. Where the primary schools seem perpetually in flow, Abi's day seems more episodic. Apart from the walk to and from school, and around crowded corridors between lessons, mostly, Abi is curiously immobile: sitting in the same position, one leg crossed over the other, only her hands fluttering over a keyboard, to write, to work something out, or to pick at the holes in her tights. The main bodily coordination of the class occurs at the end of lessons, when all students are required to tuck their chairs neatly under the desks. Young people are summoned and imagined in diverse ways by their teachers: 'boys and girls', 'guys', 'Year 10s', 'children', as of varying 'ability'. But most of all, they are addressed as individual learner subjects, prospective exam takers, as Sara's field notes record:

- Spanish teacher: 'You won't have a *controlled assessment* on [our new topic of the environment], but [it] comes up in the *reading and listening paper*. [It is worth] 20% ... The choice you have here [in your textbooks] is *just like it would be in an exam* ... This might happen *in an exam*, always listen twice'.

- Religious Education teacher, before a test: 'Look through the paper, is there any thing you can add to *get a point* [an extra mark], if something is worth six points you need to make six points'.

- Maths teacher: 'That won't *get you a mark* ... Between now and next year *when you have your exams* ... Perfect, you'll get *all your marks* ... You're not going to LOSE marks by doing that, so I say go with it ... remember *in your exam* they give you a tolerance, so if the answer is 65 and you say 66 or 67, that will be all right ... ' [our emphasis]

Thus, the teaching focuses around standardized measures of student learning, exams, testing and other attainment measures, evoking a wider culture of 'performativity' (Ball 2003) that is also evident in 'Know Your [National Curriculum] Level' posters in every classroom. Only in Science, however, is such an exam imminent; for the most part, the exams for which students are being 'readied' will be taken in the following academic year. Temporality in this case is extended, referring to a relatively remote future – 'between now and next year ... ' Even in the present, it is less precise or more stretched than in primary schools: '17 minutes to go ... Three minutes to go ... ' (English teacher). Relationships between teachers and students are generally formal and distanced, even though teachers appear kindly and to care about their charges. Rarely is group work or talking between students actively encouraged, even in classes with fewer than 20 students, underlining the sense of education organized around the investment in self, as an individual, competitive good.

Moments of sociality, emotional connection, intimacy and warmth occur mainly in the interstices of the school day: walking to school, sitting on the grass with friends at lunchtime or snatched moments in lesson time itself. Only in one lesson is Abi paired with one of her close friendship circle, as if the school does not take seriously or respect the groups that students might make for themselves (cf. Bibby 2010). In fact, she and her friends spend much of their time providing resources for each other – sharing strategies for essay-writing, looking things up, swapping digital competences – but this too is under the radar rather than explicitly legitimated by the school.

Students develop different coping mechanisms, as Sara notes in a maths lesson, spent mostly working in silence:

> Lottie, who has long highlighted blonde hair and an engaging manner, asks the teacher: 'do you get to have tea whenever you want, as a teacher?' … There follows a discussion about Earl Grey, which Lottie claims is the 'nicest tea in the world', and how many biscuits the teacher has had, what she thinks about different brands. Eventually the teacher says 'let's save our biscuit conversations for the end', although they continue a while as if both are enjoying this breach in the norm … So, the face to face is what is designated 'irrelevant', distractions from 'learning', the tasks in hand.

Lottie is clearly skilled at drawing her teachers into 'off-topic' chats to break up monotony, without actively resisting learning. Abi's resistance is partly passive, a subtle inertia; apparently a 'good' student who gets on with her work, neither threatening to bring down the school's results or being flagged as outstanding, she generally passes unnoticed. For instance, in English, she seats herself at the edges of the computer pool room so that the teacher – who towards the end of the lesson hands out detentions liberally to those (mostly male) students whose progress or web browsing he deems inappropriate – is unable to see her playing with her illicit mobile phone. She also transgresses semiotically, ripping holes in the regulation black tights of the uniform, and wearing officially forbidden Doc Marten boots (see Figure 6.4). Reading over her shoulder an essay on Carol Ann Duffy's poem *Medusa*, in which Abi stresses Medusa's *anger*, *fury*, *vengefulness*, suggests as with *The Iron Man* the capacity of literature to provide a space for articulating feelings that do not otherwise get much of an outlet in school. Abi's iPhone music also offers a commentary, as she listens to My Chemical Romance's *The Black Parade*, a concept album about death and revenge. In Abi's case, our presence – being held in someone's gaze, for once – may feel like an intervention that validates her own summation of her days: 'Boring'.

Teenage mother Jasmine's body is pre-eminent in researcher Ester's account of her day. Out of school, her weight loss is monitored and a cause for concern and correction (her foster carer plies her with food and cake). In school, she moves from having 'so much energy at the beginning of the lesson' to being 'crashed out, lethargic, exhausted'. Eventually, she goes to Physical Education (PE) and 'comes alive': 'on the mat she was smiling, laughing and grimacing as she did the exercises. When she boxes she is energized, fit and ferocious'. Ester is left worrying about whether her exhaustion is a consequence of being observed (is that a strain in itself?), or of the school, with its limited curriculum offer (a mix of 'basics', vocational, arts and 'real world' subjects – Business and Communication, English, Art, Science, PE) and teacher-directed approach (cf Thomson & Pennacchia 2016). As with Abi, Ester notes the 'The silence and absence of chatting is so notable in the school – during both lessons and break times'. Only when watching 'Vines' on YouTube is there an eruption of the sociable into schooling.

Sean's special school is very much focused on the needs and the messages carried by the bodies of the students, with staff responding quickly to signs of distress or pain with a range of therapeutic ameliorating strategies. Their days are documented not only by Liam, but also by the staff, who use photos and 'home books' to construct explicit lines of communication between home and school. This is in marked contrast to many other schools, where communication with parents occurs primarily to alert them to problems they are asked to address (Thomson & Pennacchia 2016) – as is the case with Tempest, whose family receives 'almost daily' complaints about her behaviour from school. Such juxtapositions allow us to contemplate whether schooling might be a more collaborative endeavour than currently, and what more body-attentive pedagogies might involve.

Post-digital schooling

In the introduction to this book, we explore how a saturation of digital technologies moves us beyond debates about the difference that the digital makes, towards the emergence of new kind of materialities that transcend distinctions between on- and off-line. In this section, we explore this emergent sensibility, starting with a focus on the obvious ways that, throughout, teachers and children integrate screens into their days. Our photographs reveal mainly 'traditional' desktop PCs in schools, rather than mobile technologies, and whiteboards used to focus children on the front of the class or to screen audio-visual material and electronic resources, sometimes 'off the shelf', such as a Spanish course package in Abi's case, or curated from a variety of teaching websites. In Jasmine's science lesson, we observe a simulation of learning, where screens seem to act as a screen for inactivity:

> Everyone has a tablet but they don't seem to be using it – not even for cheeky browsing on the internet. [...] The teacher is drawing the lesson to a close. He is reminding the class that this is a controlled assessment and counts for 25% of their final GCSE grade. He encourages the group to 'do your best to research this', to not rely on the knowledge gained during lessons and to 'go online to research object distance and image distance.'

He reminds the class to *save any work and log off the tablets. I am not sure that anyone has used them.* (Researcher Ester's field notes, our emphasis)

Schools operate under conditions of resource constraint: Nkosi's teacher regrets the school's lack of iPads and comments that they only get access to the computer pool once a week at the most. Lucien's teacher rewards him by putting him in charge of dispensing and collecting the 12 class laptops, with children bidding to negotiate who most 'needs' one – a labour intensive process for what amounts to a few minutes of screen time. Teachers' use of screens is risky – time spent fumbling with equipment leads the noise levels to rise and careful classroom management to falter; screening a YouTube video to one group, as Lucien's teacher does, pulls the other children irresistibly towards the screen and away from their books. But it also complements the lessons on time – screening digital versions of the analogue clock models they have in their hands, demonstrating art techniques, a child's good handwriting. Meanwhile, older technologies – textbooks and worksheets – continue to shape classroom practices.

Turvey and Pachler (2016) argue that permeability and boundary crossing are features of mobile technologies and highlight the fit and tensions between practices with Web 2.0 technologies in everyday contexts and their appropriation in school structures and cultures. There are somewhat ironic attributions and counter-attributions being made in these respects around the digital between schools and homes. Parents, for instance, assume that schools are using technology as a pedagogic resource to support children's academic development. Saffron's mother Tina tells Lucy that the school encourages the use of iPads, to blank looks from Saffron herself who sees it as only for play. Schools meanwhile suppose the same of families – for instance, that Gabriel's home would be technologically rich, enabling internet searching for homework, when in fact it is determinedly analogue. Nonetheless, many families seem to feel a need to provide their children with technologies: David is getting an iPad for his birthday, Nkosi has a new Nintendo 2DS, Megan and her brothers each have a tablet for Christmas; Saffron, who already has an iPad, is to get a PC for her birthday so she can 'do PowerPoint presentations'.

Meanwhile, in schools, the digital is often made to signify in 'domestic' ways: before their mock exam, Abi's Religious Education teacher promises that he will 'show you some YouTube, after, to relax you'; Saffron's school uses an audio clip of rainforest sounds to quieten children towards the end of the day; wet play means screening a cartoon. In other words, many of the 'meanings' of screens in school are romantic or informal (as pleasure, as relaxation) or pragmatic (as babysitter) rather than pedagogic. Tutor group time in Abi's school is spent playing games, students having identified the few that 'weren't blocked', or surfing the web. 'Official' discourses focus on digital

FIGURE 7.4 *'Once you put it online . . .'*

youth's risks rather than opportunities, for instance in the ICT classroom's poster in Abi's school menacing 'once you put an image online ... you lose control of it' (see Figure 7.4) produced by the National Crime Agency's Child Exploitation and Online Protection (and for an analysis of the normative gender policing encouraged by CEOP's campaign, see Dobson & Ringrose 2016). Both Abi's and Jasmine's schools have an official policy of banning and confiscating mobile phones, not always enforced: 'today no one has bothered' notes researcher Ester. Parents perform 'good' parenting by being careful to tell us they have 'strict rules', that their children are 'sensible' online, always 'ask before searching'; consult us over whether they should install filters; Saffron's aunt tells how she 'explained what playing an addictive game was doing to her brain' in such a way that her daughter stopped playing it. Our notes reveal Abi consulting Google many more times than she ever asks for help from a teacher, and using her phone for both learning (looking up words) or contact (with her mum). Abi's science teacher comments that she sets homework online, but that only the parents like it. 'The kids all want paper … Not a single child in this class [does it online]' she says, adding – as if to emphasize the curiousness of this – 'and they are all quite high ability, actually'. But young people may identify the digital as their own space and resist school's encroachments into it. At home, Abi alternates between doing her homework or revision, and watching YouTube or playing Quiz Up, her social media providing reward and release. Researcher Lucy observes that Saffron appears to have little time alone, in her space, either at home or at school, and that screen time, therefore, could be a place of escape, familiarity and intimacy. However, it also means that the child can become lost: during her ICT class, Saffron 'disappears', using headphones to create a protected but also isolated space that acts as a barrier to building a conversation about what she is actually doing, leaving Lucy wondering whether screen time might need more intensive monitoring and teaching in school to achieve creativity.

Surveillance technologies are both normalized and routinized. Lucien's teacher is filming his lesson with two iPod touch cameras for training purposes, although later it emerges that the sound did not record and he will have to do it again. Abi's friend Hermione tells an anecdote in which she was sick on the stairs at school, tried to blame it on someone else, but the teacher just 'knew' it was her, not by looking at her, but because she'd '*seen it on the* [CCTV] *cameras*' – an account that suggests both acceptance and overestimation of the powers of a pedagogic panopticon. However, researcher Lucy's camera produces consternation among lunchtime staff, who rush to know what she is doing and why. The regulation, suspicion and constraint around individuals' use of the visual in schools, Lucy reflects subsequently, stands in marked contrast to the ubiquity of parents' online postings of images of their children.

A screen is universally used to take the register, and opens up new questions about the digital in schools. 'Stand by the desks and wait 'til I call up SIMS' says Abi's teacher during morning tutor time, referring to School Information Management Systems. Register taking is in one sense a thoroughly routine and familiar practice. In terms of the elements of practices that Maller and Strengers identify (2013), its common understandings (the meanings and rationales that inform how, when, where and why practices should be performed), and practical knowledge (the skills and practical know-how required to perform them) are relatively stable. However, the material infrastructure (the 'stuff' – appliances, gadgets and technologies – that makes practices possible) is dramatically different from previous decades. Extensive data systems like SIMS, heavily invested in at national, local and school levels, constitute perhaps the aspect of the digital occasioning most academic debate about its meanings for education, and how the 'data dream' might be reconfiguring what education is and how it is imagined and lived (Ozga 2011). They make students' attendance, achievement and behaviour visible and man-ageable in new ways. Arguably, they provide the essential infrastructure for the dominant policy-driven 'effectiveness logic', which is enacted via actuarial comparison technologies such as inspection, league tables and test results (Thompson 2016; Thompson & Cook 2016; Williamson 2015; Selywn 2010). There are therefore questions to be asked about the implications of digital technology, the constant surveillance, recording, quantifying and evaluating that happen digitally and interpersonally in schools, for subjectivity.

Thomson, Hall and Jones (2010) and, more recently, Livingstone and Sefton-Green (2016) and Finn (2016; 2015) all identify an 'aural landscape' of National Curriculum levels permeating schools. Thomson et al. see this as the outcome of educational policies of 'raising standards' and 'closing the gap' (by focusing on key quotas of A*-C grades at GCSE), which leaves a 'good enough' student such as 'Maggie' in their study (and, we might add, Abi) under-stretched and overlooked. Livingstone and Sefton-Green argue that the 'ritualized' and arguably meaningless focus on 'moving through levels' margin-alizes questions about curriculum content or the intrinsic value and interest of learning. Finn's study of a 'data-driven school' also demonstrates the impact on students' subjectivities as they define themselves by levels. He highlights how teachers and students become tied together in specific ways: success is socialized ('we are outstanding' as the school proclaims) while failure is indi-vidualized. However, due to new mechanisms of teacher accountability, that failure belongs to the teacher as well as to the student – and ultimately, to the school, as lower overall results risk school closure, takeover, senior manage-ment job losses or falling rolls. Finn (2015) documents the school's construc-tion of 'data walls' – displays in public spaces, using photographs of students placed according to whether they are headed for 'success' (in examination terms) or failure (marked by a skull and crossbones). He wonders about the psychic dynamics and costs of a system that is nonetheless widely accepted and even welcomed by staff and young people alike.

Thompson (2016: 836) argues that 'the volume, variety and velocity of data, as it is accompanied by a perception of a social that has accelerated, has implications for how subjectivity is produced'. He describes the self in school as 'continuously and surreptitiously elicited to generate data that are stored in databases, connected, integrated and made sense of algorithmic-ally' (ibid.: 837). He and Cook (2016: 751) propose that data are changing the meaning of what it is to teach: 'in the shared physical space of the class-room, bodies cannot face each other with the same intensity. In particular, each teacher body comes to be represented through patterns extracted from databases with respect to student performances... To teach becomes an algo-rithmic projection of the likelihood that the presence of a specific external body (this teacher with that name) will correlate with improved scores on the students' parts'. Hardy's (2015) account identifies key aspects of education in Australia that are currently defined as 'risks', notably student behaviour, attainment and teacher learning. They are 'managed', he argues, by specific commodified packages of behaviour management programmes, teaching to the test, and professional development activities. How far these can be said to 'work', as Biesta (2010) has argued, depends on how far the complexity of human learning is reduced by schooling. Biesta's critique of the policy mantra of 'what works' in evidence-based policy is that it occludes both the kind and the amount of work that needs to be done to create an order in which connec-tions between actions and consequences can become more predictable and more secure. Locating learning physically, spatially and temporally within spe-cific institutions and timetables; grouping practices; curricula staged accord-ing to assumed norms; assessment forms that define what outcomes are said to be valuable, and so on, are all crucial means by which the conditions of 'effectiveness' are produced. These processes come to make learning seem a more rational, linear, contained and knowable process, but they have costs.

Our own methods, we would argue, provide insights into what these costs might be and how data practices and policy conditions might be making them-selves felt, which help substantiate these evocative arguments. While on the surface our approaches continue to reveal the face to face, the embodied, in specific contexts, they do suggest the ongoing 'work' of risk management processes in schooling. For instance, we have identified a level of homogen-eity across very different school settings, particularly in relation to behaviour management techniques. We noted the possibly problematic consequences of those techniques and of ability grouping practices for questions of inclusion or social stratification. Above all, while we might not have been able always to *observe* the dilemmas of big data or managerial approaches to schooling, we may have *felt* them. Our emotional responses to the shadowing should not be taken for granted (school was boring because school is boring), but need to be read. Sianne Ngai's work (2007) encourages us to see emotions as 'interpret-ations of predicaments' and we might wonder what predicaments contem-porary schools are facing. Her argument that 'ugly feelings' such as anxiety index 'obstructed or suspended agency' resonates in relation to our affects of tedium, anxiety, exhaustion, stress. Anxiety, Ngai argues, is a diffuse emotion with a future-oriented temporality that expects something – risk, exposure and failure – which are, arguably, precisely the threats currently held over schools (Ball 2003, Jackson 2010). Boredom, equally, might be generated by the very behavioural 'fixes' used to manage and reduce 'risk' in schooling. Classroom management techniques may appeal because they deliver to teachers the sense of agency that is undermined by centralized curricula and policy edicts. However, rather than marking the triumph of evidence-based practice, such strong explicit pedagogies may banish the chaos, unpredictability and 'beautiful risk' of learning (Biesta 2013). Affective intensities are excluded from the core activities of teaching and learning, informality reduced, and less space is allowed for children to be other than good and compliant. Instead, intensities make themselves felt elsewhere: in the poignant reluctance with which Abi's teacher curtails a conversation about biscuits, the dramas around behaviour tokens, the ripple of interest researcher Lucy detects amongst children when Saffron's teacher mentions her daughter having a bath at the same time each day, even the attention accorded by children to an unfamiliar adult. All these perhaps provide intensive moments of relationship and identification otherwise hard to find. The fatigue Jasmine expresses may have arisen from the limited curriculum on offer to her, which would have served to enable her Pupil Referral Unit to demonstrate 'progress', widely reified as a measure of effectiveness (Bradbury & Roberts-Holmes 2016). Yet, it marginalizes equity-related educational notions such as a common curriculum or of humanities, arts and social sciences as ways to make sense of the world and oneself (Thomson & Pennacchia 2016). Relegated too are larger questions – posed by philosophers such as Jacques Rancière – about the role of schooling processes in installing rather than challenging inequalities (Bingham & Biesta 2010).

Using small data to understand big data and contexts

Gibbon (2015) argues that focusing on the digital – as in, the device, the screen, the platform, or medium – reveals the narrowness of our understandings of 'technology': the body of the child is already inscribed and invaded through other, softer, behavioural technologies and biopowers such as the behaviour chart. This chapter has accordingly sought to expand perspectives, charting the ubiquity of precisely these 'other' technologies. In so doing, we have argued that our observations can tell us something about the policy, material and discursive conditions shaping current schooling practices.

'School' is both a noun and a verb; it is also a place and a concept, which is has been framed over many years through discourses of 'crisis' and 'inadequacy' (Mockler 2014), with a consequent requirement for improvement, invariably linked to audit cultures through accountability and compliance structures. Our observations suggest, as others have also argued, how educational policies of 'improvement' and their associated data practices might be part of the problem rather than the solution. Our data indicate how affects may index the 'suspension of [teachers' and children's] agency'; how anxiety about the future may make it harder for the experience of the present to be acknowledged or addressed; how the exclusion of parents may flow from an internal focus on attainment, with its associated arcane vocabularies; how constant surveillance has counter-intuitive effects (Abi is able to disappear in school precisely because she is not marked out as posing a particular challenge); how the stress on behavioural fixes and the aural landscape of 'good learning' limit the range of identities available to students and teachers, and detach pedagogy from questions of what is being learnt, why, and from whom (Biesta 2016). If 'big data' practices have tended to be individualizing and ahistorical, erasing the social context in which numbers are generated (Selwyn et al. 2015), our small data, we would argue, can in principle provide both context and relationships. In the face of our wider social amnesia about the history of the school (Hunter 1996), we might learn from Aliyah's solitary but noble endeavour (discussed in Chapter 5, see Figure 5.1) to preserve through a tie her own affectionate memory of her school as it was before poor inspection reports led to its restructuring and the repudiation of its past. Here we too have attempted to bear witness to the de-collectivization of the school and the focusing of individual management, with its attendant affective consequences, rather than allow these processes to occur unnoticed and unmourned.

8

Recipes for Co-Production with Children and Young People

Liam Berriman and Kate Howland
with Fiona Courage

In this chapter, we reflect on the role of children and young people as 'co-producers' of our research. Over the course of the Everyday Childhoods project, we held a number of events and activities aimed at involving children in the research. Each event was conceived as an opportunity to experiment with different methods of co-production, drawing and building on participants' existing skills, knowledge and competencies. These events were inspired by models of 'public sociology' that seek to engage wider communities in the co-production of research (Burawoy 2005; Puwar & Sharma 2012).[1] In this chapter, we ask how 'co-production' can generate opportunities for enrolling young people's existing skills and knowledge to become partners in research: as data creators, consultants, or as data animators. The chapter focuses on three events staged at different moments in the Everyday Childhoods project – exemplifying ways of inviting young people into research. These examples

---

[1]The 'Public Science Project' at the Centre for Human Environments at CUNY (City University of New York) is particularly emblematic of this form of collaborative knowledge exchange research: https://www.gc.cuny.edu/Page-Elements/Academics-Research-Centers-Initiatives/Centers-and-Institutes/Center-for-Human-Environments/Research-Sub-Groups/Public-Science-Project-(PSP).

showcase three strategies of co-production: a media competition (Space Invaders), the project archive (Curating Childhoods) and a hackathon workshop (My Object Stories). Although each were conceived as activities in their own right, understood collectively, they shed light on the possibilities and challenges of co-production in research with children and young people. This discussion aims to provide insights into our successes, as well as the numerous unexpected problems and complications we encountered. The events are presented in chronological sequence.[2] Echoing the approach taken in Chapter 2, we present these as recipes for co-production, revealing the resources and methods required as well as our sources of inspiration.

Models of co-production

The Everyday Childhoods project involved contributions from researchers with a range of academic expertise, including youth studies, education, archiving, sociology, media studies, and human-computer interaction (HCI).[3] This cross-disciplinarity enabled us to combine and synthesize learning across several fields. Co-production has become particularly significant in youth studies and HCI scholarship over recent years. In youth studies, this has manifested in 'participatory research' approaches that involve young people as collaborators in research. In HCI 'participatory design' has become a central methodology for engaging young people as stakeholders in design processes. Here, we give a brief overview of the parallels between approaches to co-production with young people, and how these influenced our thinking.

One of the core features of youth studies has been to recognize and promote young people's agency and capacities for action in decisions affecting their lives. This has had a strong bearing on the design of research and can be observed in the rise of research studies where young people are significantly involved in the collection, interpretation and curation of research data. This ranges from providing young people with cameras to capture photographs or videos (Wilson 2016) to running theatre workshops in which young people reinterpret and reenact excerpts of data (McGeeney et al. 2017). In these instances, researchers try to provide young people with greater say and stake

---

[2]'Space Invaders' was a media competition held prior to the Face 2 Face study in 2013 and was led by Sevasti-Melissa Nolas and others colleagues at the Universities of Sussex and Brighton. 'Curating Childhoods' was an immediate follow-on project to the 'Face 2 Face' study (2014–15) and was carried out in collaboration with the Mass Observation Archive. 'My Object Stories' took place shortly after 'Curating Childhoods' and drew on the collaboration with Mass Observation and new partners in the Sussex Humanities Lab.

[3]The authors of this chapter represent each of these backgrounds, with Berriman from sociology/ youth studies and Howland from informatics/HCI.

in different phases of a research project. This has often led to young people being explicitly defined as research 'co-investigators' or 'collaborators' (see for example with children: Bradbury-Jones & Taylor 2015; Lundy et al. 2011; and with young people: Tucker 2012).

In HCI, many researchers investigating and designing technology for children use participatory and co-design methods to ensure that the voices and ideas of potential end-users are included in the design process. Researcher Allison Druin pioneered an approach to bringing children and young people on to design teams, and characterized a continuum of roles for children in design research, which reflects increasing involvement: users, testers, informants, and design partners (Druin 2002). Druin and colleagues have strived to involve children as full design partners through their Kidsteam programme, in which children take roles on an intergenerational design team through twice weekly after-school sessions over the course of a year. Children take part as volunteers but are also given a technology gift (worth around $100) at the end of the year. Co-design and participatory design methods are now widely used by those carrying out interaction design research with young people, including hands on activities such as ideas generation and paper prototyping (Robertson et al. 2013). However, even in the most dedicated approaches to giving young people creative control, such as Druin's long-term collaborations, full equality of decision making and access to benefits from research are rarely achieved.

Outside of academic research, co-production methodologies have also been widely used in commercial product design and market research (Humphreys & Grayson 2008), including with children and young people (Berriman 2014; Buckingham 2011). Discussing new marketing techniques directed at children, Buckingham has argued that although market researchers have begun to adopt the rhetoric of children as 'active' participants in research and design, making children feel 'empowered' does not always equate to greater agency or power (Buckingham 2011: 94). Berriman likewise found in the creation of children's virtual worlds that the rhetoric of co-production was commonly found within design teams but that contributions were often highly asymmetric and uneven between children and adults and between different groups of children (Berriman 2014: 209). Though these critiques have often been levied at more commercial forms of co-production practices, the same scrutiny has not always been directed at co-production methodologies in academic research. A key concern with co-production is the extent to which its (often idealistic) rhetoric is supported by research that creates more equitable and symmetrical relationships between children and adults.

Critical discussion about participatory and co-production methodologies with children and young people have expanded over the last decade, particularly in terms of their ethical complexities (Bragg 2007). One of the key concerns has been the extent to which categories of 'adult-researcher' and 'child-research subject' persist as a default binary in research relationships – underlined by age, status and power differentials (Alderson 2008). Whilst this concern is not limited to co-production methodologies, it does bring into question how and whether existing power differentials can be surmounted. Concerns have also been raised in relation to children's compensation and reward for time spent as 'co-researchers' or 'co-designers' (Bradbury-Jones & Taylor 2015). These points have brought into question the extent to which research can be accurately labelled as a collaborative partnership when decisions and benefits from a project are unequally distributed.

Such critiques have prompted us to critically reflect on how decision making, resources, rewards and creative control have been distributed between the different parties involved in our own research activities (see Chapter 3 for a full discussion). In particular, we draw on sociologist David Oswell's (2013) argument that children's agency should be seen as distributed within wider socio-material arrangements. In this theoretical model, agency is not simply located in the individual, but rather is relationally negotiated and distributed within a socio-material arrangement. This approach provides a framework for evaluating the effectiveness of co-production in *redistributing* agency and decision making between children and adults. It prompts us to ask how co-production methods can configure roles so that each individual has the opportunity to contribute to, and benefit from, a project or event. As we reflect on each of our recipes of co-production, we will draw on this model of agency as a way of evaluating how effective our methods were in generating more equitable models of children's participation.

In the Everyday Childhoods project, we have sought active involvement from young people in generating and curating data, and in particular, have explored novel methods for including young people's voices in the communication of research findings. Each of our case studies draws on multiple disciplinary approaches and insights, and over the course of this chapter, we weigh up the success of this convergence of approaches. We have been sensitive to the ethical challenges that co-production can raise, particularly in ensuring that children and young people's involvement is rewarding and appropriately recognized, and that their time is compensated and not unduly wasted. At the same time, the legitimate need to reward can come into direct conflict with ethical concerns about coercing participation. Building on past discussions of co-production with youth, the present chapter reflects back on the strengths and limitations of different models of co-production with children and young people. In particular, we draw attention to: (1) how young people's participation varied in form, distribution and contribution across different events, (2) the distinct skills, knowledge and competencies young people brought to the research, and (3) the relevance and value of the events for the young people taking part.

The competition: 'Space Invaders'

Our first experiment in co-production was a public engagement event as part of a local festival, inviting young people's responses to public debates (particularly in the media) about the positive and negative impacts of digital technology on their lives. We asked young people to make short films as part of a competition where prizes would be awarded by a panel of judges.

Origins and inspirations

Competitions are a popular way of encouraging engagement and participation from young people, and place a clear value on the outputs. The promise of potential prizes and accolades can be effective in encouraging young people to put time and effort into producing a piece of media. With a carefully chosen brief, entrants can be encouraged to put forward their own take on issues of interest both through their message and their choice of media. However, the incentivization through prizes also brings with it difficulties of judging, including the potential for entrants to be swayed by what they think the judges wants to see and hear and the implication that some personal accounts of experiences are 'better' and more deserving of reward than others.

Our method was also partly inspired by the Mass Observation Archive's use of 'directives',[4] which invite members of the public to share their thoughts on a discussion topic of contemporary relevance (e.g. global warming or Brexit). The responses are then collated by the archive as a snapshot of opinion on the topic at that moment in time. Similarly, our method attempted to capture a snapshot of young people's perspectives on debates about digital media's role in their lives and to publish them on video sharing platforms for others to see.

Ingredients

- An online video upload platform
- Attention-grabbing advertising
- A judging panel of children and adults
- A venue for showcasing entries and awarding prizes
- Prizes

---

[4]http://www.massobs.org.uk/mass-observation-project-directives.

The event

Space Invaders was not explicitly a research activity, but a public engagement project that allowed researchers from different disciplines to experiment with ways of hearing young people's voices on the subject of digital media. It was formative in shaping the Face 2 Face and Curating Childhoods projects, influencing other forms of digital self-recording methods that we used.

To gather young people's opinions on and experiences with digital media, we devised a competition format which requested short video submissions across two different age ranges (11 and under, and 12–18).[5] Taking a deliberately open approach, we asked young people to tell us in 3 minutes how they use sites such as Facebook, Twitter and YouTube, as well as phone apps and online games. We highlighted concerns from some adults that 'children and young people are wasting their time and brains online using social and other media', and invited entrants to tell us about the good and bad in their media lives, commenting on what these media allowed them to do and how they could be improved. We placed no constraints on the formats of the videos, allowing for a wide range of filmmaking expertise. We advertised a technology prize for each age group (worth around £100), and asked for submissions to be uploaded to a video sharing site, with parents' permission, giving instructions for how to make videos private, if preferred.

We received thirteen submissions, four in the 11 and under category, and nine in the 12–18 category, all submitted via YouTube or Vimeo. The videos covered a wide range of topics, and adopted a number of different styles. The formats included videography, animation, video game footage, static graphics and audio, with most entries employing more than one of these. Many of the submissions explicitly addressed and responded to public debate around the topic of young people's use of digital media. Over half adopted documentary style formats, with voiceovers and interviews used to comment on the benefits and dangers of technologies. Home settings were most common, but there were also public and school backdrops. The submissions in the older age category of this type adopted common social media formats, such as talking head pieces to webcams, mainly in bedroom settings, spliced with other footage including that from 'real world' settings, news reports, and game video

---

[5]Information about the Space Invaders event, including links to the children's video entries, can be found here: https://circyatsussex.wordpress.com/2013/04/19/space-invaders-children-youth-and-public-spaces/. 'Space Invaders: Children, Youth and Public Space' (2013) was a project run by the Centre for Research and Innovation in Childhood and Youth (CIRCY) at the University of Sussex in collaboration with the School of Education at the University of Brighton. It was funded by the University of Sussex through the Higher Education Innovation Fund. The project was led by Sevasti-Melissa Nolas and the project team included Sara Bragg, Kate Howland, Avril Loveless and Rachel Thomson.

capture. The game footage included 'let's play' style clips with voiceover, and shorter excerpts which gave a quick view of different games.

The competitions entries adopted, subverted and satirized 'old' media approaches to reporting on technologies in young people's lives. The inclusion of 'old' media such as news reports was used in one 12–18 submission to highlight hysteria and overreactions to perceived threats from violent video games. The news report approach was also used in an 11 and under submission, but this time with the children taking on the roles of anchor persons to gently mock the gossipy style of entertainment news whilst addressing various social media topics.

In some entries there was clear frustration, and a perception that older generations point out the 'evils' of some popular technologies without really understanding how they work and how they are being used by young people. Overall, the tone was largely positive, with young people taking the opportunity to counter perceived concerns, and providing numerous examples of how these technologies can connect friends, families and even lost dogs.

The competition culminated in a public showcase and prize ceremony, in which excerpts from the videos were shown to a large audience as part of a local arts festival, and a debate on the use of social media was held by university students. The video entries were judged by an independent panel of adult experts, and young people's view were gathered through two local school visits. In these visits, we showed the entries to GCSE and A-Level media students at schools where none of the entrants attended. Following the screenings, we led facilitated discussions on the videos and asked for comments on each, as well as voting on which entry should win. The feedback from these youth panels was presented to the adult judging panel to be taken into consideration. The young people's choice for winner in each category was fairly clear, and these were ultimately agreed with by the adult panel, although there was some debate between the judges. The runner up choices were not so clear-cut, so we also awarded a 'young people's choice' commendation in each age range to recognize entries valued highly by the young judges but not awarded a prize. The prizes and commendations were taken very seriously by the entrants, and the winners were very happy. All the entrants received certificates, but it was clear that a few of those who were not awarded prizes or commendations were disappointed and we received some emails from aggrieved parents on some of the children's behalf. We also failed to realizes, until it was too late, that awarding a first prize, runner up and young people's choice commendation left only one entry in the youngest age category that wasn't singled out for specific praise. Using a competition format placed value on the work that we asked young people to do, but the awarding of prizes creates losers as well as winners.

Reflections

Through their video contributions, young people had an active involvement in setting the agenda for the Face 2 Face project around the role of screen-based technologies in young people's lives. They broadened our ideas of the kinds of technologies that were important, and reiterated the need for young people's voices and roles in debating and communicating these issues. In this model of co-production, young people were treated as competent creators, and given full control and responsibility for defining their message and choosing how to convey it. However, although we sought young people's feedback, which was taken into account, it was ultimately the adult judging panel that were given the final say on the winners. The competition format was successful in attracting considerable engagement from local young people, although the socio-cultural spread was not very wide, and around half the entrants had some form of direct or indirect link with the universities involved. The public showcase event was well attended by entrants, families, friends and others, and demonstrated the value that was seen in the work.

There were a number of ethical concerns to contend with in a competition model. The judging and prize giving elements of competitions need to be considered very carefully to avoid any indication that some entries were not valued. In the context of a research study, rather than a public engagement activity, these issues would become even more challenging, as the idea of 'judging' participant data is very problematic. In addition, consent and legal considerations must be considered very carefully. In the Space Invaders competition, parents were required to give consent and to take responsibility for uploading the videos, due to legal age restrictions on online platforms. To some extent, this necessary safeguarding may have detracted from the autonomy of the entries, as parents may have felt it necessary to vet the content, and young people in turn to moderate their messages.

Entering the archive: 'Curating Childhoods'

Our second experiment in co-production took place in partnership with the Mass Observation Archive during preparations for archiving the 'Everyday Childhoods' data collection. As Thomson describes in Chapter 3, our ethical discussions with participants often began with the archive – informing families from the beginning that their research contributions would form part of an archive. Over the course of the Face 2 Face project, it became increasingly clear that discussions about the archive (which often felt quite abstract for participants and researchers) should ultimately take place *in the archive*. This led us to our follow-on project, 'Curating Childhoods', which involved a workshop at the Mass Observation Archive aimed at providing families with a say in the future archiving of their data.

Origins and inspirations

One of the drivers for the Curating Childhoods[6] project was a desire to bring together popular and professional practices of curating and archiving childhood. Over recent decades, 'curation' has expanded from the niche practices of galleries, archives and museums, to a wider range of popular practices of cultural sorting, cataloguing and ordering (Balzer 2015; Obrist 2015). Curation has also been seen as a practice undertaken by children. In the context of digital media, education researcher John Potter (2012) has described how curation has become a new form of digital literacy through which children and teenagers learn to cultivate profiles, pin boards and timelines. In an article on the 'The Secret Lives of Tumblr Teens', journalist Elspeth Reeve (2016) describes how some young people can achieve fame through curating popular Tumblr boards of 'found' online content, including gifs, memes and videos. These feeds can attract tens of thousands of followers, providing the young people behind them with cultural celebrity status as accomplished curators[7]. Alongside these digital practices, our research also observed how children's curation practices could take place in more personal and material forms that were not always as deliberate or public facing. As Berriman describes in Chapter 5, this could take the form of collecting and preserving toys and other items of significance in shoeboxes and photo albums. In these instances, curation is more focused on cultivating personal sites of memory that materialize links to special relationships, moments or events in time. In the Curating Childhoods project, our aim was to explore how children's existing ideas and practices of curation might inform our archiving of research data.

A further source of inspiration was from a professional site of curation: the Mass Observation Archive. We were particularly inspired to work with the Archive based on its long history as a site of co-production between archivists and members of the public. Since its founding in 1937, the Mass Observation Archive collection has been sustained by long-term partnerships

---

[6]'Curating Childhoods: Developing a Multimedia Archive of Children's Everyday Lives' (2014–15) was funded by the AHRC's 'Digital Transformations' theme and was led by Rachel Thomson, Liam Berriman and Fiona Courage. The project's reports and outputs can be accessed from: http://blogs. sussex.ac.uk/everydaychildhoods/curating-childhoods/publications-and-output/.

[7]'The curator' on social media bears some similarities with the categories of 'the geek' and 'the lurker' discussed in our moral map in Chapter 4. The curator, as described in Reeve's article, highly values their privacy and is admired by others for their skill at finding and re-publishing niche and obscure content.

with volunteers who submit regular diaries responding to directives. This form of public engagement with an archive was radical at the time of the Archive's establishment, and today remains a unique curated record of everyday life. For the most part, the Archive's diarists and contributors have been adults aged 18 and above. Records of children and young people's everyday lives, on the other hand, have remained conspicuously absent from the Archive's collection, with children's diary records only occasionally being collected through schools (see Box 8.1). The Curating Childhoods project was set up with the aim of increasing the visibility of children's lives in the Archive by establishing a new 'Everyday Childhoods' collection. The collection would initially be comprised of data from the Face 2 Face project, but would then be further expanded through regular invitations for children and young people (up to 18 years) to contribute to the archive by submitting self-documented accounts of their daily lives. Central to the project was the idea that young people should play a consultative role in the creation of the Archive, and that the archive should become a space accessible to children and young people. The project proposed to set up dialogues between archivists, researchers and children to explore what the ethics, practices and responsibilities of curating records of childhood should be. In doing so, these discussions aimed to bridge the popular and private practices of young people and the professional and public data practices of the Archive.

Ingredients

- An archive with space for activities
- Flipcharts and pens
- Blank postcards
- Lunch and refreshments

The event

The 'Curating Childhoods' workshop invited children and families from the Face 2 Face study to visit the Mass Observation Archive and to discuss the public archiving and potential reuse of their data. Throughout the Face 2 Face project, the research team had regularly discussed with the children and their families the prospect of archiving the dataset and what this would entail. Our impression during these conversations was that the archive remained quite an abstract space for many young people – imagined as quiet and 'dusty'. These misconceptions weren't limited to the children, but also the research team, who were often uncertain what might happen to the project's data in the archive. Though the team had experience of depositing and accessing archive data as researchers, it was difficult for us to imagine who the full potential range of public archive users might be and to what ends they would use the data. Against a backdrop of growing archive-based scholarship (Moore et al. 2016) and secondary data analysis (Bishop 2009), we also felt it ethically necessary to explore with our participants how their data would be curated and what its potential future uses might be. Our approach was therefore to imagine our dataset as a site of co-production beyond the data collection process – whose future should be carefully negotiated between families, archivists and researchers. For MOA, the workshop was an opportunity to learn more about the expectations of children and parents for how the archive would care for and make publicly available their data. The past experience of the archive team had been that children, and particularly parents, were reticent to have their data made indefinitely public, even when anonymized (see discussion in Box 8.1). The workshop would therefore also provide the Archive with the chance to find out what reassurances children and parents might want about their data being publicly available.

Not all of the families involved in the original project were able to attend the workshop and, in total, six families (seven children and six adults) took part on the day. Of those in attendance, the majority were from the teenage research panel, who were keen to meet other children involved in the study. The workshop's first activities focused on imagining the potential audiences for an archive on Everyday Childhoods. In one exercise involving all children and adults (including archivists and researchers), scenarios were posed that asked each person to consider how 'comfortable' they would feel about anonymized archived data being accessed by different users (e.g. journalists, historians, students) and at different distances in time (ranging from a year to several decades). Participants were asked to position themselves along an imaginary scale that ranged from 'very comfortable' to 'very uncomfortable'. By encouraging all attendees to be involved in the activity, we aimed to create a reflective space in which children and adults could both directly engage and participate in discussions and where neither's viewpoint was privileged. For each scenario, participants were asked to share their reasons for their comfort or discomfort. In many cases, we observed children following their parent's lead, leading to uncertainty whether this always represented the child's own position. This wasn't the case, however, with a participant who had been accompanied by her older sister. In most scenarios, the sisters held vastly different opinions about how comfortable they would feel about research data being reused. This led to debates in which the elder sister would describe feeling more comfortable with how data was shared (e.g. with students or journalists) and the younger sister feeling less comfortable arguing 'I'd like to keep my privacy'.

Workshop participants were invited to write a postcard to an imaginary future user of the archive sharing their hopes for how the Everyday Childhoods collection would be used (see Figure 8.1). It was agreed in advance that these postcards would be archived in the Everyday Childhoods collection and would be required reading for anyone accessing the collection. This led to the postcards being treated as valuable means for communicating with the future users of the archive. Across the majority of the postcards were requests for the data collection to be treated with 'care' and 'respect', and a strong emphasis on the necessity of recognizing the original context in which the data was created. For many of the young people, and some parents, the postcards also gave voice to concerns that their words or actions might be misjudged or misinterpreted in the future. For some, this reflected a concern about historical distance and how present-day activities and interests might be viewed as 'strange' in the future. However, for a number of young people and parents, this reflected a concern that their data would be read and handled by an unknown archive user they would never meet. In discussions following the postcard activity, many of the parents described how they would be happy for the data to be used by researchers they knew, but would feel nervous about unfamiliar archive users. This provided a key learning point about the significance of careful planning in transferring care of data from researchers to archivists.

A final workshop activity split the group into sub-groups of younger children, older children, and parents, facilitated by either a researcher or archivist. The focus of these groups was to explore what individuals would be comfortable

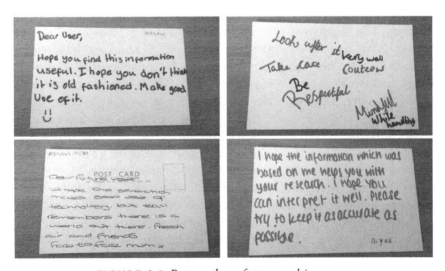

FIGURE 8.1 *Postcards to future archive users*

sharing in a public archive record of their (or their children's) everyday lives, and to reflect on who should be involved in making decisions about what can or cannot be shared. Separating the children and parents also provided an opportunity to explore different concerns and expectations about the archiving process. In the children's groups, we were particularly interested in comparing sharing with a public archive versus other everyday forms of sharing – for example, private sharing with friends or public sharing on social media. These scenarios provided particularly interesting insights into the nuanced landscapes of privacy and sharing that children and young people inhabit, particularly in terms of when they felt parents or other adults should be involved. In the case of many everyday forms of sharing, the eldest group of children portrayed themselves as confident in being able to manage what they made public and kept private – particularly amongst friends and peers, and via social media. Whilst they acknowledged they might sometimes need adult help, such as if they felt they had lost control of their privacy, they largely positioned themselves as confident sharers. When the discussion turned to the archive, however, we found that participants felt less confident about deciding what was made public. In this instance, parents were viewed as a welcome source of advice, and the children described how they had regularly discussed their involvement in the research with family members. When asked how far into the future they would still rely on their parent's advice for deciding what to archive, the young people all described being in their early or late twenties. In this instance, we were particularly struck by how presenting opportunities to shape decision making might be met with uncertainty and trepidation by the children, who may prefer the support of adults in making those decisions.

BOX 8.1 'Bringing children into the archive'. An interview with Fiona Courage, Curator of the Mass Observation Archive collection.

Liam: One of the reasons we felt the 'Curating Childhoods' project was significant and timely was the conspicuous absence of data on children's everyday lives in public archives. Prior to the current project, what records did Mass Observation have on children?

Fiona: Working with young people is an area that Mass Observation has traditionally steered clear of. In the organization's earliest phase, work in this area was limited to the observation of children by adults, and occasionally the collation of essays by teachers that were then sent in to Mass Observation as evidence of young people's opinions and attitudes. These essays were often written as part of a child's normal school work, meaning that the children may have been unaware of who they were writing for, or indeed the use that would be made of their work. Whilst these essays provide a fascinating insight into opinions of Jews in 1938 or the wardrobes of teenagers in 1947, the fact that they were written with the consciousness of school work and the eye of the teacher upon spelling and grammar means that they may not be a true representation of the individual child's life. Rather, they are a response to what opinions or experiences they believed were expected of them.

In later years, Mass Observation has begun to collect work on recording life experiences of young people in the context of specific projects such as the Children's Millennium Diary project (Blackwell 2001). The project was led by a local community publisher working with schools in the Brighton area to encourage children to keep a diary for a week during the year 2000, to be added to an archive that would be kept by Mass Observation. More recently, schools have been invited to encourage pupils to take part in the annual call for 'day diaries' that Mass Observation puts out on 12th May each year. Numbers of participants under the age of 16 has grown each year, however only in terms of those diaries returned by schools. Young people outside of the context of school are not responding 'off their own back'.

Liam: How does the 'Everyday Childhoods' collection differ from other Mass Observation collections? Do you feel that it fits with the original ethos of Mass Observation?

Fiona: The Curating Childhoods project has allowed us to explore some of these issues and has given us the opportunity to understand some of the more practical and ethical issues that have restrained Mass Observation's attempts to record the lives of young people, particularly in recent years. The data collected throughout the project has allowed the young participants to shape their responses, satisfying the original objectives of Mass Observation that saw its participants as the 'the cameras with which we are trying to photograph contemporary life' (Madge & Harrison 1938). The idea that observers would be ordinary people recording their lives without scientific or academic training was an important one, as this served to provide the element of authenticity of real lives, rather than lives seen through the lens of the researcher. The data recorded by participants could then be made available for all to see, for use by all disciplines ranging from science to the arts. In this, the Curating Childhoods project has allowed us to continue in this ethos, as although the data was collected by researchers, it has been done so in a way that allows the participants to drive what is collected, what is recorded and what is seen of their lives.

Liam: You mentioned that there have been ethical restraints for Mass Observations collection of data with children, what are the particular ethical concerns of children's data from an archive perspective?

Fiona: Curating Childhoods gave us an important opportunity to explore some of the ethical issues that have constrained our work with young people in the past. Since 1981, Mass Observation has operated on restricted funds as a Charitable Trust, reliant on project funding and royalties to be able to continue its own core project and to undertake other projects. As a result, there has been a tendency to play it safe, and to avoid ethical constraints by working with a panel made up of volunteer writers over the age of 16. As volunteers and adults, this panel is able to enter into a dialogue with the Archive to understand what use is made of their responses, and to give consent for its use. They are also able to conform to the need for anonymization, self-censoring details that may make them easily identifiable to researchers.

Liam: As part of the Curating Childhoods project, we jointly hosted a workshop at 'The Keep' Archive for children and families contributing data to the Everyday Childhoods collection. Is it common to bring data contributors into the archive? What did you learn from the workshop?

Fiona: One of the most important facets of this project was the opportunity to work closely with researchers creating and using these datasets. Understanding the way that research is driven, and taking the opportunity to discuss what both parties require to get the job done is an ideal but rare scenario. Archivists are often not present in the early stages of planning, meaning that data can be collected without the important metadata that is required to preserve it and allow its reuse in the future. Equally, they are unable to understand the drivers for research that inform how projects are designed.

The project also gave us the opportunity to work directly with young people and their carers to find out more about the understandings and concerns that they have relating to how the data that they provide for a specific project may be kept and made available for use in the future. Concerns that we had expected and that had constrained our actions in the past, were not seen as important as other aspects which took on far more significance than we had ever given credit to. Carers were more concerned about immediate reuse of data, whilst young people seemed very comfortable with this leading us to reflect on how contemporary use of social technology to 'share' life could create generational differences. More surprising to me was the response to use of data in years to come; whilst carers saw this is an opportunity to make a mark on future understandings of history, the young participants were concerned with the potential for misinterpretation and misunderstandings of their lives with the passage of time.

Reflections

One of the key learning points from the workshop was the important role of parents and family members in co-production projects with children and young people. The presence of parents and carers at our workshop may at times have influenced aspects of the children's participation – we also found that the children sometimes felt more confident making decisions with their parent's help (see also Boddy 2013). Sharing data about their lives in a public archive (even anonymously) was an important and sometimes strange request for the children at the workshop, and being able to draw on the advice of parents or family members was seen as greatly valuable in deciding what to share. Though participatory methods are often framed in youth studies research as an opportunity to recognize and integrate young people's independent decision making within a project, this case study also serves to highlight how young people may also seek to draw on the experience of others to help support with decision making. Co-production can therefore also be a method that recognizes and reflects the distributive nature of agency (Oswell 2013), with youth participation supported by wider networks of help, encouragement and advice by significant others in their lives.

The workshop also served to highlight how co-production projects can usefully support the creation of new dialogues between groups who have not traditionally worked closely together. By holding the workshop in the archive, children and families could gain a first-hand sense of how their data would be curated and made publicly available. The workshop also provided opportunities for discussions and activities that collaboratively explored the ethics and responsibilities of sharing data publicly. These discussions sought to recognize the distribution of expertise within the group – drawing on the different ways that individuals conceptualized the responsibilities of an archive in sharing accounts of children's everyday lives. At a time when archiving of research data has become a standard practice, and for many UK research funders a 'default' practice[8], these discussions provided rich insights into the ethical terrain of co-producing an archive with children and their families.

The Hackathon: 'My Object Stories'

The third and final example of co-production is a digital research workshop for young people (aged 11–16 years) hosted in collaboration with the Mass Observation Archive. The workshop invited young people to explore how research archives could become a potentially creative space for collaboration and co-production. This involved young people creating data during a morning workshop and then 'hacking' and 'reanimating' that data in the afternoon with archivists, digital artists and developers. This workshop took inspiration from

---

[8]The Economic and Social Research Council's Research Data Policy (as of March 2015) is that 'All data created or repurposed during the lifetime of an ESRC grant must be made available for re-use or archiving within three months of the end of the grant' (http://www.esrc.ac.uk/funding/guidance-for-grant-holders/research-data-policy/).

the previous events described – providing young people with the opportunity to record data about their own lives, and to be involved in the data's curation and reuse.

Origins and inspirations

The workshop was partially inspired by the recent trend in 'hackathons' – collaborative events which bring together participants with diverse digital expertise to take part in a 'design sprint'. The hackathon first emerged in the late 1990s as an intensive format for collective programming activities, becoming significantly more widespread in the 2000s (Briscoe & Mulligan. 2014). The events often have a 'competitive' element to them, with multiple teams attempting to achieve a similar goal but through different means. More recently, it has become common to assemble cross-skill teams, including participants with a broad range of non-technical expertise, such as designers and marketing specialists. Our workshop didn't entirely fit the mould of a typical hackathon, but we nonetheless drew on some of the format's key features – most notably, the emphasis on creative and intensive co-production over a short timescale in a multiskilled team. One of the recent adopters of hackathons have been archives and libraries who have used the events as a way of 'opening up' their digitized collections and to experiment with creative ways of using their collections.

The workshop also drew inspiration from recent social science and humanities approaches of 'reanimating' data using participatory methods and drama techniques. McGeeney et al. (2017) describe how methods of 'revoicing' and 'reenactment' can generate new insights by inviting research participants to reflectively explore and handle data. They draw on the work of Elizabeth Freeman (2010), who describes how methods of revoicing can give rise to queer temporalities that connect moments in time in non-linear ways. The aim of our event was to encourage children to creatively experiment with their research data, and to explore different possibilities for its reanimation – with participants employing digital tools to experiment with the representation of their raw data and reflecting on how it might 'speak' to different public audiences in different 'cooked' forms (see our discussion in Chapter 2).

Ingredients

- A suitable hackathon venue (with plug sockets, wireless internet, tables/benches)
- Hardware supplies, for example, cables, laptops, webcams, fiducials, memory sticks, tablet computers

- Software, for example, programming tools, video editing software.
- Digital mentors with a mixed range of expertise (e.g. design, programming, sound engineering)
- Lunch, snacks and refreshments

The event

The 'My Object Stories' hackathon[9] was designed as an opportunity for young people to work collaboratively with archivists, researchers and digital developers to experiment with methods of 'reanimating' research data. The workshop's promotional materials emphasized that young people weren't required to have any specific technical experience or digital skills to take part. Instead, we aimed to create activities that would be accessible to all young people regardless of their digital proficiency – providing a supportive environment in which they could confidently experiment with creative 'reanimation'. To support young people's experimentation with less familiar digital tools, we put together a group of adult 'digital mentors' who would be on hand to provide short tutorials or coaching with different tools. These included volunteers with expertise spanning 3D design, programming, sound engineering and games design. With the mentor's support, participants would be encouraged explore a range of different hardware and software tools. In contrast with Space Invaders, which asked entrants to draw on their existing skills (particularly multimedia recording and editing), the hackathon invited participants to test out or discover unfamiliar tools and techniques. A small group of archivists and researchers were present on the day and took part in discussions with young people about their data and its reanimation.

The workshop was attended by three girls and four boys, and most participants attended with a friend or sibling. The young people all described themselves as reasonably confident with digital media, and a few were particularly interested in more complex digital skills such as computer programing. This included a couple of the older boys who were undertaking computer science as subjects at schools. In the morning, the young people were invited to record their object stories to create data for the hackathon. Inspired by the methods used in the Face 2 face study, each of the young people had brought along one or more objects to share, including a guitar, a retro games console, a pair of Dr Martens shoes and a One Direction poster. Both the creation and reanimation

---

[9]The 'My Object Stories' project (2015) was co-funded by the ESRC's Festival of Social Science and the EPSRC's Communities and Culture Network +, with additional support from the Mass Observation Archive, the Sussex Humanities Lab and the Centre for Innovation and Research in Childhood and Youth. The hackathon event was co-organized by Liam Berriman and Chris Kiefer.

of the data took place in the same day. During the morning, participants were invited to record a short story about a 'favourite' personal object, followed by an afternoon of exploring new ways of reanimating the data recordings using a range of digital programmes and tools. An 'Object Stories' booth was set up in the morning for the young people to record audio and visual data and in close collaboration with a film maker and a photographer, the young people recorded short audio narratives to convey the personal value of their objects, as well as a number of still images. After their multimedia data was uploaded to a memory stick, the young people were then able to begin planning how their data might be 'reanimated' using different digital tools and techniques.

Matching young people with data reanimation activities proved to be one of the most challenging elements of the workshop – particularly in ensuring that they had enough time and support to confidently experiment with their chosen digital platforms and tools. Despite the relatively small size of the group, time was quite limited for participants to create polished animations of their data. Over the course of the workshop, we arranged for a group digital installation to be led by two digital artists, with expertise in programming and sound engineering, that all participants would be able to contribute to over the day. This more ambitious installation would recognize children's objects using motion-tracking technology, and would audio-visually project 'object story' (images and audio recordings). However, getting young people involved in the design of this installation proved challenging on the day. One of the main barriers to participation was the complex and time-consuming amounts of line-by-line programming that the installation required. Though we were keen for the young people to learn about and be involved in the installation's development, the complexity of the programming often proved a barrier for the participants to be meaningfully involved. This knowledge and skills gap resulted in an uneven sense of responsibility and ownership for the installation, with the young people's participation largely limited to observing and providing occasional feedback on the design and development.

Instead, the young people's time was primarily distributed around other data reanimation activities that required only brief learning curves and could be assembled in relatively short periods of time. These activities included reanimating their object stories data using augmented reality apps, editing short movies in video editing software, and designing prototype video games. Most of the participants chose to move between activities, briefly experimenting with each in order to explore how their object stories could be told differently. A few decided to focus their time on one activity, and dedicated the afternoon to creating more polished data reanimations of their object stories. Though we had originally aimed for each young person to have their own data reanimation to share at the end of the workshop, we found that most participant enjoyment of the workshop came through the opportunity to play

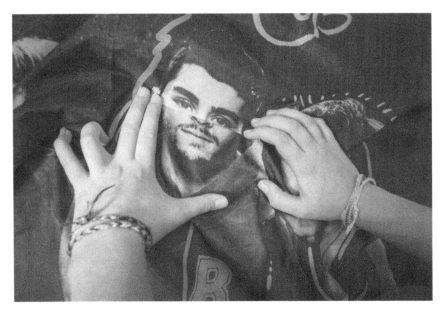

FIGURE 8.2 *Zayn Malik's face is distorted on a One Direction flag to express upset with his departure from the group*

and experiment with different tools. In this respect, their participation did not entirely match our original expectation, but as this was a co-production project, we wanted to be flexible in allowing the young people's interests to guide their choice of activities.

By the end of the day, the group had generated a variety of reanimated object stories, though still in varying stages of completion. Two participants had developed short prototype video games where object stories could gradually be 'unlocked' and pieced together by playing the game. This included a game where the aim was to collect 'rare' GameCube discs and a multiple choice adventure game about discovering the book 'The Day of the Triffids' for the first time. A few other participants had experimented with an augmented reality app which had allowed them 'to bring their objects to life' and have the object tell its own story. This included a pair of plastic toy animals who described their rescue from a bin, and a One Direction poster where the band members described fan heartbreak and anger at Zayn Malik's departure from the band (see Figure 8.2). Whilst we had sought to ensure that all of the young people had a chance contribute to the activities of their own choosing, we learnt from a parent at the end of the workshop that their child had not had a chance to take part in one activity and had been too shy to ask. Though the workshop had ended, we offered to briefly rerun the activity one-on-one for their child. As with Space Invaders, this illustrated the significant role parents can play in judging the 'fairness' and value of their child's participation in a research activity.

Reflections

Of the three examples described here, the hackathon workshop was most influenced by cross-disciplinary approaches to co-production – with young people positioned as both co-researchers and co-designers. It also most starkly illustrated the challenges of equipping all young people involved in an event with the skills and resources necessary to fully participate. In some instances, the skills threshold did prove too high and time limitations meant that young people didn't always have the opportunity to become fully involved in an animation project. However, we also found that a 'mixed economy' of participation could also be positive. Whilst some young people threw themselves into a single data animation activity, others preferred to float between different activities at their own pace. This resulted in a range of different data animations that might not otherwise have been produced by a group who all shared a similar skill level and confidence.

The hackathon also created new opportunities for knowledge exchange between the different partners involved, particularly between the young people and archivists. One of the aims of the event for was to learn new ways of working with young people to animate and bring archive data to life. For the archive team, who did not consider themselves particularly technically savvy, the event was an opportunity to learn from young people what forms of digital storytelling might be possible with archive data. Over the course of the workshop, this led to a number of interesting conversations between the archivists and young people about what stories could be told through objects and how the record of those stories might be reanimated using digital tools. Likewise, having archivists present at the workshop also provided the opportunity for young people to ask questions about why archives are interested in stories about their everyday and how those records are stored for future use.

Learning from co-production

Co-production presents a number of challenges for how we conceive children and young people's involvement in research. Over the course of the 'Everyday Childhoods' project we experimented with several different co-production methodologies as a way of opening up what young people's participation in research looks like and exploring new dynamics in the 'knowledge production' process. The interdisciplinary make-up of our project team proved valuable in allowing us to interweave different traditions of co-production. From the project's conception, we questioned how our participants could become more involved in the research process – exploring the different kinds of roles that they (and sometimes their parents and carers) might play. We also sought to bring critical awareness to our experiments in co-production – identifying not only the dividends of rethinking children's contributions to research, but also the numerous complications that arise in pursuing a co-production model.

One of the main difficulties for co-production models is assessing their success in creating more equitable models of research between children and adults. Over the course of this chapter, we have attempted to critically reflect on what we felt worked in our project events, but also acknowledging what we felt didn't. Ideas of 'distributed' agency (Oswell 2013) have proven useful in this regard, providing a means of interrogating whether and to what extent the socio-material arrangement of different co-production activities might provide more symmetrical relationships between research partners. One of the main questions we have found ourselves coming back to time and again has been the extent to which our co-production models evenly distribute contributions, decision making and, ultimately, value and recognition between researchers and participants. This question has become a useful yardstick, allowing us to interrogate whether and to what extent we have enabled young people to make substantive contributions to the shape and direction of the research, and to be able to derive and extract value from it. In bringing these criteria to bear on our three examples, we have found quite a mixed picture. In some instances, our attempts at distributing participation within a project did not unfold in the ways we had anticipated. In the Curating Childhoods project, for example, we found that children could be uncertain about contributing to decisions affecting the archiving of their data, and often looked to the guidance of their parents or carers. Similarly, we found that our sense of the value young people might derive from a project did not always match the expectations of young people or their parents. In the case of the Space Invaders project, this came through in the discontent of some parents who judged the value of their child's participation based on their success in the competition. However, there were also many instances where we were surprised when unintended forms of value were derived from the research. In the 'My Object Stories' Hackathon, participants took pleasure from different parts of the workshop, such as recording their object's story or learning how to code a basic game in Unity. Whilst in the case of the Curating Childhoods project, we subsequently learnt that one young person had taken up work experience at the archive after enjoying the workshop.

A further challenge has been the rapidly changing digital affordances of co-production. Digital practices of documentary, curation and data animation have provided new opportunities for inviting children to take part in the co-production of research. However, on occasions, these digital practices also posed barriers to participation. This became most apparent in the hackathon, when the digital coding expertise required to take part in particular aspects of the co-production process locked some or all of the young people out. In this instance, the project failed to anticipate how steep the learning curve would be and resulted in a barrier to participation. This might be indicative of a broader gulf between the digital practices of academics (researchers, designers, archivists, etc.) and the young people we seek to work with. As Thomson describes in Chapter 10, the shift towards more democratized models of research requires that we take account of the digital practices of research and curation that young people are already engaged in. However, as this chapter suggests, matching the digital practices of young people with academic research – particularly in a co-production context – can raise further challenges.

Co-production methodologies might be realistically conceived as ones in which fairer distributions of contribution, decision making, value and recognition are constantly strived for in research activities, but may not always be successful in the ways we hope or intend. It requires us to be flexible in our expectations and to be open to a model of research where the majority of insights will emerge through the process of collaboration, rather than at the final destination.

9

A Fellow Traveller: The Opening of an Archive for Secondary Analysis

Jette Kofoed with Rachel Thomson

I was invited into this study *as* a fellow traveller. I opened the archive with a dedicated intention to grasp what was going on in this particular research project. I had been part of the advisory board, and had participated in seminars and group sessions. On these occasions, I had previously seen parts of the data so I felt myself familiar with the ideas, 'takes' and overall findings of the project. I had a hunch of what to find (Berriman & Thomson 2015). Hence, it was with confidence that I accessed the archive. There are a number of similarities between this project and my own research: we share thoughts, inspirations and are on the same wavelength when reading each other's publications. Both projects focus on children and youth's digital lives and on how to develop adequate methodologies to study this issue. I expected myself to flow into the data, and to find new aspects of what I already knew from my own research. I expected to absorb myself in what I like best: diving into data.

So, I opened the archive and there I met a puzzling alteration of the researcher I am used to being. I found myself *unknowing*. I was not able to make sense of the data. At first, I read the notes and the transcriptions meticulously, carefully. But the more I read, the more I realized that I had very little sense of what was happening on the pages and in the interview situations. My reading sped up. I found myself pacing around the archive trying to make sense of what was there. I could not penetrate into the details of it. It was as if someone had stolen the keys to grasping and deciding what was at stake, a set of analytical keys that I as a pampered researcher am used to possess. Methodological and analytical skills are some of the academic traits I have been trained in over the years, and one of the skills I have taken pride in cultivating. I have taught methods classes for BA students for years; I have dwelled at developing doctoral classes with particular focus on data analysis and research methodologies. And here I was – unable to detect what was at stake. These data weren't even messy; they were just inaccessible to me. Even within the comfort zone of my own field of research, I found myself *unknowing.*

Accessing an archive

In struggling with the misfit between my own expectations and what actually happened when opening up the archive, I found myself crawling back to the data. Not only did I not know the cultural, temporal, spatial setting, neither did I know the landscape of the archive (how long are the interviews? What is the relationality between the interviewees? Who is the interviewer?). The vastness of the archive made it impossible to take it in as a whole. The lack of orientation and free movement became obvious limitations to a fellow travel-ler entering the archive. I was invited to engage, yet the immediacy of my *unknowing* slowed my engagement in a contradictory movement, because I initially fastened my pace through the archive. I could not access the ethnog-raphy of it by entering the website and the multimedia documents. Although interesting and innovative, somehow, the multimedia documents were too organized; it laid out parts of the analysis, but I wanted to enter into the data as a co-researcher. So while enjoying browsing the multimedia on the web-site, I needed to get back to the data. I needed 'raw' data to access not the researchers who had carried out the research, but the data on children and youth lives as these are transformed by media. Usually, I dislike the notion of 'raw' data, but here it suddenly made sense. A distinction between raw data and notes that I, however, later learned made up a stumbling stone of its own.

A new kind of humility grew out of this meeting between me as a *naked* researcher without contextual knowledge, without the details of the meth-odology used and without the sensory knowledge of the place and time of the interviews and the archive: what did it smell like? What did the Starbucks phone cover look like? Exactly what colour of pink was the bedcover? What did this colour of pink connote in this particular setting? I was at a loss, and found myself deprived of a kind of access that I had not even considered a privilege on previous occasions where I was involved in secondary analysis. But indeed the access to informational, political, cultural, social and sensory contextualization had been a privilege that I only understood now that I was left without such access. This proved to be an 'untried methodology', as characterized by Lapping & Bibby (2012), who reflect on methods growing out of a psycho-social conference on 'Knowing- not knowing'. In becoming a fellow traveller in this case, I had to diverge significantly from my previous research practices. It called me in as unknowing, disoriented, affectively disturbed and it urged me to develop unknown skills (Lapping & Bibby 2014).

I found myself stuck with the data and left without the sensory remembering of the interview situation that you draw upon when rereading your own data. I did not have the excess of information that spills over in ethnographies where you conducted the fieldwork yourself as, for instance, described by Hammersley and Atkinson (1983), and as demonstrated throughout anthropological literature (Emerson et al. 2011; Hastrup 2010; Hasse 2011; Fog Olwig & Gulløv 2003; Staunæs & Kofoed 2015; Winther 2013; 2015). I must have missed the chapters on secondary analysis and how to immerse myself into data that I had not participated in producing. Doing fieldwork is an embodied enterprise (Pink et al. 2016, Okely 2007; Davies & Spencer 2010) as is also data-analysis (Thomson et al. 2012; Staunæs & Kofoed 2015). So when doing fieldwork, my body is an integral part of orienting myself in the field, amongst the children and youth and in their social media landscape. Usually, I am there with the young people, sharing a perspective and closeness that allows me to co-observe their mediatized landscape. In this case, I knew neither the landscape nor the everyday settings; nor did I know the landscape of the archive, so I stumbled over voids.

Voids of knowledge

I have engaged in reading data produced by fellow researchers before. But I had overlooked the fact that, on prior occasions, the researcher who had carried out the research had always been accessible to me. S/he has been present to open the archive; mostly (I realized in this new process of opening a new archive on my own) in contextualizing the ethnography: who said this? How did she look? Blond? White? Asian? What is the context of this particular school in East London/in western Oslo/in Perth? What does it smell like? How do I (not) find my way? What are the politics around working class housing in Oslo/Copenhagen/Sussex/Adelaide? How does working class housing actually look? What does the countryside look like?) The access to this kind of contextual knowledge prevented me from meeting *what I didn't know*.

When attempting to open this archive I realized that it couldn't be opened by force, but I needed to coax my way in. I needed to open myself to the archive, rather than the other way around. In so doing, voids of knowledge presented themselves to me, not least the question of how to handle them. Was I, as a fellow traveller, allowed to fill out the void? What if the knowledge I lacked proved essential in understanding the case? These questions arise because I was engaged in co-analysis, I was not merely *reading* the data or reading someone else's analysis. Was I free to interpret the void, and if so, how does this differ from fabrication of data?

Let me offer an example. When reading part of the archive, I met Jasmine. I know her age, but not her colour of skin, not her hair, not the way she dresses or carries her child. I met Megan, who lives in 'a large old rustic country house'. Obviously, this note presents a lot of in-depth cultural and social knowledge, but I am unaware of the detail of a large old rustic country houses in the UK? What do such houses look like when not situated in Denmark? All that surfaces as relevant when reading these notes were the details I didn't know. Do they wear school uniforms? Do they bring lunch boxes? What does a 'CBA' mood entail? Voids of knowledge displayed themselves. Am I as a fellow traveller capable of filling the voids that emerge in the meeting of myself and the archive? The cultural knowledge of Copenhagen that I take for granted? Let me dwell on this by introducing an example.

Some years ago, I was engaged with a group of researchers who carried out secondary analysis on data that only one person in the group had produced. The study was UK-based. Part of the data consisted of interviews with young people about their dreams of a future. One of the participants dreamt of 'going up North'. Unaware of specific differences between a UK and a Danish setting, I assumed that 'up North' referred to going either to the northernmost part of Norway or to Greenland. As it turned out, the young girl dreamt of going to university in Newcastle. Of course, my ignorance and immediate interpretation got the cultural and social setting all wrong. But could I potentially have suggested an interpretation (not of the North as such, but of the dreaming) that could either have added, say, affective layers to what my colleagues already knew or have added questions that would have allowed the analysis to deepen beyond what we take for granted in the settings in which we feel at home? In that case, we did not pursue the promises of fellow travellers in any systematic way, but only allowed the embarrassing ignorance on my part to help us pursue more descriptive details of why 'the North' presented itself as an appealing option for this young girl. In hindsight, this void of knowledge carried the potential for more than added *descriptions*, but possibly also entry points for new *analytical* foci. Entering into the archive of the Everyday Childhoods project reminds me that there might be not-knowings of the secondary analyst that are worth allowing back into formative analysis. This recollection spurs an awareness of the relationality of primary and secondary analysis. Obviously, the researcher who carried out the fieldwork has privileged access to details and cultural, social, material and affective contexts of, in this case, the children and youth. But does the privilege of fieldwork translate into privileged positions in analysis? Of course, I cannot, as a secondary analyst, say much with certainty. But perhaps the voids of knowledge revealed to me during this travel hint at an analytical option, which could be worth pursuing, namely, the *promise held in slow-motioning* processes of inquiry, the *hesitancy* embedded in meeting what I so obviously do not know and theorizing of new questions: who guards the knowledge production? Does the responsible fieldworker in all cases carry more weight than a secondary analyst? What if the not-knowing carries potential for spurring new analysis?

Without a body

In traversing the archive, it became clear how a lack of embodiment prevents me from intuitively grasping what is at stake. The absence of my meeting 'real people', and only narrated versions of their being, is at the core. I am a fieldworker in the habit of meeting people. In this case, I meet a mediated and narrated group of youth. Not only are 'they' merely present in the archive as documentation, but my presence in the archive is invisible. I could pace around, make noise, annoy them – it wouldn't leave a trace. I could as well not have been there. So the senses that I am used to make use of when doing fieldwork are out of sync with the current enterprise of entering the archive. The records of fieldwork encounters documented in the archive required presence and immediacy on the part of both the young participants and the researchers. The liveliness of the fieldwork has been processed into transcriptions and documentation. The sense of fieldwork and the sense of youth and of social media that I have cultivated are not of much use. Quite the contrary, I need to find the liveliness of these youths in a similar way to a historian accessing an archive of texts. From the archive, the presence of the subjects emerges. Doing fieldwork is a multisensory experience, accessing an archive, however, privileges the sense of the eye. I can read the texts; initially, I cannot smell them, feel them or hear them. But gradually, in the intersection of my own unknowing, my disabled body and the texts, I start allowing the privileged eye to spur more senses. Presumably, much like a historian at work in territory that is unknown to the fieldworker.

Flowing movement

Gradually, I entered into a *flow of movement* (Jørgensen, in prep) between knowing *my own research* on cyberbullying, social media and digital youth lives, and *embedding* myself into researcher considerations and concerns that were not my own, but which served as entry points into the archive. And, finally peeking into data where bits and pieces of mediated youth life became intelligible to me.

What happened? My route involved an initial preoccupation with the researchers' notes on how they carried out the ethnography. Even though I was not particularly interested in this, I realized that I could not access the data directly but needed to go through the notes of a researcher whom I didn't even know. So I paved my way through unknown researchers' notes on their fieldwork. In that process, I became intimate in a strange *one way relationship* with the researcher who had been present in the field. I forced myself into a new doubling of him/her without having any idea of who 'Ester' would be. 'Ester' and 'Sara' became fellow travellers, fieldworkers in the midst of ethnography with all the fears, anxieties, joys and awkwardness that I know so well. I latched myself onto unknown colleagues and forced my way into data that would not otherwise open itself up to me. I needed proximity to the unknown researcher who authored the notes. I was walking in someone else's footsteps and the pace of my moving in being 'on foot' gradually opened the archive to me.

First, I rewind from the 'raw' data of transcriptions and move in through the researchers' notes. In and through these notes I stumble over unknown taken for grantedness. These slowly transformed from being obstacles to insights: of researchers' bias, researchers' positioning and cultural and social blindnesses. What at first presented themselves as stumbling stones preventing me from grasping the data, slowly became new access points from where I – not as an individual researcher – but as part of a collectivity of the imagined research team, could reinterpret the data. So rather than a process of smoothly accessing the archive, it became a process of *palimpsesting* (Lather 2007) the archive itself, the data from my own research, cultural and social knowledge of a Scandinavian youth and media field, and researcher subjectification from numerous previous fieldworks and secondary analyses. Through a process of allowing layers of data indirectly to palimpsest, the archive let me in. I was given the key to the archive, but only now found a way in. Not in any direct manner where I in any 1:1 scale could make sense of the archive, but rather in a much more humble way, coaxing the archive open to questions that, on the one hand, were consistent with the overall purpose of the research and, on the other hand, spurred new questions into the data, particularly a question of temporality. The temporality of research processes (in rewinding, slowing down, paving and palimpsesting) and the temporality of young lives. Let me unfold the latter.

A core question of temporality

In my own research, I have explored how technologically mediated youth communications entail what I have termed 'non-simultaneity' in intensity, in engagement in the ongoing conversation and affective saturation of youth life (Kofoed 2014). This is a core finding in my research on cyberbullying, where non-simultaneous investment in exclusionary practices seems to be an important vehicle in processes of inclusion and exclusions. The fact that the youth are not necessarily engaged – temporally – in the same conversation or dramas at the same time, seemed to spur dramas into more drama, as they have to endure the not knowing of who knows what about an ongoing harassment or evaluation of a specific incident. Moments of intensities thus seem to be tied together in a kind of repetitive rhythm, as I have argued elsewhere (Kofoed & Ringrose 2012; Kofoed & Stenner, 2017). Let me clarify this a bit further. In cases of cyberbullying, as these emerge among youth in school, it seems that no position can be guaranteed stability and permanence. When 13-year-old Nora logs on to Facebook to check her friend Louise's interpretation of what happened during school today, and when the next day Louise can't be sure that Nora has actually read her status update or whether she has been on Facebook, Snapchat or Instagram at all, there is a revelation of non-simultaneity in affective intensity (Kofoed 2014). Nora's reaction to Louise's update might be mediated by others commenting on it. This mediation might lead Nora to think and react differently, in a way that Louise could not understand. I have suggested conceptualizing such tumult in terms of *non-simultaneity of intensity* (Kofoed 2014).

I looked in the archive and couldn't find such non-simultaneity. The lack of obvious non-simultaneity in this archive is not significant in itself. Non-simultaneous practices might be specific to cyberbullying, or it might be spurred by particular research interests. But the interest in temporality and its particularity of non-simultaneity allowed the new awareness of *palimpsesting* to direct my attention to drama. In the archive, Jasmine is quite content with being without her phone for three months and hence without the 'drama', as she expresses it.

She says 'It was so good, like there was no drama, like you didn't have arguments with people, people wouldn't always be able to contact you so you would like, people would have to like come like and see you face to face to speak to you'.

Researcher Ester: Mmmm.
Jasmine: Life is actually stressful with a mobile phone.
Ester: So why was it, what, what made it better?
Jasmine: I don't know but it, it was nice.
Ester: And what's umm, so what's the drama, what kind of drama happens then?
Jasmine: Like everything like when people start arguing and they, like they're like, they try and get you involved and they like call your phone or they text you and they're like 'isn't it this?' and you're like 'I don't wanna get involved' sort of thing whereas if you're face to face it'll be easier to like just deal with 'cause you can go on forever on your phone.'

Palimpsesting this piece of data with findings from my own data on cyberbullying might suggest that dealing with drama in and through social media as it spurs and hastens the drama known from cyberbullying research could be worth pursuing in this UK-based data on digital youth lives. Not in order to investigate cyberbullying in particular, but in order to investigate if and how dramas are lived in digital lives amongst children and youth in this particular data set. Perhaps mediatized drama is an issue integral to digital youth life, and perhaps the 'favourite thing methodology' allows us to know more about mediatized dramas, since many of the youth mention their phone as their favourite thing?

An affective confession

A close colleague of mine witnessed a conversation some years ago in the corridors at my university. I was full of excitement readying myself for new fieldwork. A colleague responded that she was done with fieldwork and thrilled to know that her students would carry out the field work she had set up. Obviously we took two different paths in regards to ethnographic research – she rejoiced in not going 'out there' herself, I rejoiced in *being* the fieldworker. A third colleague overheard this conversation and kindly, but firmly noted: 'You will never be the head of any research project as long as you insist on doing the dirty work yourself!'. This exchange encouraged me to think through my attachments to the sensory experience of being in the field. To me, it wouldn't work if I cut off the actual fieldwork from the rest of the research process. My dedication lies with the production of empirical data, in involving my researcher body and sensory abilities in the fieldwork as part and parcel of the research process. The meeting point in the corridor distilled my understanding of different researcher subjectifications and academic strategies, operating as a turning point in my academic self-perception: I do prefer absorbing myself in fieldwork, allowing this exact scholarly activity to continuously be at the core of my academic life. Not something I am free to leave behind as I become more senior.

This particular incident and the insights cultivated from this recast itself when first hastening around the archive and later, when 'slow-motioning' my moves: the sensory aspects of academic agency *are* integral to my becoming and maintaining an academic life. My preference for meta-theoretical informed empirical research is not unique, but is shared by many, and by some described as being *possessed by data* (Thomson 2014). I share this possession – in making sense of the particularities of Snapchat and Facebook; in traversing these and other social media and in meeting and sensing the youth who hook up and who exclude each other.

This recollection throws new light on the issue of opening an unknown archive. Obviously, the paths into an archive are intertwined with others who walk the path. As established, I am a multisensory researcher who needs to saturate herself in the field. So, initially I clung to the researcher's notes as an intermediary between the unknowing associated with my own researcher body and the scholar actually present in the field. And hence, I tried to access the field – not through the field, – but in and through the stand-in-researcher who became my access-point. Through the notes, I paved my way into a blurred – and growing – understanding of Jasmine, Megan, Nathan and others. I grasped the opportunity to get a grip on what their digital lives were like, through an imagined doubling of the positioning of the researcher that was somehow impersonal and yet the very body whose senses allowed me to become part of it. *Impersonal* because I don't know whom the name covers for, yet I needed a person situated like myself in the field to *impersonate* me and through whose writing allowed my sensory vocabularies to evolve. An adequate strategy seemed to evolve: in traversing different kinds of data, I inscribed myself as an avatar via the researcher('s notes). I began by observing her/his notes, and this allowed me to co-observe the interview-situations and to enter further into the archive.

Leaving the archive

The Everyday Childhoods project addresses how media is transforming children's everyday lives. The archive turned out to *transform* my researcher subject into a different affective attuned researcher. I had to pause myself, surf my way through the different parts of the archive, allowing not knowing to surface and spur me, pause again, rewind and finally find an access point. This could be termed a *reparative* research methodology. *Reparative,* in the sense that 'the reparative reader helps himself again, and again' as Eve Sedgwick points out in her book on affect (Sedgwick 2003: 150). In being bereaved of my usual access to the field, I needed to help myself again, and again. In so doing, a vocabulary of *hesitancy, not knowing, slow motioning, palimpsesting* and *avatar* surfaced. In pointing this out, the project of secondary analysis and fellow travelling is not cast aside as insufficient or invalid but, on the contrary, it is repaired as fertile ground for cultivating new kinds of questions: how far North did she travel? What are her desires? Does ethnicity expose itself in transcripts? Does intensity? And not least: What promises do voids of knowledge hold.

In traversing this archive, I ended up amongst many imaginary minds thinking together in palimpsesting data, affects, researchers' notes and previous findings. Indeed, it ended up being many minds thinking together.

10

Researching as a Popular and Professional Practice

Rachel Thomson

In the twenty-first century, the speed of development of commercially available social media technologies has outstripped the timelines of academic social research, meaning that we have become increasingly reliant on commercial platforms such as Facebook, SnapChat, Instagram, YouTube and Google as a route through which to conduct our enquiries. As explored in Chapter 5, these platforms have become the 'everyday archives' through which lives are documented, stored and shared (Beer & Burrows 2007). Researchers cannot help but work with and through these platforms and devices, 'repurposing' them for social research, so that 'their capacities of data collection, analysis and feedback, come to be incorporated into social and cultural research' (Marres 2012: 151). For Evelyn Ruppert, the term 'big data' is not simply a question of large data sets, but rather, marks a set of practices that are now a ubiquitous part of social worlds changing our 'research relations as social scientists' as well as our everyday lives (Ruppert 2016: 15). In the introduction to this book, we cite the view of Adkins and Lury (2009) that the digital revolution changes our relationship with the 'empirical', something with practical and theoretical consequences, including the emergence of 'live methods' that involve a wider set of actors and spaces in knowledge production (Puwar & Back 2012). Noortje Marres (2017) points to the potential of tracing 'research in the wild' for understanding how researchers can form part of *experiments in living,* contributing to projects of knowledge-making and world-changing. These debates coincide, not surprisingly, with a renewed interest in the co-production of social research, emerging from campaigns by and with marginalized groups, 'public science' and community archive based activism.

Everyone it seems is involved in research. Knowing how to search and assess sources is a requirement of the National Curriculum.[1] Teachers are expected to research their own practice, and may well film classes to facilitate critical reflection. Advertising is based on research, in fact, advertising is based on knowing what we are *researching* and matching product placement with target audience. And we re/search for fun, to relax or to perhaps to work and demonstrate the kind of person we want to be. The internet is the clearing house for most research activity providing access to immense data bases and creating new data about our interests and desires. We opened this book by reference to public debates over the wellbeing of children and the consequences of an immersion in digital culture. In the face of rising anxiety and conflicting evidence, we have proposed research as a solution – inviting readers to pay attention to digitally mediated practices, socialities and materialities. We have made a case for a particular kind of slow research that notices detail, nuance, feelings of awkwardness and the passage of time. Paradoxically, we have used research in order to discover its place in everyday cultures.

What can we learn by focusing attention on everyday research practices? In this final chapter, we take 'research' as a topic of enquiry in its own right – describing and reflecting on practices of research in the everyday cultures of children and teenagers. The chapter works through a series of empirical examples. The first two capture something of the redistribution of research methods, noting their distinctive affordances and associated affects. We ask what the role of the professional researcher may be within this new division of labour, noting the potential of 'repurposing' of both traditional research methods and digital tools. A final example suggests the potential for reflexive methods that open up the project of knowledge building in surprising and generative ways.

Research as everyday practice

Lucien: Becoming an expert

Lucien presents his 10 page PowerPoint about cars. This is his topic. I keep quiet and let him do his presentation which involves reading the slides verbatim. Afterwards he tells me that he researched this all himself using Wikipedia and his car magazines. It is not homework but Lucien will 'email it to him' (his teacher), he expects it 'will surprise him'. I later discover from

---

[1] For primary school, KS2 History (www.bbc.co.uk/education/subjects/zcw76sg) and Computing (www.bbc.co.uk/education/subjects/zvnrq6f).

All About Cars

By Lucien

FIGURE 10.1 *Lucien's car project*

his parents that Lucien has been working on this for the last 6 weeks. He learned PowerPoint at school (they don't use it at home). I got a sense that he likes school and pleasing his teacher. This was my introduction to Lucien's prodigious capacity for focus and information, as long as it is his chosen topic. [Researcher field note RT]

Lucien's interest in cars was established early in the research process (see Figure 10.1). He clearly gets a great deal from accumulating knowledge about cars. His sources for this research are varied and, in the past, involved magazines and a computer game, and only recently extended to Wikipedia. Knowing about cars is one of the things that distinguishes him from other boys, and he is able to use this expertise to connect to adults. Research skills have the potential to travel across the spaces of school and home. In the following extract taken from Lucien's 'day in a life', we can see how Lucien's teacher acknowledges these research skills within an educational economy, even though the task was set by the research team rather than as homework.

9.50: Back on the carpet to reflect on the learning. 'I promise maths will get better if you concentrate and try. Let's warm down with a bit of counting. You're on fire Charles!' Senior assembly now as sounds of piano begin to draw our attention into a new space [audio]. Lining up silently, 'let's make it the best we've ever done'. As the children leave the class Mr B turns his attention to me and mentions Lucien's amazing PowerPoint presentation and asks if I have seen it. 'Great research and presentation skills'. [Researcher field note RT]

A couple of hours later, research is on the official curriculum – yet fraught with problems. Although the school endorses research skills as having educational value – it cannot provide a research friendly environment. The reflexive loop that allows teachers to record their own practice does not seem to extend to the children.

11.30: Major negotiation over laptops. Who 'needs' one to do their research. The topic is inventors – some are researching the Wright brothers, others Thomas Edison. Twelve hands go up, 'we should have enough'. Mr B gives Lucien the keys and I decide to help so that I can see the system. The lap tops are in a locked cupboard outside the door with shelfs and facilities for charging. Each machine and shelf is numbered [photos 42–3]. I unplug and pass onto Lucien and other children who gather round. Probably upsetting Mr B's system. I sit near Lucien and he tells me that yesterday Mr B had gone to a website called 'goo' rather than Google. He has also tried searching for himself and even managed to get Google in Arabic! The main source for research is Wikipedia, but he also tries others on the list. He is amused by an entry for a Wright Brothers restaurant. Others are 'educational' but full of product placement. It is interesting for me to see these websites in a school context where the advertising seems a shocking intrusion. Ads for Snickers bars flashing up alongside sites for the Wright Brothers (*they* have done their research). A couple of times Lucien's searches are blocked for no apparent reason [photo 46]. Mr B asks 'are people on computers using them to good effect' – he must be reading my mind. Some on our table are diligently copying out words from Wikipedia. Mr B shares an 'in-joke' with Lucien from across the room about searching for 'goo'. He glows. [Researcher field note RT]

As a researcher who can see across boundaries, I feel the need to answer the question of why Lucien seems so big and bold at home and so small and quiet at school. How can his car research project help us understand this? I think of the girl who shared something inappropriate at circle time at the end of the school day. Mr B had invited the children to bring something important from home and to talk about it. This girl brought a McDonald's toy, which was dismissed very quickly. It evidently had no educational value for Mr B. So perhaps Lucien's research is a kind of stealth show and tell – enabling him to secure recognition for another, bolder version of himself – revealing his hidden treasures. He is not simply recognized by his teacher, but he is also seen doing this by researchers. So cultivating 'expertise', with its gendered and classed histories, continues to be an effective strategy and a vindication of his willingness to be visible.

Abi: Cultivating obsession

If research involves 'systematic enquiry' then it is distinguished from the forms of know-how in everyday life that involve us knowing enough to get along and get by. For something to count as research suggests that it is more than the ordinary, drawing us into practices that may be seen as within the orbit of professional or expert practice. In the past, a travel agent may have 'researched' the ideal itinerary, or an estate agent may have sought to match potential buyers and sellers of property. Yet increasingly, digital interfaces and databases allow us to undertake these searches ourselves. Researching holidays and properties becomes integrated into a new kind of everyday – being as much about fantasy and pleasure as it is about securing a transaction. The epithet of 'porn' (property-porn, holiday-porn) that is attached to these new kinds of popular research suggests something about the unconscious desires that may be invoked by the practice of research and the trouble caused by transgressions of expert and popular boundaries. It warns us that research practices may be repetitive, compulsive, addictive.

The language of obsession is drawn on by Abi to narrate a succession of research projects that might, in an early era, have been describes as hobbies or interests. An 'obsession' on the book, play and film versions of Oliver Twist focused on the character of the Artful Dodger, and a desire to know and consume everything possible about the character. Being involved in a production of Alice in Wonderland prompted research into rabbits and a growing and active interest in animal care and rights. Both these passions drew Abi in new practices: travelling to the city to see a show; working as an intern in an animal shelter. Fellow fans of Oliver Twist tended to be adults. Working at an animal shelter made her cautious about dedicating her future to an area where wages are so low. An obsession with horses involved accumulating a full riding kit, yet no animal, and was unsentimentally resolved by selling the collection on eBay.

Acquiring a tablet transformed Abi's searching abilities. A nascent interest in the band One Direction initiated through hearing and memorizing songs was soon consolidated by watching films on YouTube until she exhausted the supply of material. She then set up a Twitter account, following each of the band members, discovering that by following retweets she could access a huge community of fans (see Figure 10.2). Abi explains that Twitter was decisive in turning the latest of her singular 'obsessions' into a collective practice:

> Yeah definitely because I think that is what– I think it is Twitter that does it. Because you might like you might like something, but then like if you go on Twitter it is just like mad because everyone else is on there liking it loads, and like Tweeting pictures, keeping you constantly up to date. So you just get like obsessed with it, you constantly know where they are, and stuff.

She now understands herself as a 'fangirl', gaining and sharing pleasure with others in relation to a common object of desire secured both by detailed knowledge but also imagination and curiosity:

> And then there are so many people that are like Fangirling about it. So it is just like when you talk to people who are like that too, you are just like

more and more obsessed, and mixed with the interviews and the songs
and it is just like (laughs) . . .

Drawing on another of her ongoing obsession is with YouTube stars Dan and
Phil, Abi explains to researcher Sara the phenomena of 'shipping', through
which fans (sometimes with the encouragement of celebrities) fantasize about
erotic relationships between their objects of desire. 'Phan' then expresses the
romantic joining of Phil and Dan and the role of the fan in creating this link.
Abi explains:

> **Abi:** Erm yeah Phan is their ship name.
> **Sara:** And do a lot, so a lot of Phans- erm a lot of people who like Dan and
> Phil want them to be in a relationship.
> **Abi:** Yeah, yeah.
> **Sara:** Are they in a relationship?
> **Abi:** (.) Well technically not but that's (.) well like everyone's like– most
> people that are ship Phans think that they are, but they are just not saying.
> **Sara:** Hmm.
> **Abi:** Though technically not, but you know.
> **Sara:** I was just wondering about that. I checked them out after we met,
> and I was wondering if they were gay and in a relationship, or just two
> straight guys who happened to be-
> **Abi:** Phil's bi (sexual).
> **Sara:** How do you know that?
> **Abi:** He used to go out with another You-Tuber called Charlieskies who
> used to be a girl, and is now a boy (laughs).
> **Sara** Oh right. Interesting.
> **Abi:** Yeah.

The intersection of fans, celebrities and YouTubers (who begin as ordinary
fan and turn into celebrities themselves) involves a dynamic cultural circuit
that depends on practices of search as well as the production and circulation of content by users. It is clearly a great deal of fun, as well as providing
opportunities to travel (camping out with fellow fans to see the celebrity and
to get a selfie) and to make friends with those beyond your neighbourhood.
The question of whether such practices are 'progressive or reactionary has
come to dominate much academic discussion of the phenomena. Some like
Jodi Dean (2005) suggest that 'communicative capitalism' relies on fantasies
of participation, contribution and circulation. In practice, these networks are,
for Dean, apolitical in that they are contained and literally privatized with economic value harvested by advertisers and corporations. Others, like feminist
historians Laura Cofield and Lucy Robinson, suggest that female fandom has
long been misunderstood as a reactionary cultural form rather than a site of

FIGURE 10.2 *Synchronicities: the smart phone and One Direction*

innovation and resistance (Cofield & Robinson 2016). Abi's comments suggest that her participation provides her with access to 'publics' in a new and rather slippery way, something that cannot quite be separated from her participation in a research project that seeks to understand these practices. We can glimpse this in Abi's explanation of the update accounts through which fans effectively survey the every movement of the band.

> **Abi:** Update accounts.
> **Sara:** Update accounts where they tell you where they are, and you know. And where are One Direction at the moment?
> **Abi:** I don't know actually because I haven't been on Twitter today.
> **Sara:** Where were they yesterday?
> **Abi:** I think at the moment they are in – I don't – I am scared to say this because if I get it wrong then One Direction are going to hate me!
> **Sara:** (Laughs).

Expert and popular cultures of research

The line between expert and popular practices of research has long been porous. Mass Observation is a fascinating example of the democratization of

research, inviting the public to act as informants on their own lives and investi-
gators of the lives of others. In an analysis of responses to Mass Observation
in the late 1930s, Mike Savage (2007) suggests that a particular fraction of
the 'technical middle class' looked to Mass Observation as a way of identifying themselves as intellectuals. Alongside the nascent Workers Education
Association and Pelican paperbacks, contributing to Mass Observation calls
was part of a middle class cultural claim that distinguished them from both
the working classes and the landed gentry. So social research is not simply
a mechanism through which we can find out about social class (the focus of
Savage's enquiry) it also offers a set of practices and spaces through which
classed identities can be claimed, created and expressed. Turning to contemporary research practice, we might also consider how democratic practices
of research may be taken up by particular groups as part of projects of self-
making. Following Savage, we may consider how research practices (in both
expert and popular form) may be understood as part of wider cultural formations, expressing something of the spirit of the age as well as being practices
colonized by particular groups.

During this project, we became aware that the methods that we proposed to use with young people, echoed practices that they were familiar with from popular culture. As explored in Chapter 2, our invitation to
young people to share a typical 'day' and a 'favourite thing' mapped onto
genres familiar to teenagers from the world of YouTube self-documentary
(see Figure 10.3). Aliyah's favourite thing was a memory box inspired by
YouTuber JacksGap. His memory box, collated at the age of 15, includes
a series signifiers of nonthreatening middle class masculinity: a prefect's
badge, skiing medal, BBC pass and a poem to a dead hamster. Aliyah's
box of memories included obsolete technology (her Tamagotchi) and an old
school tie – also obsolete in the face of the academization of her school –
signifying social class in a rather different way. These methods can be
understood as practices that travel between expert, popular and educational

FIGURE 10.3 *Popular genres of research: JacksGap and Tyler Oakley*

cultures, retooled in new settings and with new actors to achieve contingent purposes, yet bringing with them some vestiges and associations of these other spaces. It may be that the spaces *between* these different versions of self-documentary, and between expert and popular practices of research, are particularly revealing of the 'intensive materialities' described by Lash as a feature of the polymedia landscape. For example, we have gained much by thinking of the relationship between Aliyah's memory box and the inspiration for JacksGap, as well as thinking through the rather different stories told in Aliyah's self-made 'day in a life' (which foregrounds a common teenage culture) and the researcher-led observation (where, for example, ethnicity and religion are made visible).

Reflexive methods?

An important feature of self-documentary culture is the value generated by the passage of time. This may be expressed through the disarming nostalgia associated with changing technology (for example the 'dead' Tamagotchi or the retro-appeal of mix tapes) or the powerful effect of witnessing bodies as they grow and age as captured in the many timelapse animations that document children changing over time. The potential of film to capture the *liveness* of youth marks the birth of the cinema and remains central in its passage into the post-digital age. Vicky Lebeau (2008, 2013) suggests that our ability to film the everyday lives of children and to then control these images, even folding them back into second or third-level representations involves a 'votive epistemology'. The materiality of time becomes palpable through the documentation of 'growth'. One of the affordances of the digital is the ease with which we can access these reflexive and iterative methodologies, which fix us at the moment of recording and then refix us in new moments of consumption and display. The everyday use of recording devices as a way of documenting vitality and growth is captured in the following extract from Jasmine's 'day in a life' observation. Researcher Ester records how she uses her phone to communicate about and with her baby daughter:

> Jasmine gets her phone out to take a selfie of baby R. The carer's son runs into the room and Jasmine. makes him pose for a picture too. I take a photo of Jasmine taking a photo of baby R. The Jasmine plays me a recording that she made yesterday of a telephone conversation she had on her phone – in the conversation she is telling her friend that baby R. 'pooed' and then R. makes a noise that Jasmine says R. says 'pooed'. I can't hear it but Jasmine swears that is what baby R is saying!

Decline is also captured by these methods, and we see affinities between Jasmine's documentation of Baby R and the attentive documentation practices encountered around Sean whose deteriorating health condition had made speech almost impossible. Here researcher Liam describes the way that Sean and his carers use his tablet and digital picture frame as a methods for memorializing his body and ability as it changes:

> Sean communicates using just a few subtle body gestures during the interview, but smiles a few times when [his carers] Linda or Karen tell him jokes. One of the first objects that Linda produces from Sean's bag are four baseball caps. Apparently Sean has a large collection of baseball caps, and often wears matching caps and scarfs. Today he is wearing a bright cheque cap with a matching scarf. Two caps in particular appear to have significance for Sean, a blue Chelsea cap and a red Ferrari one. In the photographs on his digital picture frame we see him sat on the side lines of a football match, wearing his Chelsea cap and scarf. There are also photographs of Sean in various 'flashy' cars, including a Ferrari. Whilst Karen is holding up the digital picture frame for us to see the photographs, she asks Sean if he wants us to continue looking at them or to move onto another objects. He indicates with his hands that he'd like to continue looking at them. I ask if he has the digital picture frame on in his room and he indicates yes. We look at two small silver toy cars from when he was younger, and he gives a big smile as Karen drives them over his stomach and chest. We look at his tablet from home, which has a video of a care worker who has left the school to go travelling for a year. The video shows her on her last day receiving gifts from the staff and students. Sean filmed the video on his tablet by himself. Apparently he keeps in touch with the care worker whilst she is travelling by Skyping her on weekends using his tablet. According to Linda and Karen he keeps photographs and videos on his tablet to remind him of people and events

Digital research methods also have the potential for reflexivity, iterativity and surprise. In previous longitudinal research with young people, we engaged in these practices through representing young people with extracts of audio recordings of interviews that stretched back over 10 years – filming the process of them listening to and reacting to the sound of their own voices. Our shorthand for this process was sharing their 'best bits', employing a phrase familiar to us and our participants from the then relatively new reality TV show 'Big Brother', whose consolation prize to those leaving the house was to edit together their bespoke highlights from a vast body of video data. Our experience of using this as a research technique was that as the time elapse between the making and the broadcasting of these images increases, the potential for pathos is amplified. Witnessing your former self can be funny, moving, embarrassing and most importantly, 'entertaining', as demonstrated by the popularity on YouTube of reading out your old diary entries (ThatcherJoe). An exemplar from popular culture comes from YouTube star Zoella who celebrates reaching four million subscribers by using a slip screen to share a video diary that she made at 12 years old – the gap between the juxtaposed texts is both unsettling and revealing as we move between the polished 'face to camera' Zoella of the present (surrounded by products and endorsements) to a girls-eye view of packing for the holidays, naming and enjoying the consumer culture that infuses her bedroom.[2]

As a third stage of research in this study, we went back to young participants with extracts from previous interviews, with the intention of sharing the perspective that we had generated through gathering data with them over time (and thus negotiating informed consent for the research process) but also beginning the process of agreeing on a document that could be shared more publicly. We called this method the 'recursive workbook interview' because it explicitly involves engaging with material from the past in the present. For the teenagers in the research, this involved looking at extracts collected over the course of 12–18 months, but for the younger participants in the extensive sample, the 'beginning' of the research process stretched back to before their birth, when we had met their mothers in the final stages of their pregnancy. As we explored in Chapter 2, these encounters could be surprising, unnerving and creative – suggesting the potential of live digital methods to open up new critical spaces. We end this chapter with an edited extract from researcher Liam's final interview with Megan, where they review her 'day in a life' and favourite things multimedia outputs made using Prezi. Though Megan has only been involved in the study for a year, much has changed and the process of looking again at the documents created by the research and thinking about what will now happen to them focuses attention on continuities and changes, which are both spoken and unspoken.

At the beginning of the interview we discuss her involvement over the last year … She talks about how being involved was better than she thought it would be and that she had mainly been worried that it would be 'lots of questions' that she wouldn't be sure how to answer. I feel slightly unsure asking what she thinks has changed in her life over the past year as I'm aware that her home life may be in the process of significant change. We end up staying in fairly 'safe' territory by discussing her transition into secondary school. She talks with amusement about how she is taller than most of the other year 7s, and the topic of size comes up again after the

---

[2]link https://www.youtube.com/watch?v=xZvRxVbxOKo.

interview when she complains to her dad that her feet are getting too big now and that she needs 'adult' shoes … When we move on to discuss the fieldnotes it turns out that Megan hasn't really read them. They're a bit too long for her to read and so her mum has just discussed parts of it with her. Her mum says how she found them really interesting and remarks on how busy the day seems. Megan remarks how she feels primary school already feels like it's becoming a part of the past. There's some amusement at the choice of 'Megan' as a pseudonym as apparently they had originally planned to call her Megan but changed their mind [. . .]

We move on to look at the Prezi and look at each slide in turn. I ask Megan questions about the day as we go through it and she seems to remember most of it quite well. When I ask how she felt about being observed she says it was fine and that most of the time she didn't even see that I was there. It strikes me that this seems to be a characteristic of day in a life observations conducted at school. We get to the last two slides of 'day in a life' part of the Prezi which are of Megan playing Minecraft. The first one contains a recording of her describing Minecraft to me and how she came to get into it. As the recording plays she instantly hides her face in her hands with embarrassment, much to the amusement of her parents. I ask how she feels about having the recording of her voice and she says it's just embarrassing playing it here in front of everyone, but that she won't mind it going online. Megan says that she isn't as into Minecraft as she was. She still plays it but not as much as she did then … Until this point I hadn't realised that Megan had been holding her tablet the entire interview. Her parents point this out and say that she carries it with her everywhere. Later on Megan shows me that she was able to bring up the Prezi on her tablet. After going through the Prezi we talk about publishing it online and also archiving the data from the study. I try to address this to Megan as much as possible. We finish the interview with enough time for her mum to sign the consent form again with Megan and a brief discussion of the Curating Childhoods event in December. Megan seems quite excited about the event and the prospect of meeting some of the other children involved in the study.

In a critical review of 'creative methods in media research', David Buckingham (2009) is scathing about the naïve use of participatory and visual methods in research with children and young people, suggesting that it is rare to see researchers using mediation as a way to open up critical space for thinking about mediation itself. In the face of a plethora of approaches that claim the empowering potential of making and doing as forms of self-expression he challenges researchers to pay attention to the contexts through which images are produced and consumed and the kinds of identity work that being involved in research demands of its subjects – including how 'tasks' may echo other genres they are familiar with through school or popular culture. The recursive interview certainly has parallels in popular culture, as noted previously, yet it has affective affordances of a particular kind – demanding a live engagement with material from the past in the present. In Chapter 2, we presented material from the recursive interview with Lucien and his mother Monica, who together looked back over his whole lifetime revisiting a birth story that had not previously been shared. In this example, the collision between past, present and future that the situation involves is dramatic and is responded to creatively by Lucien, who moves between 'baby-talk' and a fluent performance of field notes that involve him quoting his father's words. This example involving researcher Liam, Megan and her parents is less dramatic yet equally poignant, capturing an important transition from primary to secondary school and the complicated feelings provoked by seeing an earlier version of self.

In Chapter 2, we characterize this recursive method as a form of 'performative research' within an emergent live methods tradition described by Back and Puwar (2013), a form of inventive (Lury & Wakeford 2012) or 'affirmative' method (Massumi 2002) which effectively breaks the fourth wall that distinguishes research practice from life as lived (see also MacLure 2013 and Staunæs & Kofoed 2014). We see this approach as engaging in the materiality of the media as a way of talking about things that might otherwise be hard to articulate. The recursive interview also draws participants into the research process, understanding themselves as objectified and documented, yet involved in the project of interpretation. In a similar way that the early days of video diaries appeared to provide glimpses into new critical documentary practices (Pini & Walkerdine 2011), it may be that the affordances that excite us here will soon be normalized and glossed so that the potential for the past to disrupt the present in such a visceral way is taken for granted.

Learning from researching childhood in a digital age

In this chapter, we have thought critically about what it might mean to 'research' in a digital, even post-digital age – when the incitement to research is built into our platforms and tools and takes form as new structures of feeling within the culture as we 'stalk' and 'obsess' for fun. In the face of claims of a crisis for empirical research or the discovery of research in the wild, we point to the way in which expert and popular cultures of enquiry have long been in conversation while also acknowledging the specificity of the digital and the potential it raises for new modes of engagement. Rather than seeking to preserve the specificity of the expert researcher, we are interested in the connections between popular and professional practices, asking what the spaces in between can allow for in terms of creative and critical meaning making. Mindful of critiques of naïve approaches to multimedia methods, we consider the specific affordances of the digital, its potential to generate surprise in recursive movement between past and present, and between cultural spaces. Far from collapsing the idea of research into everyday or commercial practice, we are interested in thinking how a critical and ethically engaged research practice may play a role in the creation of hybrid public spaces, ephemeral yet networked and animated by logics that may be diverse and undetermined.

This chapter brings to an end our account of researching everyday childhoods in a digital age. Throughout the book, we have drawn attention to new kinds of materialities that are part of a digitally saturated culture. This is fast moving terrain, and the examples that we showcase will soon be superseded by new applications, augmentations and adaptations. Yet, we hope to have introduced a conceptual language, a mode of enquiry and pointers for policy and practice with salience over a longer term. This includes the following.

Conceptually

- The need to move beyond the online/offline binary to think of the emergence of new kinds of materialities, socialities and forms of care.

- Understanding media as having their own biographies and understanding individual biographies as mediated in ways that are both contingent yet patterned.

- Conceptualizing media landscapes as underpinned by powerful logics of practice, for example the crosscutting imperatives of participation and in/visibility that characterize the social media landscape for young people.

- An alertness to the central role of children and teenagers for the creation and circulation of value in communicative capitalism.

- Recognition that institutional habits of 'protection' may cut across young people's capacity to participate, and to create and access 'publics'.

- Awareness of the extensive and intensive dimensions of digital culture and how these may reveal distinct challenges and sets of concern around children's well-being.

- Critical insight into the ways that old social divisions such as gender, race and class may be recalibrated and obscured in a 'post digital' landscape.

Methodologically

- Digital documentation is an everyday practice that connects professional and popular modes of research.

- We can embrace a new relationship with the empirical that acknowledges the performative/live dimensions of digital methods and the potential for collaborative experimentation.

- The value of being alert to the material and affective affordances of our different research methods.

- Recognition that research can start rather than end with an archive, opening projects of knowledge production up to a range of stakeholders.

- Understanding the value of long and slow methods for making sense in a digital age

- Realizing the multimodal potential of digital data and developing new modes of publishing that are fit for purpose.

Policy and practice

- It is important not to make assumptions about young people's digital media access and competence which is likely to be varied, and dynamic, especially among younger children;

- There is currently a strong divide between personal and popular digital cultures and educational spaces which may be understandable (having developed over time in response to circumstances) rather than defensible.

- Schools are increasingly data driven, giving rise to new kinds of pressure in the classroom. Opportunities for individual research and creativity are circumscribed.

- The current focus on risk and danger in children's digital culture obscures more ordinary modes of interaction, a concern with digital safety needs to be balanced with an awareness of young people's digital rights.

- Young people are keen to discuss and understand the practical, ethical and economic dimensions of digital media, including the competing imperatives or participation and visibility and the creation, ownership and control of content.

- Participatory research is an ideal tool for building digital literacy and debating questions of privacy, visibility, value and ownership.

Appendix 1

The Story of the Project

Rachel Thomson

The Face 2 Face project was funded by the ESRC in 2012 as a methodological innovation project focusing on qualitative longitudinal research.[1] The research team had accumulated expertise in the practice of following research participants through time. This began in 1996 with the Inventing Adulthoods project which, for over 15 years, journeyed with young people from the cusp of 'teenagehood' into adulthood, witnessing social and technological revolutions that not only transformed their lives, but also the methods of the researchers working with them.[2] What began as an interview study using analogue tape recordings ended up as a digitized archive available to other researchers for secondary analysis, and multimedia teaching resources exploring the changing shape of youth transitions. The Inventing Adulthoods study also became an exemplar for a new kind of research that was both deliberately longitudinal and qualitative which proved to be in tune with emergent theoretical interests in temporality and materiality, and the demands of a digital age. We were fortunate to collaborate with media and information professionals to create open access digital data archives and to co-produce a range of state of the art multimedia documentation.

---

[1] Thomson (PI), Howland, Bragg, Kehily and Berriman, NCRM methodological innovation project Face to face: tracing the real and the mediated in children's cultural worlds, Grant reference 512589109, final report available to download from http://blogs.sussex.ac.uk/everydaychildhoods/face-to-face/publications-and-outputs/.

[2] The Inventing Adulthoods data set is archived and available for secondary analysis from the UK data service (SN: 5777, http://dx.doi.org/10.5255/UKDA-SN-5777-1). The project website documenting the methodology is archived at http://www.restore.ac.uk/inventingadulthoods/. Publications from the project include Henderson et al. (2007) Inventing Adulthoods: a biographical approach to youth transitions (Sage) and teaching materials produced by the Open University course Youth: Perspectives and Practices including the Young Lives DVD.

When this study began in 1996, mobile phones were a luxury item and social media was in its infancy. Yet, as participants were followed through the process of leaving school and home, platforms such as Friends Reunited emerged in tandem with new needs to network and keep 'in touch' with school friends as the university experience expanded to include more and more young people. In 2002, the research team published a paper capturing the emergence of information and communication technologies in young people's everyday lives, focusing on 'new and transitory cultures of sociality associated with the use of the mobile phone'. It argued that 'mobile telephones can be understood as an individualizing technology, placing young people in the centre of social networks, yet also making them available to 'reciprocal obligations'. We cautioned 'against investing this technology with particular characteristics suggesting that distinct potentials are realized in relation to particularities of class, age, culture and circumstance' (Henderson et al. 2002: 494).

Longitudinal methods proved to be valuable in documenting the take-up of digital devices by young people, but the kinds of methods of documentation employed by researchers were constrained by a need to ensure compatibility and continuity over time. The challenge of 'obsolescence' was simultaneously technical (could we still access the data), theoretical (did we still understand the data in the same way) and ethical (did we foresee using the data in this way). Reflecting upon the importance of the tape recorder as a tool of social research Les Back (2012) reminds us that every research tool reveals 'something' perfectly, and that this is 'settled' through an interaction of the method and the theoretical frame of analysis. In 2002, our research paradigm involved revealing how individual and collective projects of self were constructed over time, relying on tape-recorded interviews, repeated in waves – with social media and digital technology used as a way of tracking and 'keeping in touch with participants' who could now screen their calls, putting unwanted researchers straight to voicemail.

In a subsequent longitudinal study which ran between 2005 and 2009, we explored how digital methods could capture lived temporalities, including different and combining prospective orientations to the new with retrospective or recursive approaches to revisiting the past (McLeod & Thomson 2009). The Making Modern Mothers project combined a cross-generational and longitudinal research design to capture the experience of families at the arrival of a new generation.[3] Expectant mothers and grandmothers shared their life stories and their hopes for the future and the research team returned to them over time to explore how their lives unfolded in relation to each other, paying attention to the interplay of the miniature, the routines and the epic. Life history interviews gave way to a series of increasingly collaborative research encounters

---

[3]The Making Modern Mothers project is reported in Thomson et al. (2001) and the multimedia website http://modernmothers.org/.

that sensitized us to the interplay of different time scales in forging family practices including observations of a 'day in a life' with mothers, and grandmothers sharing and narrating treasured objects and family reflections on fragments of data gathered from across the study and organized into 'memory books' (see Chapter 2). In collaboration, we animated digital data in such a way that we could share the perspectives generated through the project with participants and a wider audience. In this study, we both witnessed and contributed to the new ways in which digital culture was penetrating family life, providing new sources of peer expertise on birth and parenting and new ways of displaying and communicating family (Finch 2007; Dermott & Seymour 2011).

Time	1996–2005	2005–2009	2013–2014	2014–2015
Study	Inventing Adulthoods	Making Modern Mothers	Face 2 Face	Curating Childhood
Methods	Repeat interviews, Memory books, Creation of public archive and public multimedia case studies	Repeat interviews, Object interviews, Day in a life, Recursive interview, Public website with multimedia animations	Space Invaders competition, Object interviews, Day in a life, Recursive interviews	Creating and sharing digital archive. Hackathon. Public website with multimedia animations
Sample	n/a	62 first time mothers, 12 case study families	Children panel 7 yrs old. New teenage panel	Families Children Teenagers
People	Thomson, Henderson, Holland, McGrellis, Sharpe	Thomson, Kehily, Sharpe, Hadfield, Arnott & Hughes	Thomson, Berriman, Kehily, Howland, Bragg, Sharpe, Hadfield, McGeeney, Arnott & Hughes	Thomson, Berriman, Courage, Arnott & Hughes

The Face 2 Face project built on these foundations, in terms of people. technology and methodology. Initially a 12-month project, we proposed to work with two panels of young people: the children initially followed from before birth in the Making Modern Mothers study (born in 2005) and a new panel of teenagers recruited for the project. Both panels would be followed over the course of a calendar year, adapting previously used methods to focus on the digital within their everyday lives and cultural worlds. In line with our interest in the digital as both topic and resource,[4] we set out to explore how digital research methods might be used to document and share these lives. Traditionally social research leaves questions of audience and the afterlife of data open until the very end of a project, when we consider how 'findings' might be 'disseminated'. We wanted to invert the temporal structure of the project, starting with the challenge of creating ethically robust publically shareable accounts of young people's everyday lives. By embracing the affordances of digital culture, we sought to reimagine social research within a digital age – inviting young people and their families to join us in a project that began rather than ended with the idea of the archive thinking through the relationship between popular practices of self-documentation and display and those undertaken by experts as part of a wider project of public culture. Supported by an AHRC digital transformations grant we were able to explore this over another 12 months as part of the Curating Childhoods project, establishing a safe archival home for the data set in the 'Everyday Childhoods' collection at the Mass Observation[5] Archive and working with participants, their families, researchers and archivists to explore the ethical and practical dimensions of data sharing and reuse.[6]

Questions of scale in qualitative longitudinal research are mediated by time. A sample may be numerically small, yet generate a huge data set that is both intensive (documenting many encounters) and extensive (covering an extended period of time) (Yates 2003). In this project, we worked with just 14 young people (6 children and 8 teenagers), yet our contact was both intensive and for some extensive, with considerable 'backstory' provided by the Making Modern Mother project. Our research team was also extensive, connecting the MoMM team with a new group of researchers with specialist interests in digital childhoods. In keeping with good practice in QLR we took care of established research relationships with individual researchers following the same child over time. Yet coming together with each other and with project advisors in analysis workshops that focused on distinct methodological tools. One full

---

[4]Including the Space Invaders public engagement project that involved the authors and Sevasti Melissa Nolas http://www.sussex.ac.uk/esw/circy/research/completedresearch/spaceinvaders.

[5]The Everyday Childhoods website provides detail of both the F2F and Curating Childhoods projects as well as direct access to the multimedia case studies http://blogs.sussex.ac.uk/everydaychildhoods/.

[6]The Everyday Childhoods collection can be accessed through the following website http://blogs.sussex.ac.uk/everydaychildhoods/.

time researcher (Berriman) undertook the bulk of fieldwork with teenagers, Sue Sharpe conducted fieldwork with three of the children while the rest of the team focused on single cases and/or analysis. Work with media professionals Susi Arnott and Crispin Hughes focused initially on the extensive panel (children) and the creation of multimedia documents animating data collected as part of the favourite things and 'day in a life' methods. The creation of multimedia documents of teenage lives was led by Liam Berriman using freely available web platforms. In practice, there was a great deal of collaboration and knowledge exchange between the media professionals and amateurs, which was productive in terms of thinking through how and why researchers and filmmakers approach the task of documentary making – and this is something that we discuss explicitly in Chapter 2. Participants from both panels and all researchers were invited to be part of the Curating Childhoods stage of the study.

The question of scale also raises the question of who are this sample of children, young people and families, what apart from themselves do they 'represent' and how we might move from their particularity to think about wider trends, typicalities or generalizations? These are questions that are central to the validity of qualitative research and become visible as attempts are made to 'scale up' qualitative research through linking studies in different ways (see Mason 2002, Henwood & Lang 2005, Weller, Davidson & Anna 2016). As a discipline, sociology has a changing relationship with the particular, the case study or case history, with the ascendancy of the random or representative sample being a motif of post-war social science. Yet the case study also has an honourable sociological history mobilizing an alternative logic of validity that values depth over breadth and moreover understands depth as a route to generalization.[7] Qualitative research benefits from thoughtful sampling. Small qualitative samples can for example be drawn from broader data sets with cases selected purposefully to represent something of interest, or we may deliberately construct a sample so that the cases are 'emblematic' of established phenomena/trends or aspects of the wider case.[8] In this study, certain cases were inherited from the previous Making Modern Motherhood project, the case studies for which were selected from a wider volunteer sample in order to reflect a diversity of situations of mothering, meaning that the sample enabled us to see how issues of social class, ethnicity, sexuality and locality might shape experience. The children of these families thus extend

---

[7]For an interdisciplinary review of the case study see Platt (1992), for a humanities perspective see Berlant (2007) and for an inspiring discussion of the distinction between variable and narrative logics in case study research see Abbott (2001).

[8]So for example in *Unfolding Lives* I selected 5 longitudinal cases from a wider sample of 100 on the basis that they were emblematic of trends in youth transitions that were condensed into particular figures such as the high achieving minority ethnic working class girl (Thomson 2011).

the extensive family case studies, which now include at least three generations. The teenage sample is much more 'shallow' in terms of back-story and
was again selected in order to explore diversity with a particular focus this
time on the affordances of technology. In generating the teenage sample, we
deliberately included young people with physical disabilities while also seeking to maintain diversity around social class, family formation, ethnicity and
place. The details of the sample are laid out below.

Designing an ethical project

> A key objective of the project is to work collaboratively with co-researchers
> and a media partner to see what kind of ethically sensitive open access
> documents of everyday childhoods-over-time it might be possible to create.
> In doing so we will contribute to the development of ethical understand-
> ings in researching children's lives, informing critical debates concerning
> the tensions between child protection and participation in researching
> childhood in a digital age. (Ethical Review Application (ER/RT219/1), p. 1)

One of the starting points for this project was our awareness of a growing
asymmetry between commercial supported public spaces – such as those
facilitated by social media platforms where young people would share data
and represent themselves freely – and publically funded spaces such as
archives and social research where the figure of the child seems to be disappearing in the face of growing anxieties about safeguarding. We set out then
to deliberately 'push the envelope', working against the grain to explore how
ethically robust research might be conducted with young people that recognized and respected their vulnerability without falling into a set of risk avoid-
ance practices unthinkingly. This meant that we had to prepare a well thought
through case for the research at the point of ethical review. Our thinking on
the key issues required by the review process is outlined here:

INFORMED CONSENT
All participants involved in this research will be given a detailed information
sheet explaining the aims of the research, the methods to be employed
and how the resulting data will be stored and used. In principle, we consider that young people aged between 8 and 5 have the capacity to consent to and dissent from taking part in research. In this project, we will be
seeking to undertake research within household settings and with parents/
carers. We will therefore also secure consent from at least one parent/
carer responsible for the young person involved in the research.

(2) All interviewees will be asked to provide written consent for the recording, transcription and use of interview data.

(3) Off-line observations: The researchers conducting 'day in a life' observations will explain their role as appropriate to those observed as part of the ethnographic part of the research. Field notes will not include real names or identifying information and will be anonymized before they are archived. Where visual data is produced, this will be negotiated with the consent of the co-researchers, who will have the opportunity to edit the data record before display/ publication or archiving.

(4) Online observations: Data capture of online activity is an important part of this project. We will seek to realize a principle of informed consent in this respect, ensuring that material is recorded with the consent of all parties involved. Where it is not possible to secure such consent, we will edit material retrospectively in line with our ethical commitments.

(5) Data display: A key aim of this project is the creation of public documents of young people's everyday lives. From the earliest stages of the research, we will communicate this to potential participants and their families. We will work with participants and our media consultant to negotiate what is acceptable and appropriate in these documents, including issues of confidentiality and anonymity. We will not publish these multimedia documents without gaining the agreement of our research subjects.

(6) Archiving of data: It is our intention to archive data from this research with the Mass Observation archive. Choosing what is possible to archive, in what form, under what access arrangements, will be part of our negotiations with research participants. Given the exploratory nature of this project, we will not seek consent to archive until the end of the project when researchers and participants are fully aware of what the data record entails. The attached archiving consent form is a draft and will be refined during the project.

RIGHT OF WITHDRAWAL: All participants will have the right to withdraw from the study and to remove their data from the project and, ultimately, from the archive. In longitudinal research, issues of attrition are well explored and there is evidence of research participants withdrawing from studies and then returning to them. We will explain to participants that they are able to withdraw data up until the point of publication.

SAFEGUARDING & HARM: Our overall intention in this research is to have no harmful impact on participants and ideally to enhance well-being and the development of skills and insight through participation in an interesting project. All adults involved in fieldwork will have an enhanced DBS. When working in institutional settings, we will follow the safeguarding policy of the organization if we are concerned about potential harm to any of the young people or those close to them. Researchers conducting field-work will be well informed about local support services and will be encour-aged to share this information with young people if needed. In general, we would aim to respect young people's confidentiality and would only break with this where we had concerns about their safety or that of others. If we felt it was necessary to do this, we would always talk to the young person about this first, and if possible secure their consent for disclosure. This will be explained to young people and to parents/carers as part of the informed consent process.

CONFIDENTIALITY AND ANONYMITY

(a) Confidentiality: Our duty of care to participants means that we will make clear to participants the limits of confidentiality within the research relation-ship, explaining that if we hear or see anything that raises concerns about the safety of participants or others close to them, then we will pass on our concerns to appropriate agencies such as youth workers, social workers and head teachers. Ideally, we would only do this with young people's con-sent, and always with their knowledge. A key objective of the study is the exploration of confidentiality in an age of performative visual methods, and as a team, we hope to extend and elaborate good practice in this arena. By inviting them to curate the open access multimedia documents that are a key outcome of the study, we will support them in thinking through the potential audiences for materials generated in the research (and to the other digital records that they make of their lives in their engagement with social media). Whether or not documents generated in the research process are suitable for archiving and sharing will also be negotiated with co-researchers. Issues of internal confidentiality are especially pertinent in relation to the extensive case study panel, where we will be using extracts from interviews from different family members in the 'recursive scrap-book' method. Here we will seek consent for reuse of data from the per-son whose data is used to avoid unintentional breaches of confidentiality. A draft of the 'scrap-book' will be given to a parent in advance of the inter-view to ensure suitability and to secure consent.

(b) Anonymity: The use of visual and indexical digital methods means that it is impossible for us to promise full anonymity to participants. At the very least, they will be recognizable to those who know them already, and it is neither possible nor productive to completely disguise places. However, it is not our intention to expose individuals through this research, and we will pursue an approach that consistently does not focus on indi-vidual identities, by focusing on what people do rather than who they are;

avoiding photographs of faces; the inventive use of audio and involving participants in the editing process. Co-researchers may willingly forgo anonymity, wishing to own and present their own work and ideas. We are open to this as a possibility and have successfully negotiated this in a previous project where four young people from a sample of 100 forwent their anonymity to take part on a film based on the ESRC Inventing Adulthood study (Thomson 2013).

DATA PROTECTION: The core research team will have access to personal data in this study. This includes the principle and co-applicants, the research fellow, the research assistant and the project secretary. Personal information will be shared with the project consultants as necessary. Our consent form explains the limits of the confidentiality that we can promise to participants in the face of any serious concerns about safety.

All data will be kept safely in locked filing cabinets and/or password protected files. Data archived with the Timescapes and/ or Mass Observations repositories will be kept indefinitely. Data that is not archived in this way is likely to be destroyed after a period of up to 10 years due to the cost of preservation and storage. Any web-based resources arising from the project considered to have lasting value will be submitted for digital archiving through the ReStore project of the National Centre for Research Methods.

[extracts from Ethical Review Application (ER/RT219/1)]

Appendix 2

The Cast

Liam Berriman

Research participants

Abi – We first met Abi when she was 14 years old and living in a terraced house with her mother (a lecturer) and younger brother in a semi-rural town where she attended a local comprehensive 11–16 secondary school. She initially took part in the study's pilot panel and subsequently became a full participant in the study. Abi's family come from a white British background.

Aliyah – We first met Aliyah when she was 14 years old and living with her family (including three older and two younger siblings) in a semi-detached house in a suburb of a large city, where she attended a local comprehensive secondary school that had recently reopened as an Academy. Aliyah's father worked in property management and her mother was a homemaker. Aliyah and her family are practising Muslims, and her parents migrated from Bangladesh before she was born.

David – We first met David as a baby, as part of the Making Modern Motherhood study. When we revisited David aged 7, he was living as an only child with his father, who works long hours in a non-professional role, and mother in a flat in a large inner city area, where he attended a local primary school. David's father Richie has a Guyanan heritage and his mother Anastasia, a Romanian/Russian background.

Funmi – We first met Funmi when she was 15 years old and living with her family (including two older brothers and two younger twin brothers) in a semi-detached house in a suburb of a large city, where she attended a local comprehensive secondary school. Funmi's mother was a mature student and clothes designer and her father was a professional musician. Funmi's family come from a black British background.

Gabriel – We first met Gabriel as a baby, as part of the Making Modern Motherhood study. When we revisited Gabriel aged 7, he was living with his mothers Kay and Nadia (who were both public sector professionals) and younger brother in a provincial city, where he attended a local primary school. Gabriel's family come from a white British background.

Jasmine – We first met Jasmine when she was 15 years old and living with her newborn daughter R and her older sister in a large urban area. Jasmine moved on two occasions during the project and, in our final interview, she and her daughter were living with a foster family. Jasmine attended a short-stay community school, which had an on-site nursery for pupils with young children. Jasmine's family come from a mixed race British background.

Lucien – We first met Lucien as a baby, as part of the Making Modern Motherhood study. When we revisited Lucien aged 7, he was living in a terraced house with his father Jamie and mother Monica (both civil servants) and younger sister in an inner city area undergoing gentrification, where he attended a local primary school. Lucien's family come from a white British background.

Megan – We first met Megan when she was 10 years old and living in a large house in a rural setting with her father (an interior decorator) and mother (an artist). Megan was one of a set of triplets (with two brothers) and had one older brother. At the beginning of the study, Megan attended a Church of England primary school and, by the end, had graduated to a local comprehensive secondary school. Megan's family come from a white British background.

Nathan – We first met Nathan when he was 13 years old and living in a terraced house in a residential suburb of a large city, where he attended a local comprehensive secondary school. He lived with his mother (a social worker) and an older brother. Nathan's family come from a black British background.

Nkosi – We first met Nkosi as a baby, as part of the Making Modern Motherhood study. When we revisited Nkosi aged 7, he was living with his mother Lorraine (a chef) and younger sister in a large city, where he attended a Catholic primary school. Nkosi's family come from an African Caribbean background.

Saffron – We first met Saffron as a baby, as part of the Making Modern Motherhood study. When we revisited Saffron aged 7, she was living as an only child with her mother Tina (an administrator) and father (self-employed) in modern house in a new town with family living nearby. She attended a local primary school. Saffron's family come from a white British background.

Sean – We first met Sean when he was 13 years old and living in a semi-detached property in a small rural town. Sean lived with his father and mother (his full-time carer) and his older brother. Sean attended a non-maintained school for children with complex disabilities and health needs. Sean had originally been in mainstream schooling, but after the onset of a muscular degenerative condition, had moved to a school providing one-to-one care and support. Sean's family come from a white British background.

Tempest – We first met Tempest as a baby as part of the Making Modern Motherhood study. When we revisited Tempest aged 7, she was living in a household of seven with her mother Kim and her extended family on an estate in a new town, where she attended a local primary school. Tempest's family come from a white Anglo-African background.

Please note: a further two participants took part in the research but withdrew over the course of the project. These included Tim (13 years old) and Luc (13 years old).

Pilot participants

Andrew – a 15-year-old living in a semi-rural town with his mother and sister.
Claire – a 13-year-old living in a medium-sized city with her mother and brother.
Emily – a 7-year-old living in a medium-sized city with her mother and father.

The researchers

Susi Arnott and Crispin Hughes – Filmmaker and photographer respectively, Susi and Crispin had previously collaborated with Rachel Thomson on the multimedia outputs accompanying the Making Modern Motherhood study. This collaboration resumed in the Face 2 Face study, where they provided expert advice on multimedia recording to the project team, and helped to develop the project's multimedia outputs. They also provided multimedia support for the Curating Childhoods project and the My Object Stories Hackathon.

Liam Berriman – A sociologist, Liam was the full-time researcher on the Face 2 Face project and a lead investigator on the Curating Childhoods project. He primarily worked with the intensive cohort of the Face 2 Face project, particularly, Aliyah, Funmi, Megan, Nathan and Sean. Liam also led the 'My Object Stories' Hackathon in collaboration with the Mass Observation Archive.

Sara Bragg – With an academic background in education and youth studies, Sara was a lead investigator on the Face 2 Face project and worked primarily with the intensive cohort, particularly Abi. She was also closely involved in the Space Invaders and Curating Childhoods projects.

Fiona Courage – the lead Curator of the Mass Observation Archive, Fiona collaborated with the project teams on both the Face 2 Face and Curating Childhoods project.

Lucy Hadfield – Having previously worked as a researcher on the Making Modern Motherhood study, Lucy returned to work with Saffron and her family as part of the Face 2 Face study.

Kate Howland – Bringing an academic background in informatics and design, Kate was a lead investigator on the Face 2 Face project and worked primarily with the intensive cohort. She worked with one member of the pilot study (Claire) and another participant who withdrew from the project. Kate was also closely involved in the Space Invaders and Curating Childhoods projects.

Mary Jane Kehily – With an academic background in childhood and youth studies, Mary Jane was a lead investigator on both the Face 2 Face and Making Modern Motherhood studies. She resumed her relationship with Tempest and her family as part of the Face 2 Face study.

Ester McGeeney – A youth researcher and practitioner, Ester worked closely with Jasmine as part of the Face 2 Face study.

Sue Sharpe – Having previously been involved in the Making Modern Motherhood study, Sue returned to work with David, Gabriel, Nkosi and their families as part of the Face 2 Face study.

Rachel Thomson – A sociologist with an extensive background in qualitative longitudinal research, Rachel was the lead investigator on the Face 2 Face and Curating Childhoods projects. Rachel had previously led the Making Modern Motherhood study and resumed her relationship with Lucien and his family on the Face 2 Face project.

Glossary

Cbeebies A UK public service television channel and brand aimed at children of pre-school age and run by the BBC.

Facebook A global social network platform founded in 2001 by Mark Zuckerberg. The service includes the ability to create a personal profile, connect with networks of 'friends', and to share and 'like' content.

Fraping The infiltration of another's social media account in order to post irregular content or messages to shame or embarrass. Typically, by accessing a device that has been unintentionally left unattended (e.g. an unlocked mobile phone).

Friends Reunited A no longer existent networking platform that preceded most contemporary social media platforms. It provided opportunities to reconnect with old school friends or workplace colleagues.

Furby An interactive toy that can be 'taught' different words and actions.

Happy slapping The filming of random acts of violence on a mobile phone to be shared online.

Instagram A platform for sharing photographs either publicly or privately. The platform is owned by Facebook.

Legend of Zelda A Nintendo published fantasy adventure computer game series.

Majorettes A group who meet for parades and competitions to demonstrate synchronized baton twirling whilst marching.

Minecraft A social multiplayer game combining survival and sandpit construction genres.

Moshi Monsters Originally an online game where monsters are levelled up through games and activities (including arithmetic), but later expanded to include collectible figurines and other merchandise.

Naruto A Japanese anime series about a group of young ninjas-in-training.

Nintendo DS A popular handheld games console operated via a touchscreen, created by the Japanese electronics firm Nintendo.

One Direction A British-based boy band who achieved a high level of global fame. During our study, the band lost two of its members.

PlayStation A games console series created by Sony.

PowerPoint A facility by Microsoft Office for displaying content as slides.

Prezi A platform for displaying digital content on a large canvas. Primarily intended for presentations.

School vocabularies In England, children begin Reception class in primary school during the year of their fourth birthday. Year 1 is the first compulsory complete year of schooling, during which children turn five, and so on. Secondary school generally begins in year 7. GCSE (General Certificate of School Education) examinations are taken in Year 11, and A-(Advanced) Levels in years 12 and 13. The school leaving age is now 18. Schools funded by Local Authorities are required to follow the National Curriculum, while the rapidly growing sector of Academy schools – independent of Local Authority control – are not. Schools may have specific faith characteristics. Most schools require students to wear a specific school uniform. At the time of our research, many schools assessed students with reference to National Curriculum 'Levels'. Pupil Referral Units are state-funded provision for students who cannot cope in mainstream schooling for reasons of behaviour, health or circumstance (such as young mothers). Special Schools provide specialist services for children with complex disabilities. Ofsted refers to the Office for Standards in Education, Children's Services and Skills, inspecting all state-funded schools. Adverse reports may result in a change in how schools are run and by whom.

Sexting   The exchange of sexual body images via text or personal social media platforms.

Skype   An online platform for making audio or video calls.

Snapchat   A photo messaging platform where images appear for short periods of time before self-destructing.

Tamagotchi   A pocket-sized 'virtual pet' that was popular in the 1990s/2000s.

Top Gear   A BBC programme focused on 'fast' cars. At the time of our research, the programme was still fronted by its original presenting team, led by Jeremy Clarkson.

Twitter   A 'micro blogging' social media service which allows users to publish short posts or messages called 'tweets' that are restricted to 140 characters.

Union J   A British-based boy band. The band rose to fame after their appearance on the UK television programme *The X Factor*.

Vines   A social media service for sharing six-second-long video clips on a loop. Owned by the same company as Twitter it was discontinued in 2017.

WhatsApp   A messaging app that allows for one-to-one messaging or group 'chats'.

Xbox   A games console series created by Microsoft.

YouTube   A platform for uploading and broadcasting video content. Used by both individuals and brands.

YouTuber   An individual who maintains their own YouTube channel, with regularly uploaded videos. Whilst anyone with a YouTube channel can call themselves a YouTuber, the term was largely used as a reference in our study to YouTube 'celebrities' who had achieved large audience viewing figures.

References

Abbott, A. (2001) *Time matters: On theory and method*, Chicago: University of Chicago Press.

Adkins, L., and Lury, C. (2009) 'Introduction' *European Journal of Social Theory* 12 (1): 5–20.

Alasuutari, M., and Kelle, H. (2015) 'Documentation in childhood' *Children & Society* 29 (3): 169–241.

Alderson, P. (2008) 'Children as researchers: Participation rights and research methods' in P. Christensen and A. James. (eds) *Research with children: Perspectives and practices* (2nd ed.), New York and London: Routledge, pp. 276–290.

Alderson, P., and Morrow, V. (2004) *Ethics, social research and consulting with children and young people*, Barkingside: Barnardos.

Alderson, P., and Morrow, V. (2011) *The ethics of research with children and young people: A practical handbook*, London: Sage Publications Ltd.

Altick, R. D. (1998) *The English common reader: A social history of the mass reading public 1800–1900* (2nd ed.), Columbus, OH: Ohio State University Press.

Appadurai, A. (1986) *The social life of things: Commodities in cultural perspective*, Cambridge: Cambridge University Press.

Ariès, P. (1962) *Centuries of childhood*, New York: Vintage.

Back, L. (2012) 'Live sociology: Social research and its futures' *The Sociological Review* 60 (S1): 18–39.

Back, L., and Puwar, N. (2012) *Live methods*, Oxford: Wiley-Blackwell.

Bailey, R. (2011) *Letting children be children: Report of an independent review of the commercialisation and sexualisation of childhood.* Vol. 8078: Norwich & London: The Stationery Office.

Ball, S. (2003) 'The teacher's soul and the terrors of performativity' *Journal of Education Policy* 18 (2): 215–228.

Balzer, D. (2015) *Curationism: How curating took over the art world and everything else,* Toronto: Coach House Press.

Barad, K. (2007) *Meeting the universe halfway: Quantum physics and the entanglement of matter and meaning*, Durham and London: Duke University Press Books.

Barthes, R. (1981) *Camera lucida: Reflections on photography*, London: Macmillan.

BBC News. (2012) 'NeverSeconds blogger Martha Payne school dinner photo ban lifted' [15 June 2012]. URL: http://www.bbc.co.uk/news/uk-scotland-glasgow-west-18454800.

Beer, D. (2016) *Metric power*, London: Palgrave.

Beer, D., and Burrows, R. (2007) 'Sociology and, of and in web 2.0: Some initial considerations' *Sociological Research Online* 12 (5): 17.

Bengtsson, T. T., and Mølholt, A-K. (2016) 'Keeping you close at a distance: Ethical challenges following young people in vulnerable life situations' *Young* 24 (4): 359–375.

Bennett, J. (2010) *Vibrant matter: A political ecology of things*, Durham, NC: Duke University Press.

Berlant, L. (2007) 'On the case' *Critical Inquiry* 33 (4): 663–672.

Berriman, L. (2014) '"Activating" young people in the production of virtual worlds' in A. Bennett and B. Robards (eds) *Mediated youth cultures: The internet, belonging and new cultural configurations*, Basingstoke: Palgrave, pp. 197–212.

Berriman, L., and Thomson, R. (2015) 'Spectacles of intimacy? Mapping the moral landscape of teenage social media' *Journal of Youth Studies* 18 (5): 583–597.

Berry, D., and Dieter, M. (2015) *Post-digital aesthetics: Art, computation and design*, London: Palgrave.

Bettelheim, B. (1987) 'The importance of play' *The Atlantic* https://www.theatlantic.com/magazine/archive/1987/03/the-importance-of-play/305129/.

Bibby, T. (2010) *Education – An 'impossible profession'?: Psychoanalytic explorations of learning and classrooms*, London and New York: Routledge.

Biesta, G. (2013) *The beautiful risk of education*, Boulder: Paradigm Publishers.

Biesta, G. (2016) 'The rediscovery of teaching: On robot vacuum cleaners, non-egological education and the limits of the hermeneutical world view' *Educational Philosophy and Theory* 48 (4): 374–392.

Biesta, G. J. (2010) 'Why "what works" still won't work: From evidence-based education to value-based education' *Studies in Philosophy and Education* 29 (5): 491–503.

Bingham, C., and Biesta, G. (2010) *Jacques Ranciere: Education, truth, emancipation*, London and New York: Continuum

Bishop, L. (2009) 'Ethical sharing and reuse of qualitative data' *Australian Journal of Social Issues* 44 (3): 255–272.

Blackwell, J. (2001) *Children's millennium diary anthology*, Brighton: QueenSpark Books.

Blaise, M. (2005) *Playing it straight: Uncovering gender discourse in the early childhood classroom*. London and New York: Routledge.

Boddy, J. (2013) 'Ethics tensions in research with children across cultures, within countries' in H. Fossheim (ed.) *Cross-cultural child research: Ethical issues*. Oslo: Childwatch International, pp. 71–96.

Boddy, J., and Oliver, C. (2010) *Research governance in children's services: The scope for new advice*, London: Institute of Education.

Bollas, C. (1987) *The shadow of the object: Psychoanalysis and the unthought known*, London: Free Association Books.

Bourdieu, P. (1999) *Weight of the world: Social suffering in contemporary society*, Cambridge: Polity.

Bourdieu, P., and Wacquant, L. (1992) *An invitation to reflexive sociology*. Chicago: University of Chicago Press.

boyd, d. (2007) 'Why youth [heart] social network sites: The role of networked publics in teenage social life' in D. Buckingham (ed.) *Youth, identity and digital media*, Cambridge, MA: MIT Press, pp. 119–142.

boyd, d. (2014) *It's complicated: The social lives of networked teens*, New Haven and London: Yale University Press.

boyd, d., and Marwick, A. (2009) 'The conundrum of visibility' *Journal of Children and Media* 3 (4): 410–419.

Bradbury, A., and Roberts-Holmes, G. (2016) 'Creating an Ofsted story: The role of early years assessment data in schools' narratives of progress' *British Journal of Sociology of Education.* URL http://www.tandfonline.com/doi/full/10.1080/01425692.2016.1202748.

Bradbury-Jones, C., and Taylor, J. (2015) 'Engaging with children as co-researchers: Challenges, counter-challenges and solutions' *International Journal of Social Research Methodology* 18 (2): 161–173.

Bragg, S. (2007) *Consulting young people: A literature review* (2nd ed.), London: Creative Partnerships.

Bragg, S. (2014) '"Shameless mums" and universal pedophiles: The sexualization and commodification of children' in C. Carter, L. Steiner and L. McLaughlin (eds) *The Routledge companion to media and gender*, London and New York: Routledge, pp. 321–331.

Briggs, M. (2009) 'BBC children's television, parentcraft and pedagogy: Towards the "ethicalization of existence"' *Media, Culture & Society* 31 (1): 23–39.

Briscoe, G., and Mulligan, C. (2014) *Digital innovation: The Hackathon phenomenon*, London: Creativeworks London Work Paper, 6.URL http://www.creativeworkslondon.org.uk/wp-content/uploads/2013/11/Digital-Innovation-The-Hackathon-Phenomenon1.pdf.

Brown, B. (2001) 'Thing theory' *Critical Inquiry* 28 (1): 1–22.

Brookshaw, S. (2009) 'The material culture of children and childhood' *Journal of Material Culture* 14 (3): 365–383.

Buckingham, D. (2009a) '"Creative" visual methods in media research: Possibilities, problems and proposals' *Media, Culture and Society* 31 (4): 633–652.

Buckingham, D. (2009b) *The impact of the commercial world on children's wellbeing: Report of an independent assessment*, London: Department for Culture, Media and Sports and the Department for Children, Schools and Families.

Buckingham, D. (2011) *The material child: Growing up in consumer culture*, Cambridge and Malden, MA: Polity Press.

Buckingham, D., and Scanlon, M. (2003) *Education, entertainment and learning in the home*, Buckingham: Open University Press.

Bull, M., and Back, L. (2003) 'Into sound' in B. Bull (ed.) *The auditory cultures reader*, Berg, Oxford & New York: pp. 1–6.

Burawoy, M. (2005) 'For public sociology' *American Sociological Review* 70 (1): 4–28.

Burn, A., and Richard, C. (2014) *Children's games in the new media age. Childlore, media and the playground*, Farnham: Ashgate.

Byron, T. (2008) *Safer children in a digital world: The report of the Byron Review: Be safe, be aware, have fun.* London: Department of Culture, Media and Sport.

Campbell, M. (2013) *Out of the basement: Youth cultural production in practice and in policy*, Montreal and Kingston: McGill-Queen's University Press.

Carpentier, N. (2011) *Media and participation: A site of ideological-democratic struggle*, Bristol: Intellect.

Castañeda, C. (2002) *Figurations: Child, bodies, world*, Durham: Duke University Press.

Castañeda, C. (2010) 'The child as a feminist figuration: The case for a politics of privilege' *Feminist Theory* 2 (1): 29–53.

Chase, K., and Levenson, M. (2000) *The spectacle of intimacy: A public life for the Victorian family*, Princeton, NJ: Princeton University.

Christensen, P. H. (2002) 'Why more "quality time" is not on the top of children's lists' *Children and Society* 16: 1–16.

Clarke, A. J. (2004) 'Maternity and materiality: Becoming a mother in consumer culture' in J. S. Taylor, L. L. Layne and D. F. Wozniak (eds) *Consuming motherhood*, New Brunswick, NJ and London: Rutgers University Press, pp. 55–71.

Cofield, L., and Robinson, L. (2016) '"The opposite of the band": Fangrrrling, feminism and sexual dissidence' *Textual Practice* 30 (6): 1071–1088.

Cohen, D. (2004) 'Digital history: The raw and the cooked' *Rethinking History* 8 (2): 337–340.

Cook, D. T. (2004) *The commodification of childhood: The children's clothing industry and the rise of the child consumer*, Durham, NC: Duke University Press.

Corsaro, W. (1992) 'Interpretive reproduction in children's play' *American Journal of Play* 4 (4): 488–504.

Cousins, M. (2006) 'The aesthetics of documentary' *Tate Etc* 6 (Spring): 41–47.

Crow, G. (2012) 'Community re-studies: Lessons and prospects' *Sociological Review* 60 (3): 405–420.

Crow, G., and Wiles, R. (2008) 'Managing anonymity and confidentiality in social research: The case of visual data in community research' *NCRM Working Paper. ESRC National Centre for Research Methods*. URL http://eprints.ncrm. ac.uk/459/.

Crow, G., Wiles, R., Heath S., and Charles V. (2006) 'Research ethics and data quality: The implications of informed consent' *International Journal of Social Research Methodology* 9 (2): 83–95.

Davies, J., and Spencer, S. (eds) (2010) *Emotions in the field – The psychology and anthropology of fieldwork experience*, Stanford: Stanford University Press.

Day-Good, K. (2013) 'From scrapbook to Facebook: A history of personal media assemblage and archives' *New Media & Society* 15 (4): 557–573.

Dean, J. (2005) 'Communicative capitalism: Circulation and the foreclosure of politics' *Cultural Politics* 1 (1): 51–74.

Dermott, E., and Seymour, J. (2011) *Displaying families: A new concept for the sociology of family life*, New York: Springer.

Dobson, A. S., and Ringrose, J. (2016) 'Sext education: Pedagogies of sex, gender and shame in the schoolyards of tagged and exposed' *Sex Education* 16 (1): 8–21.

Dolphijn, R., and Tuin, I. V. D. (2012) '"Matter feels, converses, suffers, desires, yearns and remembers": Interview with Karen Barad' in R. Dolphijn and I. V. D. Tuin (eds) *New materialism: Interviews & cartographies*, Michigan: Open Humanities Press, pp. 48–70.

Druin, A. (2002) 'The role of children in the design of new technology' *Behaviour and Information Technology* 21(1) 1–25.

du Gay, P., and Hall, S. (1996) *Doing cultural studies: The story of the Sony Walkman*, London, Thousand Oaks and New Delhi: Sage.

Edwards, R., and Mauthner, M. (2002) 'Ethics and feminist research: Theory and practice' in T. Miller, M. Birch, M. Mauthner and J. Jessop (eds) *Ethics in qualitative research*, London: Sage, pp. 14–28.

Edwards, R., and Weller, S. (2010) 'Your space project – Learning about young people's lives' London South Bank University. URL: https://www.youtube.com/watch?v=El0ph9yVl3I.

Egan, R. D. (2013) *Becoming sexual: A critical appraisal of the sexualization of girls*, Cambridge: Polity Press.

Eichhorn, K. (2013) *The archival turn in feminism*. Philadelphia: Temple University Press.

Elliott, H., Ryan, J., and Hollway, W. (2012) 'Research encounters, reflexivity and supervision' *International Journal of Social Research Methodology* 15(5): 433–444.

Emerson, R. M., Fretz, R. I., and Shaw, L. L. (2011) *Writing ethnographic fieldnotes*, Chicago: University of Chicago Press.

Erickson, Mark (2016) *Science, culture and society: Understanding science in the 21st century* (2nd ed.) Cambridge: Polity Press. ISBN 9780745662251.

Finch, J. (2007) 'Displaying families' *Sociology* 41 (1): 65–81.

Finn, M. (2015) *Education, data and futurity: A data-based school in the North East of England*, doctoral thesis, Durham: Durham University.

Finn, M. (2016) 'Atmospheres of progress in a data-based school' *Cultural Geographies* 23 (1): 29–49.

Fisk, N. W. (2016) *Framing internet safety: The governance of youth online*, Cambridge, MA: MIT Press.

Fox, N. J., and Alldred, P. (2013) 'The sexuality-assemblage: Desire, affect, anti-humanism' *The Sociological Review* 61 (4): 769–789.

Freeman, E. (2010) *Time binds: Queer temporalities, queer histories*, Durham, NC: Duke University Press.

Frosh, S., Phoenix, A., and Pattman, R. (2002) *Young masculinities*, Basingstoke: Palgrave.

Gabb, J. (2011) 'Troubling displays: The affect of gender, sexuality and class' in E. Dermott. and J. Seymour (eds) *Displaying families: A new concept for the sociology of family life*, Basingstoke: Palgrave, pp. 38–60.

Gabb, J., and Fink, J. (2015) 'Telling moments and everyday experience: Multiple methods research on couple relationships and personal lives' *Sociology* 49 (5): 970–987.

Gabrys, J. (2011) *Digital rubbish: A natural history of electronics*, Ann Arbor: University of Michigan Press.

Gaver, W. W. (1991) 'Technology affordances' in *Proceedings of the SIGCHI Conference on Human Factors in Computing Systems*. New York: ACM Press, pp. 79–84.

Gergen, K. J. (1984) 'An introduction to historical social psychology' in K. J. Gergen and M. M. Gergen (eds) *Historical social psychology*, Mahwah, NJ: Lawrence Erlbaum, pp. 3–36.

Gibbons, A. (2015) 'Debating digital childhoods: Questions concerning technologies, economies and determinisms' *Open Review of Educational Research* 2 (1): 118–127.

Gill, R., and Pratt, A. (2008) 'In the social factory? Immaterial labour, precariousness and cultural work' *Culture & Society* 25 (7–8): 1–30.

Gillies, V. (2016) *Pushed to the edge: Inclusion and behaviour support in schools*, Bristol: Policy Press.

Gillies, V., and Edwards, R. (2012) 'Working with archived classic family and community studies: Illuminating past and present conventions around acceptable research practice' *International Journal of Social Research Methodology* 15 (4): 321–330.

Gitelman, L. (2013) *Raw data is an oxymoron*, Cambridge, MA: MIT Press.

Goddard, R. (2009) 'Towards engagement with the ideas of Ian Hunter: An argument for an overdue encounter' *Changing English* 16 (2): 181–191.

Grodin, M. A., and Glantz, L. H. (1994) *Children as research subjects: Science, ethics, and law*, New York: Oxford University Press.

Gulson, K. N., Clarke, M., and Petersen, E. B. (2015) *Education policy and contemporary theory: Implications for research*, London and New York: Routledge.

Gutman, M., and Coninck-Smith, N. (2008) *Designing modern childhoods: History, space, and the material culture of children*, New Brunswick: Rutgers University Press.

Hammersley, M. (2010) 'Creeping ethical regulation and the strangling of research' *Sociological Research Online* 15 (4): 16.

Hammersley, M., and Atkinson, P. (1983) *Ethnography: Principals in practice*, London: Tavistock Publications.

Hardy, I. (2015) 'Education as a "risky business": Theorising student and teacher learning in complex times' *British Journal of Sociology of Education* 36 (3): 375–394.

Harvey, L., and Ringrose, J. (2015) 'Sexting, ratings and (mis)recognition: Teen boys performing classed and racialized masculinities in digitally networked publics' in E. Renold, J. Ringrose and R. D. Egan (eds) *Children, sexuality and sexualization*, London: Palgrave Macmillan, pp. 352–367.

Hasse, C. (2011) *Kulturanalyser i organisationer: Begreber, metoder og forbløffende læreprocesser*, Frederiksberg: Samfundslitteratur.

Hastrup, K. (2010) *Ind I verden – en grundbog i antropologisk metode*, København: Gyldendal akademisk.

Hebdige, D. (1979) *Subculture, the meaning of style*, London: Methuen.

Henderson, S., Taylor, R., and Thomson, R. (2002) 'In touch: Young people, communication and technologies' *Information, Communication & Society* 5 (4): 494–512.

Henwood, K., and Lang, I. (2005) 'Qualitative social science in the UK: A reflexive commentary on the "state of the art"' *Forum: Qualitative Social Research* 6 (3). URL: http://www.qualitative-research.net/index.php/fqs/article/view/16/35.

Himmesoëte, M. (2011) 'Writing and measuring time: Nineteenth-century French teenagers' diaries' in A. Baggerman, R. Dekker and M. Mascuch (eds) *Controlling time and shaping the self*, Boston, MA: Brill, pp. 147–168.

Hoggart, R. (1957) *The uses of literacy, aspects of working class life*, London: Penguin.

Hohti, R. (2016a) 'Children writing ethnography: Children's perspectives and nomadic thinking in researching school classrooms' *Ethnography and Education* 11 (1): 74–90.

Hohti, R. (2016b) 'Now – and now – and now: Time, space and the material entanglements of the classroom' *Children & Society* 30 (3): 180–191.

Holland, P. (2003) *We don't play with guns here*, London: McGraw-Hill Education.

Hollway, W. (2015) *Knowing mothers: Researching maternal identity*, London: Palgrave Macmillan.

Hope, A. (2014) 'Schoolchildren, governmentality and national e-safety policy discourse' *Discourse: Studies in the Cultural Politics of Education* 36(3): 343–353.

Humphreys, A., and Grayson, K. (2008) 'The intersecting roles of consumer and producer: A critical perspective on co-production, co-creation and prosumption' *Sociology Compass* 2: 963–980.

Hunter, I. (1994) *Rethinking the school: Subjectivity, bureaucracy, criticism*, St Leonard's, NSW: Allen and Unwin.

Hunter, I. (1996) 'Assembling the school' in A. Barry, T. Osborne and N. Rose (eds) *Foucault and political reason: Liberalism, neo-liberalism and rationalities of government*, London and New York: Routledge, pp. 143–166.

Hurdley, R. (2013) *Home, materiality, memory and belonging: Keeping culture*, Basingstoke: Palgrave Macmillan.

Ito, M. (2012) 'Introduction' in M. Ito, D. Okabe and L. Tsuji (eds) *Fandom unbound: Otaku culture in a connected world*, New Haven, CT and London: Yale University Press, pp. xi–xxxi.

Ito, M., Baumer, S., Bittanti, M., Cody, R., Herr-Stephenson, B., Horst, H. A., Lange, P. G. et al. (2010) *Hanging out, messing around, and geeking out: Kids living and learning with new media*, Cambridge, MA: MIT Press.

Jackson, C. (2010) 'Fear in education' *Educational Review* 62 (1): 39–52.

James, A. and Prout, A. (1997) 'Re-presenting childhood: Time and transition in the study of childhood' in A. James and A. Prout (eds) *Constructing and reconstructing childhood* (2nd ed.), London and New York: RoutledgeFalmer.

James, A., and James, A. (2008) 'Changing childhood in the UK: Reconstructing discourses of "risk" and "protection"' in A. James and A. James (eds) *European childhoods: Cultures, politics and childhoods in Europe*, Basingstoke: Palgrave Macmillan, pp. 105–128.

Johnson, V., Hart, R., and Colwell, J. (eds.) (2014) *Steps to engage young children in research: Volume 2, The researcher toolkit*, Bernard Leer Foundation, pp. 26–130. URL: https://www.brighton.ac.uk/_pdf/research/ssparc/steps-for-engaging-young-children-in-research-volume-2-the-researcher-toolkit.pdf.

Kehily, M. J. (2012) 'Contextualising the sexualisation of girls debate: Innocence, experience and young female sexuality' *Gender and Education* 24 (3): 255–268.

Kirby, P. (2018 forthcoming) An Exploration of children's agency in the on task primary classroom, PhD thesis, University of Sussex.

Kofoed, J. (2014) 'Non-simultaneity in cyberbullying' in R. M. Schott and R. M. Søndergaard (eds) *School bullying: New theories in context*, Cambridge: Cambridge University Press, pp. 159–184.

Kofoed, J., and Ringrose, J. (2012) 'Travelling and sticky affects: Exploring teens and sexualized cyberbullying through a Butlerian-Deleuzian-Guattarian lens' *Discourse: Studies in the Cultural Politics of Education* 33 (1): 5–20.

Kofoed, J., and Larsen, M. C. (2016) 'A snap of intimacy: Photo-sharing practices among young people on social media' *First Monday* 21(11). URL: https://firstmonday.org/ojs/index.php/fm/article/view/6905/5648.

Kofoed, J., and Stenner, P. (2017) 'Suspended liminality: Vacillating affects in cyberbullying/research' *Theory & Psychology* 27 (2): 167–182.

Kousholt, D. (2015) ' "An old lady among the wild boys": Examine the work of gender in research practices', paper presented at the Work of Gender in the Lives of Children and Young People at Tromsø, Norway.

Kücklich, J. (2005) 'Precarious playbour: Modders and the digital games industry' *The Fibreculture Journal* 5. URL: http://five.fibreculturejournal.org/fcj-025-precarious-playbour-moddersand-the-digital-games-industry/.

Kuhn, A. (2002) *Family secrets: Acts of memory and imagination*, London: Verso.

Lacey, K. (2013) *Listening publics: The politics and experience of listening in the media age*, New Jersey: Wiley & Sons.

Lapping, C., and Bibby, T. (2014) 'Journal as methodological archive: Introduction to a cataloguing system for insecure knowledge' *Pedagogy, Culture & Society* 22(1): 1–8.

Lash, S. (2010) *Intensive culture: Social theory, religion & contemporary capitalism*, London: Sage.

Lather, P. (2007) *Getting Lost: Feminist efforts toward a double(d) science*, New York: State University of New York Press.

Lebeau, V. (2008) *Childhood and cinema*, London: Reaktion Books.

Lévi-Strauss, C. (1969) *The Raw and the cooked*, J. Weightman and D. Weightman (trans.), New York: Harper & Row.

Lévi-Strauss, C. (1978) *Myth & meaning*, London & New York: Routledge and Keagan Paul.

Lincoln, S. (2012) *Youth culture and private space*, Basingstoke: Palgrave Macmillan.

Lincoln, S., and Robards, B. (2014) '10 years of Facebook' *New Media & Society* 16 (7): 1047–1050.

Livingstone, S. (2008) 'Taking risky opportunities in youthful content creation: Teenagers' use of social networking sites for intimacy, privacy and self-expression' *New Media & Society* 15: 393–411.

Livingstone, S., and Haddon, L. (2009) *EU Kids Online: Final report*. LSE, London: EU Kids Online.

Livingstone, S., and Helsper, E. (2013) 'Children, internet and risk in comparative perspective' *Journal of Children and Media* 7 (1): 1–8.

Livingstone, S., and Sefton-Green, J. (2016) *The class: Living and learning in the digital age*, New York: NYU Press.

Livingstone, S., and Third, A. (2017) 'Children and young people's rights in the digital age: An emerging agenda' *New Media & Society* 19 (5): 657–670.

Lucas, M. (1992) 'Special things: The management of an individual provision within a group care setting for emotionally disturbed children' *Therapeutic Communities* 13 (4): 209–219.

Lundy, L., McEvoy, L., and Byrne, B. (2011) 'Working with young children as co-researchers: An approach informed by the United Nations Convention on Children's Rights' *Early Education and Development* 22 (5): 714–736.

Lupton, D., and Williamson, B. (2017) 'The datafied child: The dataveillance of children and implications for their rights' *New Media and Society* 19 (5): 780–794.

Lury, C., and Adkins, L. (2009) 'Introduction: What is the empirical?' *European Journal of Social Theory* 12 (1): 5–20.

Lury, C., and Wakeford, N. (2012) *Inventing methods: The happening of the social*, London and New York: Routledge.

MacLure, M. (2013) 'Researching without representation? Language and materiality in post-qualitative methodology' *International Journal of Qualitative Studies in Education* 26 (6): 658–667.

Madge, C., and Harrison, T. (1938) *Britain by mass observation*, Harmondsworth: Penguin.

Madianou, M., and Miller, D. (2012) 'Polymedia: Towards a new theory of digital media in interpersonal communication' *International Journal of Cultural Studies* 16 (2): 169–187.

Madsen, A. K., Flyverbom, M., Hilbert, M., and Ruppert, E. (2016) 'Big Data: Issues for an International Political Sociology of Data Practices 1' *International Political Sociology* 10 (3): 275–296.

Mahoney, N., Newman, J., and Barnett, C. (2010) *Rethinking the public: Innovations in research, theory, and politics*, Bristol: The Policy Press.

Maller, C., and Strengers, Y. (2013) 'The global migration of everyday life: Investigating the practice memories of Australian migrants' *Geoforum* 44: 243–252.

Marres, N. (2012) 'The redistribution of methods: On intervention in digital social research, broadly conceived' *The Sociological Review* 60 (S1): 139–165.

Marres, N. (2017) *Digital sociology: The reinvention of social research*, Cambridge: Polity.

Marsh, J. A., and Bishop, J. C. (2014) *Changing play: Play, media and commercial culture from the 1950s to the present day*, New York: McGraw Hill.

Marwick, A. E. (2013) *Status update: Celebrity, publicity, and branding in the social media age*, New Haven and London: Yale University Press.

Marwick, A. E., and boyd, d. (2014) '"It's just a drama": Teen perspectives on conflict and aggression in a networked era' *Journal of Youth Studies* 17 (9): 1187–1204.

Marwick, A. E., Diaz, D. M., and Palfrey, J. (2010) 'Youth, privacy and reputation' *Harvard Law School Public Law & Legal Theory Working Paper Series*: 10–29.

Mason, J. (2002) *Qualitative researching*, Thousand Oaks: Sage.

Massey, D. (1993) 'Power-geometry and a progressive sense of place' in J. Bird, B. Curtis, T. Putnam and L. Tickner (eds) *Mapping the futures: Local cultures, global change*, London and New York: Routledge, pp. 60–70.

Massumi, B. (2002) *Parables for the virtual: Movement, affect, sensation*, Durham, NC: Duke University Press.

Mauss, M. (1950 [2002]) *The gift*, London and New York: Routledge.

Mauthner, N. S. (2012) 'Accounting for our part of the entangled webs we weave': Ethical and moral issues in digital data sharing' in T. Miller, M. Birch, M. Mauthner and J. Jessop (eds) *Ethics in qualitative research* (2nd ed.), Thousand Oaks: Sage, pp. 157–177.

Mauthner, N. S., and Parry, O. (2013) 'Open access digital data sharing: Policies, principles and practices' *Social Epistemology* 27(1): 47–67.

Mayer-Schönberger, V. (2009) *Delete: The virtue of forgetting the digital age*, Princeton: Princeton University Press.

Maynard, M. (1994) 'Method, practice and epistemology: The debate about feminism and research' in Maynard, M. and Purvis, J. (eds.) *Researching lives from a feminist perspective*, Oxon: Taylor & Francis, pp. 10–27.

McGeeney, E., Robinson, L., Thomson, R., and Thurschwell, P. (2018) 'The cover version: Researching sexuality through ventriloquism' in P. Boyce, A. Cornwall, H. Frith, L. Harvey, H. Yingying and C. Morris (eds) *Sex and sexualities: Reflections on methodology*, London: Zed Publisher.

McLeod, J., and Thomson, R. (2009) *Researching social change: Qualitative approaches*, London, Thousand Oaks & New York: Sage Publications.

McRobbie, A. (2011) 'Re-thinking creative economy and radical social enterprise' *Variant* 41: 32–33.

Miller, D. (2009) *The comfort of things*, Cambridge: Polity.

Miller, D. (2010) *Stuff*, Cambridge: Polity.

Miller, D. (2011) *Tales from Facebook*, Cambridge: Polity.

Miller, D. (2013) *Future identities: Changing identities in the UK – The next 10 years.* London: Government Office for Science.

Miller, D., and Sinanan, J. (2014) *Webcam*, Cambridge: Polity Press.

Miller, D., Costa, E., Haynes, N., McDonald, T., Nicolescu, R., Sinanan, J., Spyer, J., Venkatraman, S., & Wang, X. (2016) *How the world changed social media*, London: UCL Press.

Mockler, N. (2014) 'Simple solutions to complex problems: Moral panic and the fluid shift from "equity" to "quality" in education' *Review of Education* 2 (2): 115–143.

Mol, A., and Law, J. (2002) *Complexities: Social studies of knowledge practices*, Durham, NC: Duke University Press.

Moore, N. (2006) 'The context of context: Broadening perspectives in the reuse of qualitative data' *Methodological Innovations Online* 1: 2. URL: http://erdt.plymouth.ac.uk/mionline/public_html/viewarticle.php?id=27.

Moore, N. (2012) 'The politics and ethics of naming: Questioning anonymisation in (archival) research' *International Journal of Social Research Methodology* 15 (4): 331–340.

Moore, N., Salter, A., Stanley, L., and Tamboukou, M. (2016) *The archive project: Archival research in the social sciences*, London and New York: Routledge.

Morrow, V. (2005) 'Ethical issues in collaborative research with children' *Ethical Research with Children* 12: 150–165.

Morrow, V., and Richards, M. (1996) 'The ethics of social research with children: An overview' *Children and Society* 10: 90–105.

Morrow, V., Boddy, J., and Lamb, R. (2014) 'The ethics of secondary data analysis' *NCRM working paper.* URL: http://eprints.ncrm.ac.uk/3301/.

Moss, D. (2010) *Children and social change: Memories of diverse childhoods.* London and New York: Continuum.

Muir, S., and Mason, J. (2013) 'Capturing Christmas: The sensory potential of data from participant produced video' *Sociological Research Online* 17 (1). URL: http://www.socresonline.org.uk/17/1/5.html.

Nayak, A., and Kehily, M. J. (2013) *Gender, youth and culture: Young masculinities and femininities* (2nd ed.), Basingstoke: Palgrave Macmillan.

Neal, S., and Murji, K. (2015) 'Sociologies of everyday life: Editors' introduction to the special issue' *Sociology* 49 (5): 811–819.

Neale, B., and Flowerdew, J. (2003) 'Time, texture & childhood: The contours of qualitative longitudinal research' *International Journal of Social Research Methodology* 6 (3): 189–199.

Neale, B. A., and Bishop, L. (2012) 'The Timescapes archive: A stakeholder approach to archiving qualitative longitudinal data' *Qualitative Research* 12(1): 53–65.

Neale, B. A., and Hanna, E. (2012) 'The ethics of researching life qualitatively through time' *Timescapes Methods Guide Series* No. 11. URL: http://www.timescapes.leeds.ac.uk/assets/files/methods-guides/timescapes-series-2.pdf.

Ngai, S. (2007) *Ugly feelings*, Cambridge, MA: Harvard University Press.

Nielsen, H. B. (2016). 'The arrow of time in the space of the present: Temporality as methodological and theoretical dimension in child research' *Children & Society* 30 (1): 1–11.

Nolas, S. M. (2015) 'Children's participation, childhood publics and social change: A review' *Children & Society* 29 (2): 157–167.

Nora, P. (1989) 'Between memory and history: Les lieux de mémoire' *Representations* 26: 7–24.

Obrist, H. U. (2015) *Ways of curating*, London: Penguin.

Okely, J. (2007) 'Fieldwork embodied' *Sociological Review*, 55 (S1): 65–79.

Olwig, K. F., and Gulløv, E. (eds) (2003) *Children's places: Cross-cultural perspectives*, London: Routledge.

Opie, I., and Opie, R. (1959) *The lore and language of schoolchildren*, Oxford: Oxford University Press.

Osgerby, B. (1998) *Youth in Britain*, Oxford: Blackwell.

Oswell, D. (2002) *Television, childhood and home: A history of the making of the child television audience in Britain*, Oxford: Clarendon Press.

Oswell, D. (2006) 'When images matter: Internet child pornography, forms of observation and an ethics of the virtual' *Information, Communication & Society* 9 (2): 244–265.

Oswell, D. (2013) *The agency of children: From family to global human rights*, Cambridge: Cambridge University Press.

Ozga, J. (2011) 'Governing narratives: "Local" meanings and globalising education policy' *Education Inquiry* 2 (2): 305–318.

Papadopoulos, L. (2010) *Sexualisation of young people review*, London: Department for Education and Employment.

Parikka, J. (2013) *What is media archaeology?* Polity: Cambridge.

Piaget, J. (1951) *Play, dreams and imitation in childhood*, Oxon: Routledge.

Pini and Walkerdine (2011) 'Girls on film: Video diaries as autoethnographies' in P. Reavey (ed.) *Visual methods in psychology*, Hove: Psychology Press, pp. 139–152.

Pink, S. (2012) *Situating everyday life: Practices and places*, Thousand Oaks: Sage Publications.

Pink, S., Horst, H., Postill, J., Hjorth, L., Lewis, T., and Tacci, J. (2016) *Digital ethnography: Principles and practice*, Thousand Oaks: Sage.

Platt, J. (1992) '"Case study" in American methodological thought' *Current Sociology* 40 (1): 17–48.

Ponsford, R. (2002) 'I don't really care about me, as long as he gets everything he needs" – Young women becoming mothers in consumer culture' *Young Consumer* 15 (3): 251–262.

Postman, N. (1982/1994) *The disappearance of childhood* (2nd ed.), New York: Vintage Books.

Potter, J. (2012) *Digital media and learner identity: The new curatorship*, Basingstoke: Palgrave.

Prior, L. (2008) 'Repositioning documents in social research' *Sociology* 42 (5): 821–836.

Pugh, A. (2004) 'Windfall childrearing: Low-income care and consumption' *Journal of Consumer Culture* 4 (2): 229–249.

Puwar, N., and Sharma, S. (2012) 'Curating sociology' *Sociological Review* 60 (S1): 40–63.

Reavey, P. (2011) 'The return to experience: Psychology and the visual' in P. Reavey (ed.) *Visual methods in psychology,* London and New York: Routledge, pp. 1–13.

Reay, D. (2002) 'Shaun's story: Troubling discourses of white working-class masculinities' *Gender and Education* 14 (3): 221–234.

Reeve, E. (2016) 'The secret lives of Tumblr teens', *New Republic*. URL: https://newrepublic.com/article/129002/secret-lives-tumblr-teens. (Retrieved 2 September 2017).

Renold, E. (2005) *Girls, boys and junior sexualities: Exploring childrens' gender and sexual relations in the primary school*, London: Routledge Falmer.

Renold, E., Ringrose, J., and Egan, R. D. (2015) *Children, sexuality and sexualisation*, Basingstoke: Palgrave Macmillan.

Reynolds, S. (2011) *Retromania: Pop culture's addiction to its own past*, Basingstoke: Palgrave Macmillan.

Ringrose, J., Harvey, L., Gill, R., and Livingstone, S. (2013) 'Teen girls, sexual double standards and "sexting": Gendered value in digital image exchange' *Feminist Theory* 14: 305–323.

Rinkinen, J., Jalas, M., and Shove, E. (2015) 'Object relations in accounts of everyday life' *Sociology* 49 (5): 870–885.

Robards, B. (2010) 'Randoms in my bedroom: Negotiating privacy and unsolicited contact on social network sites' *Prism* 7: 1–12.

Robards, B. (2012) 'Leaving MySpace, joining Facebook: "Growing up" on social network sites' *Continuum* 26: 385–398.

Robertson, J., Good, J., Howland, K., and Macvean, A. (2013) 'Issues and methods for involving young people in design' *Handbook of Design in Educational Technology* pp. 102–111.

Rose, N. (1998) *Inventing our selves: Psychology, power and personhood*, Cambridge: Cambridge University Press.

Rose, N. (1999) *Governing the Soul: The shaping of the private self* (2nd ed.), London and New York: Free Association Books.

Rosenthal, G. (2002) 'Veiling and denying the past: The dialogue in families of Holocaust survivors and families of Nazi perpetrators' *The History of the Family* 7 (2): 225–238.

Rosenthal, G. (2010) *The Holocaust in three generations: Families of victims and perpetrators of the Nazi regime* (2nd ed.), Opladen and Farmington Hills: Barbara Budrich.

Ross, N. J., Renold, E., Holland, S., and Hillman, A. (2009) 'Moving stories: Using mobile methods to explore the everyday lives of young people in public care' *Qualitative Research* 9 (5): 605–623.

Ruppert, E. (2016) 'Big data economies and ecologies' in L. McKie and L. Ryan (eds) *An end to the crises of empirical sociology? Trends and challenges in social research*, London and New York: Routledge, pp. 13–28.

Salmon, P., and Reissman, C. K. (2008) 'Looking back on narrative research: An exchange' in M. Andrews, C. Squire and M. Tamboukou (eds) *Doing narrative research*, Thousand Oaks: Sage.

Savage, M. (2007) 'Changing social class identities in post-war Britain: Perspectives from Mass-Observation' *Sociological Research Online* 12 (3): 6.

Savage, M. (2010) *Identities and social change in Britain since 1940: The politics of method*, Oxford: Oxford University Press.

Scott, S. (2009) *Making sense of everyday life*, Cambridge: Polity.

Sedgwick, E. K. (2003) *Touching feeling: Affect, pedagogy, performativity*, Durham and London: Duke University Press.

Seiter, E. (1993) *Sold separately: Children and parents in consumer culture*, New Brunswick, NJ: Rutgers University Press.

Selwyn, N., Henderson, M., and Chao, S. H. (2015) 'Exploring the role of digital data in contemporary schools and schooling – 200,000 lines in an Excel spreadsheet' *British Educational Research Journal* 41 (5): 767–781.

Shove, E., Trentmann, F., and Wilk, R. (2009) *Time, consumption and everyday life: Practice, materiality and culture*, Oxford and New York: Berg.

Silverstone, R. (2007) *Media and morality: On the rise of the mediapolis*, Hoboken, NJ: Wiley & Sons.

Skeggs, B. (2009) 'The moral economy of person production: The class relations of self-performance on "reality" television' *Sociological Review* 57 (4): 626–644.

Smart, C. (2007) *Personal life*, Cambridge: Polity.

Spence, J. (1986) *Putting myself in the picture: A political, personal and photographic autobiography*, London: Camden Press.

Stanley, L., and Wise, S. (2010) 'The ESRC's 2010 framework for research ethics: Fit for research purpose?' *Sociological Research Online* 15 (4): 12.

Staunæs, D., and Kofoed, J. (2015) 'Producing curious affects: Visual methodology as an affecting and conflictual wunderkammer' *International Journal of Qualitative Studies in Education* 28 (10): 1229–1248.

Steedman, C. (1995) *Strange dislocations: Childhood and the idea of human interiority*, London: Virago.

Stewart, K. (2007) *Ordinary affects*, Durham: Duke University Press.

Stewart, S. (1984) *On longing: Narratives of the miniature, the gigantic, the souvenir, the collection*, Baltimore: John Hopkins University Press.

Stiegler, B. (1998) *Technics and time, 1: The fault of Epimetheus*, Stanford: Stanford University Press.

Stockton K. B. (2009) *The queer child, or growing sideways in the twentieth century*, Durham and London: Duke University Press.

Sutton-Smith, B. (1986) *Toys as culture*, Hove: Psychology Press.

Taylor, R. (2015) 'Beyond anonymity: Temporality and the production of knowledge in a qualitative longitudinal study' *International Journal of Social Research Methodology* 18 (3): 281–292.

Thompson, G. (2016) 'Computer adaptive testing, big data and algorithmic approaches to education' *British Journal of Sociology of Education* 38(6): 827–840.

Thompson, G., and Cook, I. (2016) 'The logic of data-sense: Thinking through Learning Personalisation' *Discourse: Studies in the Cultural Politics of Education* 38(5) 740–754.

Thompson, J. B. (2011) 'The shifting boundaries of public and private life' *Theory, Culture & Society* 28 (4): 49–70.

Thomson, M. (2013) *Lost freedom: The landscape of the child and the British post-war settlement*, Oxford: Oxford University Press.

Thomson, P., and Pennacchia, J. (2016) 'Hugs and behaviour points: Alternative education and the regulation of "excluded" youth' *International Journal of Inclusive Education* 20 (6): 622–640.

Thomson, P., Hall, C., and Jones, K. (2010) 'Maggie's day: A small-scale analysis of English education policy' *Journal of Education Policy* 25 (5): 639–656.

Thomson, R. (2007) 'The qualitative longitudinal case history: Practical, methodological and ethical reflections' *Social Policy and Society* 6 (4): 571–582.

Thomson, R. (2011) *Unfolding lives: Youth, gender and change*, Bristol: Policy Press.

Thomson, R. (2012) 'Qualitative longitudinal methods as a route into the psychosocial' *Timescapes methods guide* 13. URL: http://www.timescapes. leeds.ac.uk/assets/files/methods-guides/timescapes-r-thomson-ql-methods.pdf.

Thomson, R. (2014) 'Possession: Research practice in the shadow of the archive' in C. Smart, J. Hockey and A. James (eds) *The craft of knowledge: Experiences of living with data*, Basingstoke: Palgrave Macmillan, pp. 39–55.

Thomson, R., and Holland, J. (2005) '"Thanks for the memory": Memory books as a methodological resource in biographical research' *Qualitative Research* 5 (2): 201–219.

Thomson, R., and Kehily, M. J. (2011) 'Troubling reflexivity: The identity flows of teachers becoming mothers' *Gender and Education* 23 (3): 233–245.

Thomson, R., and Arnott, S. (2015) 'Day of our lives: Making and sharing multi-media documents of everyday mothering' *Studies in the Maternal* 7(1): 1–7.

Thomson, R., and Baraitser, L. (2017 forthcoming) 'Thinking through childhood and maternal studies: A feminist encounter' in R. Rosen and K. Twamley (eds) *Feminism and the politics of childhood*, London: UCL Press.

Thomson, R., Kehily, M. J., Hadfield, L., and Sharpe, S. (2011) *Making modern mothers*, Bristol: Policy Press.

Thomson, R., Moe, A., Thorne, B., and Neilsen, H. B. (2012) 'Situated affect in traveling data: Tracing processes of meaning making in qualitative research' *Qualitative Inquiry* 18 (4): 310–322.

Thorne, B. (2009) 'The 7 Up films: Connecting the personal and the sociological' *Ethnography* 10: 327–340.

Tifentale, A., and Manovich, L. (2015) 'Selfiecity: Exploring photography and self-fashioning in new social media' in D. Berry and M. Dieter (eds) *Postdigital aesthetics*, Basingstoke: Palgrave Macmillan, pp. 109–122.

Tinkler, P. (2008) 'A fragmented picture: Reflections on the photographic practices of young people' *Visual Studies* 23 (3): 255–266.

Tucker, S. (2012) 'Considerations on the involvement of young people as co-inquirers in abuse and neglect research' *Journal of Youth Studies* 16 (2): 272–285.

Turkle, S. (2007) *Evocative objects: Things we think with*, Cambridge, MA: MIT Press.

Turkle, S. (2015) *Reclaiming conversation: The power of talk in a digital age*, New York: Penguin Random House.

Turvey, K., and Pachler, N. (2016) 'Problem spaces: A framework and questions for critical engagement with learning technologies in formal educational contexts' in N. Rushby and D. W. Surry (eds) *Wiley handbook of learning technology*, Chichester; Malden, MA: Wiley & Sons, pp. 113–130.

Tyler, I. (2013) *Revolting subjects: Social abjection and resistance in neoliberal Britain*, London: Zed Books.

Tyler, I., and Bennett, B. (2010) '"Celebrity chav": Fame, femininity and social class' *European Journal of Cultural Studies* 13 (3): 375–393.

Uprichard, E. (2008) 'Children as "being and becomings": children, childhood and temporality' *Children & Society* 22 (4): 303–313.

Urwin, C., and Sternberg, J. (eds) (2012) *Infant observation and research: Emotional processes in everyday lives*, Hove: Routledge.

Valentine, G. (1996) 'Children should be seen and not heard: The production and transgression of adult's public space' *Urban Geographies* 17 (2): 205–220.

Valentino-Devries, J. (2010) 'Do young people care about privacy online?' *Wall Street Journal*, April 9. URL: http://blogs.wsj.com/digits/2010/04/19/do-young-people-care-aboutprivacy-online.

Vygotsky, L.S. (1976) 'Play and its role in the mental development of the child' *Soviet Psychology* 5: 6–18.

Walkerdine, V., and Lucey, H. (1989) *Democracy in the kitchen*, London: Virago.

Warner, M. (2005) *Publics and counterpublics*, New York: Zone Books.

Warr, D., Guillemin, M., Cox, S., and Waycott, J. (2006) *Ethics and visual research methods theory, methodology and practice,* Basingstoke: Palgrave Macmillan.

Whitty, G., and Wisby, E. (2006) 'Moving beyond recent education reform – And towards a democratic professionalism' *Hitotsubashi Journal of Social Studies* 38 (1): 43–61.

Wiles, R., Crow, G., Heath, S., and Charles, V. (2006) 'Anonymity and confidentiality' *NCRM Working Paper Series* 2/06.

Williamson, B. (2015) 'Governing software: Networks, databases and algorithmic power in the digital governance of public education' *Learning, Media and Technology* 40 (1): 83–105.

Williamson, B. (2016) 'Digital education governance: Data visualization, predictive analytics, and 'real-time' policy instruments' *Journal of Education & Policy* 31 (2): 123–141.

Wilson, S. (2016) 'Digital technologies, children and young people's relationships and self-care' *Children's Geographies* 14 (3): 282–294.

Winther, I. W. (2013) 'Children's everyday lives (re)constructed as variable sets of field bodies. Revisiting the exotic remote island – a case study' *Nordic Studies in Education* 33: 112–123.

Winther, I. W. (2015) 'To practice mobility – On a small scale' *Culture Unbound* 7: 215–231. Published by Linköping University Electronic Press. URL: http://www.cultureunbound.ep.liu.se.

Woodfield, K., and Morrell, G. (2013) *Blurring the boundaries: New social media, new social research? NCRM Methodological Review Paper*, URL: http://eprints.ncrm.ac.uk/3168/1/blurring_boundaries.pdfing.

Woodyer, T. (2013) 'Play' in S. Bragg and M. J. Kehily (eds) *Children and young people's cultural worlds*, Bristol: Policy Press.

Yates, L. (2003) 'Interpretive claims and methodological warrant in small-number qualitative, longitudinal research' *International Journal of Social Research Methodology* 6 (3): 223–232.

Young, I. M. (2005) 'House and home: Feminist variations on a theme' in S. Hardy and C. Wiedmer (eds) *Motherhood and space*. Basingstoke: Palgrave, pp. 134–164.

Index